Cowboys and Cultivators

Cowboys and Cultivators

The Chinese of Inner Mongolia

Burton Pasternak
and Janet W. Salaff

Westview Press

BOULDER • SAN FRANCISCO • OXFORD

DS
793
M7
P34
1993

Photos courtesy of Janet W. Salaff

Copyright © 1993 by Westview Press, Inc.

Published in 1993 in the United States of America by Westview Press, Inc., 5500 Central Avenue, Boulder, Colorado 80301-2877, and in the United Kingdom by Westview Press, 36 Lonsdale Road, Summertown, Oxford OX2 7EW

A CIP catalog record for this book is available from the Library of Congress.
ISBN 0-8133-1877-7

Printed and bound in the United States of America

The paper used in this publication meets the requirements
of the American National Standard for Permanence of Paper
for Printed Library Materials Z39.48-1984.

10   9   8   7   6   5   4   3   2   1

To our fathers,
Philip and Heinz

Contents

Tables

Preface

The data upon which this study is based were collected during two visits to Hulunbuir League (*meng*), in Inner Mongolia. We conducted surveys in four localities during the summer of 1988 and returned for in-depth interviews to three of those sites in the summer of 1990. Unless otherwise indicated, the quantitative data in tables and text are from our surveys. Wherever we assert a "significant" difference or relationship between variables, the reader can assume a statistical test of p=.05 or less.

The league is an administrative division corresponding to a prefecture in interior China. The next unit below the league is the *qi*, or banner (equivalent to a county), and below that are *zhen* (urban towns), and *sumu* or *xiang* (rural townships). *Sumu* is a Mongol term for areas that they control; *xiang* is used in Han areas. The unit below the *sumu* is a *gacca*, which is equivalent to a *cun* or village in Han areas. In general, *zhen* and *sumu* were formerly communes, and *cun* and *gacca* were brigades. The abbreviation FBIS refers to the U.S. Foreign Broadcast Information Service. A few equivalences for Chinese terms used at various points in the text may also be of use:

fen = when used as a measure of area, it is one-tenth of a *mu*, or 66.7 square meters; when used as a measure of money, it is one-tenth of one *mao*.

jin = a measure of weight equivalent to 0.5 kilograms.

liang = a measure of weight equivalent to 50 grams.

mao = a unit of money equivalent to one-tenth of 1 RMB.

mu = a measurement of land equivalent to .0667 hectares.

RMB or *renminbi* = a unit of money equivalent to .172 US dollars (in December, 1992).

We wish to acknowledge the help of colleagues and students at the Institute of Sociology and Anthropology, Beijing University, and of local officials in Inner Mongolia. They generously gave their time and patience during our visits, and we could not have completed this research without their support. We are especially grateful to Professor Fei Xiaotong, whose inspiration and encouragement made our work possible, and to Professors Pan Naigu and Ma Rong, who cleared stones from the path and joined

their interests and energies with ours in the field. We benefitted greatly
from their advice, insights, and tireless efforts on behalf of our common
endeavor. We are deeply indebted to the people of Sandhill, Great Pasture,
Middle Village, and Tranquillity for their indulgence and their willingness
to teach us about themselves. We have tried to present what we learned
from them in the most accurate, balanced, and sensitive manner possible.
Nonetheless, there may well be points of difference between our interpreta-
tion and that of our Chinese colleagues and hosts. It is important to stress
at the outset, therefore, that this study represents our views and not
necessarily theirs. We also acknowledge the generous support provided for
our work in Inner Mongolia by the National Science Foundation, the
Committee on Scholarly Communication with the People's Republic of
China, the Research Foundation of the City University of New York, and
the Social Science and Humanities Research Council of Canada.

Burton Pasternak
Janet W. Salaff

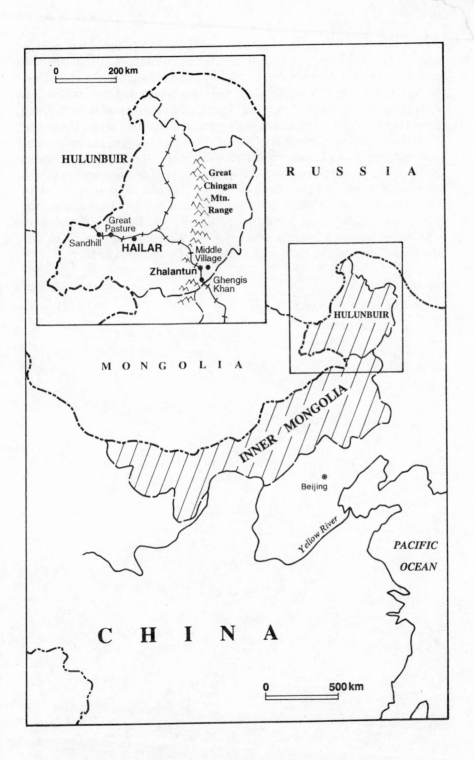

PART ONE

Introduction

1

Economy, Labor, and Family
in Inner Mongolia

There developed a perpetual antagonism, which demanded a decisive choice of every people and state that in the course of history overlapped the Great Wall Frontier, whether its founders were Chinese or non-Chinese -- the choice between agriculture of a notably intensive form and nomadism of an especially dispersed form. Of the repeated attempts to create societies or states that could integrate both orders not one succeeded (Lattimore 1962:39).

This book is about Han Chinese who dared to cross over the Great Wall of China, to make a life for themselves on the northern frontier. It is about their adjustment to life on the grasslands, and about their response to a government which has, in recent years, tried to shape the nature and direction of change in their lives. It is to some extent, too, about the frontier people they met on the other side. This is a study of how cultural tradition and economy interact to define ways of life on the Inner Mongolian frontier.

China is a large and varied nation, diverse in climate, topography, and culture. There are seven main Han Chinese dialects, and distinct regions with their own ecologies and subcultures. The Chinese government has defined and granted special rights to 55 National Minority groups (Dryer 1976). Some, like the Mongols discussed in this study, have ruled the nation. Yet ever since the Chinese state unified the populace 5,000 years ago, spread a script and consolidated rule, we have recognized a common "Chinese Way" of life. The features of this singular way of life seem timeless and uniform. Chinese culture absorbs and reshapes the cultures of those with whom it has come in contact. Thus, Fairbank described the assumption that long guided Chinese policy toward frontier peoples.

The Chinese were impressed with one fact: that their superiority was not one of mere material power but of culture. . . . So great was their virtue, so overwhelming the achievements of the Middle Kingdom in art and letters and

3

4

the art of living, that no barbarian could long resist them. Gradually but
invariably the barbarian in contact with China tended to become Chinese.
. . . After centuries of solitary grandeur as the center of Eastern Asia, the
Chinese developed what may be called, by analogy to nationalism, a spirit of
"culturism." Those who did not follow the Chinese way were *ipso facto* inferior
(cited in Bodde 1959:61).

The Chinese Way is associated with an economy based on dense
settlement and intensive farming. China is an "involuted" society (Geertz
1970). Peasants transfer increasing population pressure to the land. They
apply ever more labor and attention to squeeze marginal increments out of
limited space. Long ago the Chinese found an adaptation that worked most
of the time. To get the workers needed for this labor intensive regime,
farmers favor the patrilineal-patrilocal extended family, and strongly prefer
sons. This adaptation allowed the Chinese to fill all areas of China
possible, and her long history testifies to that success.

But there were also limits, places the Chinese Way might intrude but not
really vanquish. There were areas hostile because of their harsh environ-
ments. It was at just such a border that the Chinese state drew its line of
stone. The emperors built a Great Wall to mark the end of the civilized
world as well as to keep out the barbarians beyond. Those that could not
easily be brought to the Chinese Way, became "a badly digested morsel in
the stomach of the Chinese state" (Wiens 1954:263). Chinese might venture
across the line from time to time but it was, in the end, a frontier beyond
which they could not long survive as Chinese. At least that is what many
believed.

In this book we travel to the north, across the Great Wall and into the
northeastern reaches of Inner Mongolia. There we visit Han who found a
home where they could farm and carry out their Way. These Chinese
farmers, whose recent ancestors took the first step across the frontier,
settled where they could still use hoes, plows drawn by draft animals, and
other familiar north Chinese farming tools and techniques. Then we look
at Han who ventured further into a land which demanded new skills for
dairying and shepherding. We cross the Daxingan (Great Chingan)
mountains to the west and enter the vast grasslands that run to Siberia and
Outer Mongolia. As the terrain changes, so does the Chinese Way. There
is a contest of wills between culture and continuity, between culture and
ecology. Here the homogenizing power of the Chinese state meets a real
challenge.

In following Han settlers into the grasslands we will see how their
cultural inventory has adjusted to new and very different ecological
challenges. We will compare their adaptation to that of the Mongols living
with them. Has the common stimulus forced Han settlers to abandon their

Way so that, in time, they came to live more like Mongols than like Han farmers tilling sandy fields at the fringes of the grassland? And what became of the others as they settled among Han farmers? What form of cultural meeting occurred? We find a give and take between Han and Mongols on the grasslands, while the Chinese Way prevails in the villages.

Technology, Economy, and Diversity

Writers have long underscored the power of the Chinese state to override local differences in social structure. Social historians have explored how the centralized system of water works shaped the local class system.[1] In this view, technology created uniformity. More so in post-1949 China where, to an unprecedented extent, the state has extended its administrative apparatus downward to all aspects of life. At no time before in Chinese history has the government so controlled where people lived, where they worked, what they might grow, what they could eat or buy, when they could marry, and even when and how many children they could have. There are impressive uniformities, despite ecological variation. These policies levelled many of the traditional differences among Chinese.

Yet, in recent years, a number of studies have described how ecology and technology create diversity, and how the crops people grow, and the division of labor that results, affects family organization. Myron Cohen (1976) showed how farming techniques used in tobacco cultivation on Taiwan created a continuous demand for the labor of adult women.[2] Family division, which required a diversion of female labor from tobacco processing to domestic tasks, was postponed. Pasternak (1972, 1983, 1985) also observed how changes in environment led to new ways of earning a living and forming a family. Rainfall dependant farming shortened the time for field preparation, which intensified the need for male labor. This mode of tilling the land, which put a premium on the labor of men, deterred family division and led to matrilocal marriage and high fertility. Then, when dependable irrigation works were built and families no longer needed so much labor, family structure changed (see also Huang 1985, 1990). Our study, too, will explore how the demand for women or men's labor shapes the family they form.

We now know that in Mainland China in the 1960s and 1970s, ecology headed off the powerful pressures for uniformity of state imposed collective agriculture. When the new economic reforms were announced, around 1979, local conditions, the kinds of crops people grew, and levels of productivity they achieved shaped cadre and peasant acceptance of family production. Response to China's strict family planning measures also varied

6

with local need for family labor (Croll 1987:107; Freedman, et al. 1988; Parish 1985).

If the way people made their livings in the collective era shaped behavior, now that the economy is decentralized we expect even more varied local responses. As the move toward a market oriented economy loosens centralized control, traditional patterns reappear. In this book we study how local ecological conditions underlie these varied patterns.

The Present Study

The connection between environment and behavior should be easiest to study on China's frontiers where local conditions are physically extreme. When Han moved onto the Inner Mongolian grasslands, or into the mountainous regions of southwestern China, it was not uncommon that after a few generations they were unrecognizable as Han, having completely assimilated to indigenous cultures (Lattimore 1962; Wiens 1954). When ethnic minority peoples crossed the other way, they were drawn to the Chinese Way.

Within the Chinese Way there are and have always been Chinese Ways. It is about the sources of diversity that this book is written. We focus on how ecological challenges invite cultural adjustments. We mark changes that take place as Han cross the great frontier, including shifts in the values, norms, and ideologies that guide the Chinese Way. Yet the Way is not erased. Carried in the minds of Han settlers, preexisting rules and understandings channel responses to new challenges. In fact, culture has some power to shape these reactions.

To highlight how ecology constrains behavior this study, based on surveys and intensive interviews, contrasts Han and Mongol herders with farmers. We do not argue that Han cease to be Chinese when they give up farming for herding on the Inner Mongolian frontier. But if they are to make their livings here, they must adjust. And where the choices are few, the solutions will be similar. In some areas of Inner Mongolia, Han farmers tried to impose the Chinese Way on the frontier and converted pasture to farmland. Most such efforts to tame the frontier failed, and in recent years the Han have been more inclined to take the grassland as is. In areas where pasture was destroyed, people try to reclaim it. Where pasture was undisturbed, they use it. In doing so, they become more like the Mongols with whom they live. The frontier tamed the Chinese, and the Chinese profit from their compliance.

If the way labor is deployed shapes a way of life, then we should find differences between Han cultivators and pastoralists in Inner Mongolia. To see how they changed as they moved from dirt farming to herding, and how

Mongols shifting to settled agriculture adopted life ways that fit, we begin with the economy.

Farming and herding are distinct in many ways, and we stress here that the resource base, the timing, and the places of work determine how households assign tasks to women and men of different ages. Cultivators, who depend on a limited amount of land, can only work it harder. While farming is labor intensive, it features marked busy and slack periods. Farming on small plots of land near home can easily make use of women's labor. They can still manage to do their household work as well. Women can work alongside men, and do much the same tasks. However, conflicts arise where villagers toil at two labor intensive activities at the same time, and we explore these here.

In contrast, grassland resources are expandable, and herding offers greater rewards with less work. Pastoralism has an ongoing, repetitive work routine. Apart from milking, herding and haying and the rest of pastoral work must be done some distance from town homes. Women cannot do pastoral work elsewhere, and milk the cows and run the household at the same time. The continuous care livestock need and the continuous work done in distant places makes it hard for people to do two things at the same time. Thus, women and men do specialized herding work. Such features of the pastoral life shape how women and men, the elderly and the young, use their time.

In contrasting the two work settings, the concept of labor "substitutability" proves useful. By substitutability of labor we mean flexibility in what family members do and their ability to take over each other's work. Since people cannot be in two places at the same time, they can combine only certain activities.[3] The rigidity or flexibility of their jobs will also vary. Since cultivation and pastoralism force different choices in the use of time and space on rural families, we propose that not only will the work of farmers and cowboys differ, but so will family members' ability to help each other. Whether or not family members can stand in for each other, in turn, affects economic strategies. Thus, the substitutability of work makes it possible for farmers to do a range of nonfarming tasks. It sets the need for labor, which affects family structure and even births, within the narrow limits allowed in China today. The two labor profiles we study here shape the lives of women and men, their ability to get an education, try different jobs, and the ages at which they marry and bear children. Our study will add to the literature that links variation in the options of Han women and men to their economic functions (Andors 1983: Stacey 1983; Whyte 1984; Wolf 1985).

Despite strong pressures for uniformity, we find both cultural persistence and regional variation, and explore their sources. But since the economic and political policies in the regimes we are studying are not static, we also look at how changing policies affect variations.

Privatization: Deliverance or Scourge?

After years of repressing private enterprise, the Chinese government began in 1979 to dismantle the rural collective economy. The communes had promised economic security and increased productivity through mechanization and deployment of mass labor power allowed by economies of scale. Higher output would give rise to equality. Yet, these twin goals of equality and production, the basic objectives of the collective economy, were in tension. There were limits to production improvement within the collective. Ultimately, the system designed to reduce socioeconomic disparities also hampered the further development of production. After two decades the communes were abandoned, a move completed in the region we studied by 1983.

Hoping to expand local initiative apart from state investment, the government now encourages citizens to enter new economic niches and innovate ways to increase their incomes. One cost of the family based contract and responsibility system is class differentiation. The old slogan "everyone eating out of the same big pot," the ideological foundation of collectivization, has given way to "some will get rich first."

This is a profound change in rural China, and writers understandably dispute the consequences. Central to this dispute is whether the move towards a private economy can reconcile a commitment to equality with the concern for increased production. As China tilts towards a market economy, how has the distribution of wealth changed (Nee 1989)? Mark Selden (1985), studying one collective over a decade, finds with the dissolution of the commune increased economic activity and higher rural incomes.[4] Selden is aware that there have been losses as well. Rural education, health care, and welfare benefits, which had previously been their responsibility, have weakened. Income differences within communities arouse tension. On balance, however, he feels that "the rapid increase in income and opportunities for most farmers may more than offset any feeling of injustice among the great majority of the rural population" (Selden 1985:212; Selden 1988; Friedman et al. 1991).

A study of rural villages in Guangdong province by Sulamith and Jack Potter also gives recent developments a plus. The Potters are aware of class divisions between capitalist investors and peasant workers, the differentiation between peasant holdings, land fragmentation, and a technological regression in agriculture. Still, they document increasing prosperity, measured in real changes in per capita income, and in the use of money for public purposes, such as bettering transport, communications, and water systems. The improved infrastructure then aids further economic development (Potter and Potter 1989:339).

Others find the responsibility system lacking on just these issues. The agronomist William Hinton is most pessimistic. First is the problem of low labor productivity. He fears that agrarian productivity will decline with the fragmentation of holdings into plots too small to support machines, and will throw awry the precarious balance between people and land. Low labor productivity, combined with new and increasing opportunities elsewhere, must inevitably draw able bodied workers to seek work away from home and community. They leave less productive family members behind, the very old and young, who cannot profitably work the land. In the end "Land is abandoned by peasants who are unable to cope" (Hinton 1990:113-14).[5]

Hinton also faults the system for social polarization. He further predicts an unleashing of "get rich quick" attitudes. This eagerness to get rich, now warmly endorsed by the Chinese state, has led to "an unprecedented attack on the environment." Families despoil land and water for immediate profits. In cultivating regions, farmers grow crops on fragile hillsides. On the grasslands, pastoralists think only of increasing the number of animals they graze, disregarding the effects on pasture. With abandonment of the commune, the authority structure cannot restrain these depredations or improve the environment. Beyond this, increasing prosperity has also been associated with a resurgence of what Hinton rather ethnocentrically refers to as "gruesome customs," elaborate ancestor worship, birth, marriage, and death rituals.[6]

Finally, writers raise questions about the status of women that remain behind, tilling the land as their men folk flock to jobs in urban centers. Croll (1984, 1987b) fears that women will bear a triple burden of farming, the age old task of reproduction of the household, and in addition the new demands of handicrafts, husbandry, or other local money making ventures.

We can ask what opportunities has the new economic climate in this remote Great Wall frontier opened for herders and farmers? Who are the people that start the entrepreneurial undertakings that are now possible? We find that the combination of domestic undertakings varies with ecological regime. The options largely depend upon the division of labor, the deployment of women and men, and on the substitutability of their labor. Within each area, too, the work women and men do shape household size and structure and, in turn, the ease with which families diversify. These all affect socioeconomic stratification, wealth and poverty.

The world watches closely as the Chinese try another tack, and there is much at stake for us all. If present efforts are an overall success, an elusive prosperity will come to China, and a useful model may become available for others to modify and use. If the attempt ends in failure, we are likely to witness another bitter struggle. In the meanwhile, the more we can learn about the progress of this dramatic shift the better. It is our hope to open several windows and observe the experiment underway.

Chinese on the Inner Mongolian Frontier: The Setting

Inner Mongolia is a rich and varied region, with cultivated land and pasture, forestry and fishing, mining and mineral resources. This offers an exceptional setting to explore the way ecology shapes the division of labor and, through it, marriage and family structure. We choose from this diversity two modes of production, pastoralism and cultivation, to compare how households organize their livelihood. More, we locate subvarients of these two basic types. Pure farming versus mixed cultivation with dairying, limited versus extensive pastoralism offer a range of living styles to explore. But the diversity available to us is not confined to differences in technology and economy. Ethnic differences also condition response.

The Inner Mongolian Autonomous Region in northeastern China, the first established for national minority peoples (1947), covers 1.18 million square kilometers. The Region, with 21.4 million people, contains nine leagues (districts), and three municipalities. Its northern and eastern three-quarters, 1,000 meters above sea level, are part of the Mongolian Plateau. A natural grassland for pasturing, the plateau becomes arid to the northwest, reaching the Gobi Desert to the north. The Yin Mountains, with some peaks rising to 2,100 meters, divide this territory from the fertile plains of the Yellow River. The Yellow River turns east and flows about 300 kilometers across Inner Mongolia. The climate is harsh and continental, rain irregular, and floods and droughts are common. Only 5 percent of the total land area is arable, of which 3 percent is actually cultivated. Nevertheless, its resource diversity is nearly unparalleled in China.

Hulunbuir League, our study site, lies at the northeastern end of Inner Mongolia.[7] Covering an area of 250,000 square kilometers, Hulunbuir comprises one-fifth of Inner Mongolia, with a population of 2.4 million (1982). Its low population density, 9.1 persons per square kilometer in 1982, is half that of Inner Mongolia as a whole, due to the sizable grassland. It has nine banners (counties), two of which are agricultural. Thirty-six percent of Inner Mongolia's population is urban, and Hulunbuir has an even higher proportion of urban population (57 percent). Its four main cities, Hailar, the seat of league government, Yakeshi, Zhalantun, and Manzhouli, the largest inland port city in China, are all along the railway.

The league shares its 1,685 kilometer border with Heilongjiang province to the east, the (former) Soviet Union to the northeast, and Mongolia to the northwest. This strategic location renders it politically sensitive. Previously closed to nonresidents, including Han from China's heartland, parts of Hulunbuir have recently been opened to outsiders. The pastoral sites we visited continue to be closed to non-Chinese, however, so a great deal of advance negotiation had to be done to work there.

Hulunbuir embraces three different ecozones, two of which we studied. To the east of the Daxingan mountains is the agricultural zone, mainly grassy marshlands, where families make their livings by farming or by combining farming and husbandry. The main cultivating area is south of the mountains and west of the Nenjiang River. This important grain area produces over 2.5 percent of the annual national grain total with only 1 percent of China's population. With 582,000 hectares of cultivated land, the main crops are maize, wheat, soybeans, potatoes, and sugar beets.[8] China's cultivation depends closely on weather, and Hulunbuir's seasons are among the most extreme in China. The winters are cold and long, the summers cool and short. Spring is arid and windy, and Autumn brings rapid temperature decline and early frost. In January the temperature dips to -22 degrees celsius in the cultivating area and -28 degrees in the grasslands. Even in July, the temperature only reaches 21 degrees. Because the frost-free period is less than 135 days, farmers can only produce one crop. The technology that might extend the growing season -- like green houses or controlled irrigation -- is beyond their means.

Once an area of forest, large scale cutting during the first half of this century has left few trees. The loss of tree cover has permitted erosion in the cultivating regions and has threatened the grasslands with encroaching desert. Seasonal sand-bearing wind storms sweep through. Farm soils are sandy, and nature is capricious, with either too much or too little rain. The rivers and streams that thread their way through village fields often flood, destroying crops and eroding nearby farmland.

The lush grassland west of the mountain chain supports both sedentary and nomadic pastoralism. The grasslands of Hulunbuir, covering an area of 100 million hectares, constitute one of the largest natural pasture lands in the world. They comprise one-eighth of all the pasture in Inner Mongolia and nearly half the total land area of Hulunbuir League. Livestock are mainly sheep and cattle. As animal husbandry and dairying in particular has become increasingly profitable, the number of animals raised has increased rapidly.[9]

The quality of grassland can be uneven, and some worry about overstocking and overgrazing (Leeming 1985).[10] In one of our study sites cadres told us that, because the available grassland is limited and only "middle to lower in quality," they will soon have to restrict the number of animals households can raise. But this concern is not uniformly shared. In our second pastoral site there is so much high quality grass that residents raise sheep, dairy cows, and also export hay. Cadres there have begun to regulate pasture use but not herd and flock sizes. League officials assured us that the grazing area can support several times the number of animals presently raised.

Climate affects pastoral production as well. Sudden changes in weather can quickly reduce herd and flock size, a long term loss to herders since future reproductive contributions are lost as well. Rains or chills can claim many lambs in short order. Most dangerous are "white disasters," heavy or early snowstorms that threaten new lambs and prevent sheep from pawing for grasses beneath the snow. Then there are "black disasters," when snowfall is so light that there is little water for the animals to drink and grasses are poor.

Hulunbuir's third zone, which we did not visit, includes the rich mineral and forest resources along the mountains and foothills of the Daxingan range, where forestry is paramount. Here lie nearly 10 percent of China's total forest reserves. Hulunbuir produces over 7 million tons of raw coal a year, and has more than 100 billion tons in shallow layers suitable for open cut mining. There are ferrous metals, nonferrous metals, and minerals. Hulunbuir's rivers and lakes rank first in all of Inner Mongolia. Fishing is an important money making sideline in some areas, including the two pastoral communities covered in this study. Hulunbuir already has about 1,000 enterprises in the industrial sectors of forestry, coal mining, electric power, paper making, sugar refining, dairy products, meat processing, hide tanning, fur processing, brewing, and construction materials. Nevertheless, there is poor quality control. Thus, although the dairy industry is quite developed, with 30 milk processing plants, the dried milk quality is uneven and its shelf life limited (*Hulunbuir* 1988:3, 31).

Despite these rich resources, rural Inner Mongolia continues to be one of the poorest of China's provinces and autonomous regions.[11] In 1989, rural income per capita was only 478 RMB, compared to 602 RMB in rural China generally. Only six of China's 30 provinces, municipalities, and autonomous regions had lower average income (*Statistical Yearbook of China* 1990:314). Hulunbuir is better off than much of the region. Its position is likely to improve further in the years to come because the central government, in 1988, designated Hulunbuir an "experimental zone for economic reform." This places most of the burden of investment and reform on the league itself. But economic units can forge contracts and make alliances, and thus chart new economic directions. There has been investment in the airport and highways. Nonetheless, transportation and communications are only basic, and much of the league's rich animal and mineral resources remain to be developed.

Income has risen slowly in recent years. Much of the region continues to be remote, undeveloped, and sparsely peopled. In part because of Inner Mongolia's poverty, families in the four sites we visited welcomed the shift to family production. Our study explores some of the outcomes of this profound economic shift.

Population, Migration, and Inter-Ethnic Relations

According to the 1990 census, Inner Mongolia has a large ethnic minority population, most of whom (3.4 million) are Mongols. But Han are 80.6 percent of the population. Like the Autonomous Region of which it is a part, the people of Hulunbuir League represent 31 state defined National Minority groups -- Mongols, Han Chinese, Daur, Ewenki, Orogen, Manchus, Hui, Koreans, Russians, and others. Half of all the ethnic minority people in Hulunbuir are Mongols. A high proportion of the population, 83.4 percent, are Han.[12] They are mainly farmers and foresters, but growing numbers are herders, the cowboys of our study.

The movement of Han to Inner Mongolia has been a long process, propelled by the interests of several Chinese states.[13] Manchu policy limited migration and Han-Mongol contact. Then, at the turn of the century, moving eastward from Siberia, Russians entered, settled, and cut dense forest for fuel, housing, and lumber. They built the railway that runs by our research sites and connects Moscow with Beijing. The new telephone poles and lines alarmed the Mongols. In one of our pastoral sites, where nomadic herdsmen had been the sole inhabitants, armed resistance broke out. When the Russians sent soldiers to pacify the area, the Mongols turned to guerrilla warfare. Eventually, Russian forces crushed the poorly armed Mongols, opening the way for more settlers. Along their railway grew the cities of Harbin, Manzhouli, and Hailar.

Russians continued to manage the railway and tend cattle, until a border dispute in 1906 led to the arrival of Manchu forces. Concerned about foreign encroachment, Manchu rulers began to encourage a "migration of people to secure frontiers," to counter the Russian threat from the North. In 1911, China's new rulers further encouraged Han to move to the frontier with their families, lifted restrictions on Han-Mongol intermarriage and allowed Mongols to learn Chinese (Ma 1987:134-35). Heavy Chinese migration to Inner Mongolia began.

The railway reoriented the economy of Inner Mongolia toward China and away from the steppe. As Lattimore notes:

From the east and south the railways dispatched into Inner Mongolia even more Chinese colonists than Chinese traders, because rail transport reversed the direction of grain export, making the Chinese market more profitable than the steppe market.

Firearms emphasized the change by altering in their own way the ratio between nomad mobility and agricultural immobility. The old method of adjustment, by which border communities tended to break away from China and gravitate to the steppe when changes from intensive to extensive economy had created a suitable degree of mobility, was now impossible. Although colonization, as it pushed into the steppe, distorted more and more severely the Chinese economy and with it the Chinese family and social system ... this new extensive-economy China remained linked uncomfortably to the old intensive-economy China by the alien devices of steel rails and firearms (1990:99).

Continuous civil war and agricultural disruption in central China propelled impoverished, landless peasants from nearby northeastern provinces to the region. Settlers came mainly from the coastal regions of China south of Beijing (called *Shanghai Guan*), to build the railway, work for Russian cattle families, or trade. Han movement into Hulunbuir League sped up in the early 1930s, but slowed again during the period of Japanese aggression and civil war between Communist and Nationalist Chinese forces (1937-1949) (See *Hulunbuir* 1986; Ma 1987:136-38).

In Sandhill, one of our pastoral sites, most of the earliest Han settlers were single men but, by the 1940s, there were enough families present to launch an elementary school. They held classes in a small yurt (*ger*), a movable Mongol tent. Japan controlled the area briefly, but in 1945 the Chinese Red Army recovered it. Nearly half the local Mongol population left for Outer Mongolia at that time. Their departure was soon followed by that of nearly all the Russians still living in Sandhill.

And so Han Chinese in Inner Mongolia increased steadily. At the turn of this century, the population of Inner Mongolia, 2 million, already favored them.[14] Mongol population had been in decline, from 1.09 million in 1790 to only .84 million by 1949. Many men were celibate Lama Buddhist monks. Others served the Manchu court and were away from home for long periods, which also lowered fertility. Sanitation and health care were primitive.[15] Infant mortality was nearly 300 per thousand, and average life expectancy only 20 years in the 1940s. Venereal disease was endemic in Inner Mongolia until the early 1950s (Ma 1987:112).

Han reached 5.2 million by 1949 and, principally through immigration of farmers, 16.3 million by 1982 (Ma 1987:111). As Han converted eastern pasture to farmland, many Mongols turned to agriculture until, by 1949, over two-thirds of those in eastern Inner Mongolia were farmers (Ma 1987:121).

The period after 1949 was marked by rapid socioeconomic development. A welfare support system was put in place and employment prospects opened. Health care improved, and infant mortality declined. From 1949 to 1961, the state tried to expand the population and herds in this area of Inner Mongolia, under the slogan "let people and animals prosper" (*ren chu liang wang*). In Hulunbuir, the state encouraged women to bear more children, and those with many were designated model mothers and given awards.[16] This, in addition to the in-migration, contributed to a much larger population by the 1960s. The most severe family planning efforts that were pressed in interior China in 1982-1983 were not imposed on the Mongols here. The birthrate in 1990 was 20.1 per thousand and the death rate 5.8.[17] The Mongol population has clearly risen.

However, some of recent growth is due to changes in nationality registration (Gladney 1991:211-22; Ma 1987:112-13). Being Mongol promises political and economic advantages, and even Han invent Mongol ancestors to change their nationality status. These gains include disproportionate political representation, favored admission to educational institutions, and the prospect of avoiding the more severe constraints on reproduction imposed on Chinese families under the strict "one child" family limitation program (Jankowiak 1992).

Patterns of Han migration to Inner Mongolia have also changed. In the 1950s, much migration was state arranged to new industrial centers, rather than "spontaneous" (unofficially sanctioned). From 1960, the government curtailed migration to urban areas throughout China, and most Han migrants since have been rural people going to rural destinations. Here, however, the rapid increase in Chinese rural settlers created ecological and inter-ethnic problems. Not only did the number of farmers grow, but their conversion of grassland into farms in the early settled, southern areas damaged the traditional grazing lands. This prompted a pastoral retreat. Ma describes the problem as follows:

> When the semi-sand areas are cultivated and then abandoned, the roots of perennial grasses are destroyed. Crops cannot grow well to cover the surface of the land, and the strong wind and dry climate of the Mongolian plateau turn the sands (once fixed by perennial grass) into moving dunes. The deterioration of ecological conditions since the last century has become an increasingly serious problem in Inner Mongolia (1987:155-57).

Ethnic conflict over land reached such an extent that the government made special efforts to stop all spontaneous movement. This was especially important during 1960-1962, referred to as the "three disaster years," because conditions here were somewhat better than in nearby provinces. Many unofficial migrants entered our farming sites to escape famine during those years. The period 1963-1965 was one of recovery, when rural-to-urban migration was strictly controlled throughout China to ensure urban supplies. The ensuing period of economic and geographic stability also limited rural-to-urban migration across provincial boundaries.[18] Controls on migration loosened again during the chaos of the Cultural Revolution and its aftermath from 1966-1976, and there was a large inflow and outflow.[19]

Han movement into Hulunbuir was still at a low level when restraints on migration were imposed during the 1950s and 1960s. The area east of the Daxingan mountains, where Han converted wild land and forest into farms, did not attract herdsmen, who preferred the more ample grasslands to the west. Further, that area of Hulunbuir, close to the Soviet border and strategically sensitive, was more tightly controlled. So, Mongol herdsmen living in rural Hulunbuir experienced less competition than elsewhere. However, during the Cultural Revolution many Han moved into Hulunbuir and threatened the fragile balance between Han and Mongol interests even there.

Great pains had been taken to train a corp of devoted communist Mongol cadres. Mongol culture and religion were still intact and active during the 1930s. It has been said that it was largely these anticlerical communist workers who wiped out religious expression in the early years of communist rule. During the first years of the Cultural Revolution, moreover, Mongol cadres vehemently conducted revolution and rejected Mongol culture. Then, as the Cultural Revolution unfolded, they themselves came under attack. Their enthusiasm waned. They were accused of secretly reviving the "Inner Mongolian Revolutionary Party," an outlawed nationalistic organization set up during the late 1940s (Jankowiak 1988). The balance struck between Han and Mongols in the early 1950s shifted, and the rift between them widened.

As Han cadres, eager to welcome Han settlers, replaced many Mongol cadres, the Mongols could no longer contest Han in-migration. At the same time, fear of Soviet attack prompted administrative changes that made migration easier. The central government placed Inner Mongolia's three eastern banners under Han administration in Heilongjiang province to improve its military capacity. In-migration to Hulunbuir then became intraprovincial and therefore easier. While many of the Han who had moved into Inner Mongolia during the Cultural Revolution left, only in 1979 did Mongol leadership recover the portions of Inner Mongolia that had earlier been reassigned to Han dominated provinces. Now spontaneous Han in-migration is more effectively monitored.

With the death of Mao, the fall of the "Gang of Four," and the pragmatists' ascension to power, Mongols have more authority in Inner Mongolia and greater control over events. However, the abuse of once loyal Mongol cadres has disillusioned them, and pushed them to identify more closely with their own people.

A precarious balance has been struck between Han and Mongol interests. Yet, in this politically sensitive region bordered by two rapidly changing socialist nations, one entirely Mongol and the other with serious ethnic problems of its own, the issue of Mongol separatism (or even simply regionalism) is not at an end. Mongol administrators protect their culture and interests. This includes concern for the environment. But where Han perceive that efforts purportedly advanced to develop the grasslands in effect serve Mongol interests, they express resentment.[20] Thus, during the aftermath of the 1989 Tiananmen democracy movement, issues of regionalism and separatism arose once again in Inner Mongolia. Several Mongol spokesmen who called for greater cultural independence and increased protection of the environment have been punished.[21] Even ecological issues provide a context for symbolic and political contest.

Centuries of state imposed cultural and political separation have left a legacy of misunderstanding and ill will among ethnic groups in Inner Mongolia. The massive intrusion of Han after the turn of this century and their displacement of pastoral peoples magnified the problem. The heavy handed imposition of policies designed to create a Chinese version of socialist uniformity during the Cultural Revolution brought the problem to a head. Although Mongols have been gained greater autonomy in recent years, suspicions remain on both sides. We see this most in our pastoral sites, where Han and Mongol cultures confront most sharply.

Site Selection

Since much of Hulunbuir has been closed to casual visitors, it is a part of Inner Mongolia about which little has been written.[22] It was partly for that reason, and because development of the region will likely increase, that the anthropologist Fei Xiaotong suggested that work be done there. Fei hoped to learn about the conditions that might foster the kind of small scale development, with local products and in small towns, that he has long advocated. And so, colleagues from the Institute of Sociology at Peking University were eager to join our work as well, to pursue Fei's interests as well as ours.

In choosing sites for study, we drew upon official statistical sources and advice from local authorities in Hailar City and lower level governments. We selected locations on both sides of the Daxingan mountain chain that divides the cultivating and pastoral areas of Hulunbuir. All of them are near the trans-Siberian railroad. An hour and a half by train from our western-most pastoral site, on the (former) Soviet border, is Manzhouli; Hailar lies an hour and a half from our second pastoral site. Another of our sites is not far from the train to Zhalantun City. Apart from the railway, few roads link towns. People travel earthen roads by jeep, tractor, horse, or camel-drawn cart. Being near the railway, these sites had long been open to Han migrants. They would also be most likely to develop private enterprises in the new climate since 1979.

18

The different ecological characteristics of these sites let us explore the relationship between economy and social organization. They offer a cultural range from pure Han and Mongol cultivators, to Han cultivators who, to increase their income, also tended milk cows in sheds, to dairying Han and Mongols living in a pastoral town, and on to Mongol and Han shepherds in grassland yurts. Although we were less concerned with typicality than contrast, our locations are average for their banners (counties) both economically and demographically. When our work was done we had surveyed four sites.

We collected the materials for this book during the summers of 1988 and 1990. During our first summer, we surveyed households in all sites. During the second summer we returned to three locations for qualitative interviews.

1.   We looked at labor intensive farming in Tranquillity Village. Administratively part of Genghis Khan town and Zhalantun City, Tranquillity Village (formerly brigade) consists of several small hamlets. The population is mainly Han, but there are also Mongols, Manchus, and Koreans.[23] The village is 7 km from Genghis Khan and its railroad station, and 21 km from Zhalantun (population in 1984, 384,335). According to the 1990 census, there were 813 people (184 households) in Tranquillity, of which 78 percent were Han.[24]   From these, we surveyed 634 people in 131 households; 13 households were Mongol. Persons registered as non-agricultural headed only 3 percent of our households. We restudied 17 households during our return visit. These are our dirt farmers.

Many villagers, and all their near ancestors, had arrived as migrant farmers during the mid-1930s. They came mainly from China's northeast, from Liaoning and Jilin, or from Shandong and Heilongjiang, all provinces at the margins of the grasslands. On arrival, as Lattimore observes, they replicated their agrarian ways and culture. In recent years access to urban markets, although limited (via a few daily trains), has given a modest push to sideline industries. So we study Tranquillity to learn how villagers organize their household economies to meet the twin demands of farming and sidelines.

2.   Middle Village (brigade), under Daur township (formerly commune) and Zhalantun City, is named after one of China's smaller National Minorities.[25]   It consists of four small natural villages or hamlets, of which we studied two. We surveyed 135 households; 96 percent were Han. This is the only site to which we did not return for further interviews in 1990. Middle Village is of interest because Zhalantun, with the only nearby train station, is 28 kilometers away, too far to provide a market. As a result, wages and sideline enterprises are of little importance here. Instead, villagers combine their farming with dairying. Cows are a recent addition to the economy and life still responds mainly to the demands of cultivation,

although 65 percent of households supplemented their farming with milk sales in 1987. Middle Village lets us explore how people do two labor intensive activities at the same time.

3.   Sandhill is a pastoral town and administrative center. Despite limited pasture and grassland, most people earn their livings from small dairy herds, a few from small flocks of sheep. In contrast to the other sites, wages supplement income here. Sandhill is home for 2,939 townspeople (709 households), nearly two-thirds of whom are registered as nonagricultural. Two-thirds of the population is Han, most of the rest Mongols. Included are the families of people who work in three nearby railway stations, although we sampled only those connected to the Sandhill station. Altogether we surveyed 184 households (68 percent Han, 30 percent Mongol).[26] We reinterviewed 25 households during our second visit. From Sandhill we learn how herders without extensive grassland work their livestock, and how they combine herding with some wage earning.

4.   The economy of Great Pasture township (formerly Commune) is based on extensive pastoralism and abundant pasture and grassland. Sheep and dairy cows are both raised in large numbers. Hay cutting and fishing augment pastoral income, but wages and sidelines are insignificant. The township population was 4,232 (in 1,025 households) in 1989, 53 percent Han, 42 percent Mongol. Nearly everyone has rural registration here. The township consists of five villages (brigades), three of which we surveyed. One was mainly Han, two smaller ones exclusively Mongol.

Members of the larger Han brigade, with 679 people in 165 households, live in town. Many members of the smaller Mongol brigades (one has 212 persons in 49 households, the other 254 people in 60 households) live all or part time on the open grassland near town. Altogether we surveyed 138 households (725 people). All specialize in shepherding or dairying. The percentage Han in our sample was 58; Mongols made up 35 percent, other ethnic minorities the rest. While most Mongols in the two smaller brigades live on the open grassland, our survey includes a disproportionate number of town families. It was harder to reach families grazing sheep on the open grassland; many were on the move to summer pasture during both our visits. We reinterviewed 11 households during our second visit. These are the cowboys of our study.

Methodology

We administered two questionnaires to a sample of families drawn from the household registers of each research site.[27] The first focused on household and family composition, domestic economy, division of labor. We obtained longitudinal information about migration, education, occupation, and marriage. The second questionnaire, directed to the married women in our sample, got more detail on their marriage and fertility, and their children's education, occupation, marital status, residence, and frequency of contact.

Local cadres and local people cooperated fully with us on the surveys, a familiar technique. Our second visit coincided with the annual animal head count for tax assessment, followed a few days later by China's fourth population census. We found that local statistics and our survey data corresponded closely on size and ethnic composition of the populations, and gave similar economic measures as well. In those regards, our surveys represent the communities studied. This gives us reason to believe that other things we have to say on the basis of our sample are also representative.

We returned to conduct our second set of more extensive, qualitative interviews during the summer of 1990, armed with information and experience from our earlier work, and smoothed by the relationships already formed. We concentrated on the three sites with greatest ecological contrast. We interviewed households with various combinations of income from pastoralism, cultivation, wages, and sidelines, and different labor resources, and raised questions suggested by the earlier surveys. We discussed economic strategies, the way families used labor, as well as kinship and marriage patterns. During these visits we also spoke with cadres about local history and economy, and collected local statistics.

We focused our qualitative interviews on family formation, farming and herding procedures, and division of labor in families we had already surveyed. We did not have the occasion to get detailed life histories from most respondents, and we managed to interact with only a few in informal settings. For the most part we conducted "naturalistic interviews," directed conversations in natural settings. We chose households to reinterview that could better help us understand economic processes and their effects on social life over time. We present pieces of these interviews in later chapters to give the dynamics of how several households negotiate the shoals of change.

In our research we seek to understand how Han Chinese organize their lives to meet the different demands of herding and farming. Our methods were therefore suited to a focus on division of labor, domestic economy, and production styles. We could not look closely at the construction of women's and men's, or Han and Mongol, cultural identity. The important topic of shifting relations in both domains needs participant observation and lengthy unstructured interviewing (Gladney 1990, 1991; Jankowiak 1992). Such an understanding would also require a familiarity with the Mongol language and idiom that we and our Chinese research colleagues lacked. As a result, the issue of how women and men, the old and the young, and

Han and Mongols construct their world views, while important in its own right, remains outside our research agenda. We urge others to pursue these lines of inquiry.

Doing Fieldwork in Inner Mongolia

Since 1979, when fieldwork opportunities opened in China, many foreigners have done local studies. All have had to come to terms with the politically controlled environment. Some have written about their experiences; others conveyed their frustrations, disappointments, and sadness more quietly in off-the-cuff conversations. It was in such a climate that we conducted our fieldwork in Inner Mongolia. That we did our research in a strategically sensitive border region, where problems of political balance were intense, complicated matters further. The fault lines, sensitivities, anxieties were not laid open to our view, but we were aware of them in the shadows. The long term apprehension Chinese had about the intentions of their Great Bear (Russian) neighbors to the north did little to allay anxieties about the motives of foreigners in general. Our colleagues from Beijing were concerned as well about changes going on in China's distant heartland, changes that might later color the political correctness of our visit.

Because of proximity to the railway, the people we visited may be more tied into the world than other grasslanders. Even so, there were constant reminders that we were working in one of China's more underdeveloped regions. If our Chinese hosts had somehow to come to terms with foreign visitors in their midst, we had to adjust as well. The pastoral sites were reminiscent of the early North American western frontier. Problems of water, sanitation, climate, isolation, pose formidable challenges. They called for adjustments on many fronts, on the part of the local inhabitants but also on our part.

Water was a problem, both too much and too little of it. In this newly settled frontier, there is no systematic delivery or removal of water, no pipes or sewers. In both pastoral sites, earthen roads are muddy, and during the rainy season, many are impassible. Paradoxically, water is also a precious commodity. It is particularly scarce on the open grassland, but even Great Pasture lacks domestic wells. There, water is carted home from a central well and stored in large jars. In our small hostel the jars were, in short order, empty. Heating water is no easy matter, done by kettle on simple stoves, and only in the evening. We had to contend constantly with the fine, wind blown earth which covered everything, including our computers. Bathing was episodic, a big treat from a small pan. When our team went off to interview on the open grassland, living conditions became more spartan still, and there was no water at all for bathing.

Other familiar conveniences were also absent. In the towns we visited, we made use of all too frequently overwhelmed public outhouses and backyard pits. On the open grassland there were no designated latrines at all. For Mongols that is no problem; they simply squat under their long robes. But for visitors wearing trousers it was more complicated on the unobstructed plain, without rock or tree. One can see for miles there.

On the grassland, yurt encampments were far apart. We split up and moved from one to the other by tractor, or sometimes by horse drawn cart. If meal time coincided with our visit, our hosts felt obliged to kill a sheep in our honor. We consumed large quantities of milk-tea, wine, dried sheep's milk cheese, mutton fat, and noodles during our stay on the grassland. Eating mutton the Mongol way took some getting used to. The meat was boiled in a large pot, after which pieces, especially the choicest fatty parts, were pressed on the guests. The parts were all quite recognizable -- rib cage, lower jaw, etc.

In the villages, we had water and a more varied diet. There we took our meals in private homes or in nearby restaurants, creations of the new responsibility system. On our arrival in Middle Village, and in our honor, a dog was killed for us to eat. That too took some getting used to, especially since we had seen someone blow torching its fur. And it was somewhat disconcerting to see one of the cadres assigned to arrange our visit removing the caps of beer bottles with the pistol he carried "to defend us."

Political sensitivities constituted more formidable obstacles. Given that the Soviet border was only an hour or so away by train, Hulunbuir officials are sensitive to the presence of outsiders. Local people found having foreigners and visitors from Beijing in their midst both interesting and a bit intimidating. Having outsiders in their uncertain political climate introduced an element of troublesome unpredictability. What if something happened to the foreigners? Who would be responsible if the Russians chose to cross the border to assassinate us just to create a rift between the Chinese and American peoples? Although we were not there to study Han-Mongol relations, what might we say about these matters later? Would we portray our hosts as backward, primitive people? What if, after we left, we wrote uncomplimentary things, or published controversial materials or pictures? What if unsuspecting townsfolk revealed aspects of local life, or of recent history, that might upset officialdom above?

We can convey some sense of what was involved in doing fieldwork in Inner Mongolia by describing events that took place during the first few days of our stay in Sandhill, the first of the sites we visited. The way had already been prepared, so we believed. During a dinner given by the local leadership a couple of days after our arrival, however, we learned otherwise. Our host was called from the room in the midst of our festive dinner and returned shortly thereafter with ashen face and much altered mood. He had a short conversation with one of our Chinese colleagues, during which he conveyed his somber mood. After dinner our Chinese colleagues met separately and we knew a storm would soon break.

Finally it did. Our colleagues returned to tell us of serious trouble. Clearances for our project should have passed down through three separate chains of command -- government, Party, and security. Apparently the security clearance had gotten stuck somewhere along the way. We had already been walking about talking to people for two days without clearance. Local officials now felt we had better return to the League capital on the next train. It took some doing to persuade them to let us remain while one of our Chinese colleagues returned to clear the administrative blockage. We were allowed 24 hours to get the matter resolved and, in the meantime, we foreigners would have to confine ourselves to our rooms (grounded).

The matter was finally worked out, and clearances obtained. Our hosts, apologetic, reminded us that the Russian border was only one hour away by car and that this region is normally closed to foreigners. We were told that local cadres are even suspicious of their own people. If someone went fishing in the river along the Russian border and came back empty handed, for example, there would be many questions to answer. But we were foreigners wandering, without advance notice, into the local middle school and other places. We were taking photographs of homes, including some rather picturesque (shabby looking) Russian homes, which might create the "wrong" impression.

Better we limit our conversations and visits to persons and places agreed upon in advance. Sensitive issues having to do with the Cultural Revolution, family planning, Han-Mongol relations, or corruption had to be avoided or dealt with carefully, so as not to threaten our local hosts or the Chinese colleagues working with us. Were we to write critical things, they would have to answer for it after we left.

As a result, even where local leaders were eager to cooperate, it was not always possible for us openly to pursue issues our colleagues viewed as politically difficult. Thus, cadres were eager to tell us how they complied with birth control policies. But since our simplest questions on these policies reminded our colleagues of the vocal international pressure against China's one child family policy, we had to pursue data on this topic in roundabout fashion. On the other hand, they obliged us with unpublished data from the new census, not seen as controversial.

Local cadres were far from the political center of China, and news reached the periphery only slowly. It was not easy to know which way the winds were blowing at any particular time. These were concerns that were naturally very frustrating but, as time passed, they became less burdensome. So at first, we were not to take pictures or visit people in a casual fashion. And for our safety's sake we were not to swim in the river or ride horses. In Middle Village we were reminded not to cross certain bridges that led into townships for which we had no clearance. Luckily, after our presence was accepted and no longer a novelty, we wandered, visited, and photographed everywhere more freely. The heavy restrictions first imposed relaxed as we became familiar faces. Our 1990 return visit to the three sites was pleasant on both sides. We were happy to meet once again the friends made earlier. The unfolding of the fieldwork process, its extended nature, greatly improved the quality of relations.

Still, during our second visit to Inner Mongolia, a time of particular uncertainty, political concerns loomed greater yet. Recent changes in the international arena, the wrenching disintegration of allied socialist states, and the violent release of pent up ethnic tensions in the Soviet Union and in Mongolia just across the border, deepened Chinese sensitivities to shifting political currents. There were problems with National Minorities in Tibet.

There were also new local issues. In Sandhill we had to try to keep from becoming involved in factional struggles that had nothing to do with us. There were Han-Mongol divisions, and simple political disputes that we had to negotiate and avoid. In Great Pasture there was the young Mongol cadre, new on the job, who worried that the foreigner must be a spy, a threat. There were all the signs -- the small radio, the computer, the camera. It took a while and a few drinking bouts to come to terms with that suspicion.

Our "gatekeepers" were our collaborators in research, faculty and students in the Institute of Sociology, Peking University. They tried to ease our project as much as possible. There was a lot of paperwork and people-work, and back as well as front doors to visit, just to get us and our entourage from Beijing to Hailar, to our research sites, and then home again to Beijing. Our colleagues also had to negotiate our gaffes. They worked hard to help us communicate and overcome cultural differences. They spent many hours ensuring that we understood the complexities and nuances of the area.

Let us turn, now, to what we learned. The chapters to follow begin with a discussion of cultivators who, crossing into Inner Mongolia first, pressed that adaptation on the land. These dirt farmers give us a more traditional base line against which we can measure the deep changes that occurred when Han moved into areas less hospitable to cultivation. There they shifted gears entirely, gave up farming for a way of life akin to that of their Mongol neighbors. We follow their pursuits in Chapters 6 to 10.

Notes

1.   See for example, Chi Ch'ao-ting (1963), and Wittfogel (1957). However, with evidence based on local ecological variations, Wolfram Eberhard (1965) disputes Wittfogel's views on the uniformity of state controlled waterworks. Bringing this debate to the present, Huang (1990) contrasts two kinds of village communities. Irrigated agriculture, a network of waterways, high tenancy, and extensive commercialization in the Yangzi Delta differs from the North China plain with its harsh, agrarian regime, wells, structural poverty, and ecological instability. "Village communities were shaped powerfully by their interaction with the state: the differing land tenure patterns of the delta and North China produced very different relations with state power and, as a result, very different community organizations to cope with that power" (Huang 1990:144).

2.   Rural sociologists use the same terms for farming and dairying production as for manufacturing cycles. Thus, dairying production is organized around individual cows (each is milked separately), similar to discrete "batch" production. This contrasts with row-crop farming, where planting, cultivating, and harvesting is organized around the crop. Production activities in each phase are continuous, set by the production machinery (Simpson, et al. 1988:147). We stress that the timing of the work process in unirrigated, rainfall agriculture is not continuous. Thus, to avoid confusion, we apply the term "continuous" to animal care, and contrast this with "peaks and troughs" in cropping.

3.   A cross-cultural study found that family extension in precommercial societies is especially likely where the various tasks a woman must accomplish are mutually exclusive (Pasternak, Ember & Ember 1976). We apply this concept of exclusivity in task performance to all family members.

4.   According to Selden,

All villages did prosper between 1978 and 1983. Including earnings in off-farm activities, remittances from cities and other miscellaneous sources of income, per capita rural income increased from an annual average of 134 yuan in the first year to 310 yuan in the last. There was a tremendous jump in prosperous peasants -- the percentage of families with a per capita income exceeding 400 yuan jumped from less than one-half of a percent in 1978 to over 23 percent in 1984. But the poor profited as well -- while one-third of all families had per capita incomes below 100 yuan in 1978, less than two percent were this poor in 1984. The net result, as measured by Gini coefficients, was that overall income inequality declined steadily since 1978, from a high of .28 to a low of .22 in the most recent year. With this increased equality China may well have moved toward the egalitarian countryside which many people long thought it to have (1985:212).

Other writers also find an improved rural standard of living, especially between 1978 and 1983: Croll (1987b:114-120), Lardy (1984) and Vermeer (1982).

5.   Unger and Xiong (1990) paint a similarly dismal picture of reforms in a poor and backward area of Yunnan province. Although they note remarkable rises in rural living standards, they sound alarms about the direction of economic differentiation. In some villages, poor farmers cannot even produce enough grain to feed themselves, and government policies that are designed to "bet on the strong" cause much of the problem.

6.   As Hinton puts it,

Next to social polarization, the most striking consequence of reform was the far-reaching cultural regression. Privatization, by returning the rural economy to something closely resembling pre-revolutionary China (even to the generation of large contractors who subcontracted the extended land-use rights they usurped just as subletting landlords of old had done) brought with it, a revival of all the worst features of the old society. . . . In the cultural sphere, old customs, old habits, old ideology, and old superstitions, all bearing a distinctly feudal flavor, also surfaced. On their own once more, without the collective strength to tackle the challenges of the environment, families tended to fall back on the cultural props of the past, such as shrines to the earth god, the kitchen god, the fertility god, and others. They also revived in ever more blatant form all the traditional ceremonies that mark progress through life from birth to death, paying more exorbitant brideprices, arranging more lavish weddings and more extravagant funerals, building more elaborate tombs and borrowing more money at more usurious rates to pay for all these excesses (Hinton 1990:20).

7.   The discussion of Hulunbuir which follows combines data from *Hulunbuir* (1988), and *Hulunbuir* (1986).

8.   Inner Mongolia produces 800,000 tons of grain, exports 50,000 tons of soybeans, and more of potatoes every year (*Hulunbuir* 1988:24-25).

9.   In 1987 the league had 1.97 million head of livestock, 740,000 of which were larger animals like cows and horses. The league produced 31,910 tons of beef, mutton, and pork each year, 120,000 tons of fresh milk, and 1,963 tons of wool (*Hulunbuir* 1988:4-5).

10.   The fragile loess plateau environment is overall not well suited to farming, except under special conditions in valleys and basins. The problem is lack of water. For a general discussion of past policies that encouraged overcultivation, associated problems of erosion, and current efforts to preserve the area, see Leeming (1985:144-57).

11.   Another obstacle in the way of greater rural industrialization in this area is limited fuel and electricity. The Chinese press recently noted that, between 1981 and 1987, the region's agricultural and industrial production grew an average of 15 percent a year, but power supply increased at a rate of only 4 percent a year ("Inner Mongolia Suffers Electricity Shortage," Beijing, *China Daily*, Sept. 13, 1989:4, *In* FBIS-CHI-89-177, Sept. 14, 1989:46-47; see also Leeming 1985:183).

12. Ma (1987), finds about three-quarters of the nation's total Mongols lived in the region in the 1980s; there were another 1.6 million in Mongolia, and 0.8 million in the former USSR. Proportions reported here are based on the 1982 census (Ma 1987: 101-102). According to the recent 1990 census, there were 4.8 million Mongols in all of China (*Peoples' Daily* [overseas edition], Nov. 14, 1990).

13. Much of the discussion of Chinese migration to Inner Mongolia which follows is based on Ma (1987).

14. Around 1800, Han constituted only 28 percent of Inner Mongolia's population, Mongols 71 percent; but by 1912 Han were 57 percent. They constituted 81 percent of the population by 1937, and 85 percent in 1949 (Ma 1987:111).

15. A sample survey conducted in Chenbarhu Banner of Hulunbuir League (one of the banners in which we did research) found a natural increase of minus 66 per thousand as late as the 1940s.

16. The source for this discussion of demographic developments in Hulunbuir is *Hulunbuir* 1986.

17. The natural increase is 14.3. These rates are close to those for the country as a whole, for which the figures were: birthrate, 21.0; death rate, 6.3; and natural increase, 14.7.

18. Net rural-to-urban in-migration during this period was only 60,000, although more had arrived and were sent back. Rural in-migration was also low, only 65.7 thousand spontaneous migrants, of which nearly all were returned (Ma 1987:144).

19. The government lost control of spontaneous migration during this period. In an attempt to diffuse the urban violence of 1968-1972, it sent large numbers of urban students to rural areas. Although many went to rural Inner Mongolia, most subsequently left (Ma 1987:144-145).

20. Ecological deterioration is still a problem, although some short sighted farmers still are not concerned about it. During the last 10 years, based on the advise of scientists and agricultural experts, the government has started to restrict the cultivation of new land, and to encourage the planting of trees and special shrubs to control moving dunes. Legislation and the financial aid aimed at protecting the grassland have greatly improved the ecological situation (Ma 1987:155-57).

21. "Two Inner Mongolian Intellectuals Arrested for Organizing Society to Study Mongolian Culture and Protect Grassland," Hong Kong *Ming Pao* June 11, 1991:8, *In* FBIS-CHI-91-115, June 14, 1991:45. The banned society purportedly studied Mongol culture and criticized the regime for playing down the importance of the Mongolian people, for violating human rights, damaging the environment, and providing such a "backward" educational system for Mongols that they could not redress their problems.

22. However, there is a recent doctoral thesis on migration and economy in Chifeng, a nearby area mainly inhabited by Han cultivators, the progeny of earlier migrants (Ma 1987).

23. *Hulunbuir* (1986:49). Our 1988 census found a similar ethnic breakdown (78 percent Han, with Mongols and Manchus each comprising 11 percent of the survey population.) In terms of ethnic composition, then, our survey sample is representative of the larger community.

The town was only recently renamed *Chengjisihan* in honor of the renowned Mongol leader, Genghis Khan. The change reflects a growing national pride on the part of Mongols, and perhaps a greater tolerance of that pride on the part of Chinese authorities as well, since previous administrations did not view Genghis Khan as admirable. We use the more familiar term Genghis Khan.

24. Government records find that population has changed little in recent years. The village population rose from 858 in 1985 to 879 in 1988, and then dropped to 825 a year later. But these figures must be viewed with skepticism since recorded births, deaths, and figures on in and out migration do not balance.

25. The township contains nine administrative villages (brigades), and 42 small natural villages. It covers an area of 602,738 *mu*, of which 60 percent is forest, 30 percent grassland, and 8 percent cultivated land.

26. The proportions of nonagricultural Han and Mongol were nearly the same: Han 63 percent, Mongols 71 percent.

27. We used an equidistant sampling procedure (with a random start), to choose households for survey from the household registers of each locality.

PART TWO

Cultivators: The Chinese Way

2

Chinese Farmers:
Tranquillity and Middle Villages

The bias toward intensive agriculture thus imparted at the very beginning continued to develop because the regions into which the Chinese expanded, though somewhat different in geography and climate, and some of them naturally more fertile than the original center of diffusion at the Yellow River bend, also responded favorably to an intensive agriculture based on irrigation. Some of them might have developed successfully under a different economic and social order, but the special Chinese trend had the advantage of being the first to assert itself, and thereafter it was easier to develop toward uniformity then toward multiformity (Lattimore 1962: 38).

The North Chinese grain growing village exemplifies the "Chinese Way." All the land in this Inner Mongolian region is "upland," which means that rainfall, rivers, and ponds provide irrigation. Lines of millet, soybeans, and corn wait for rain to moisten the hot summer ground, and for farmers to apply compost. Although the fields are larger than the rice paddies of South China, into which man-made canals gradually dispense water and nutrients, cultivation is just as intensive. There is too little land to let any rest for a season.[1] Cultivation demands much labor. Unable to reclaim new land, peasants put more effort into the land they have, ever trying to squeeze a bit more out of their small holdings by working each plot more carefully. Because farmers all depend on rainfall to soften and irrigate their land, they rush to work it at the same time. It is this production regime that sets the division of labor in our two Inner Mongolian villages.

Tranquillity is a farming village with nonagricultural sidelines. In Middle Village dairying adds to farming income. Our study of the division of labor in both first explores how land and labor were managed during the days of collective agriculture. We then consider how farmers, still subject to traditional constraints, handle their limited resources under the new family responsibility system. We were impressed by similarities in the use of

31

resources under commune and present day household farming. In the next chapter we will show how the division of labor affects the standard of living and family life in these Inner Mongolian villages.

Tranquillity Village

Tranquillity is in a region of Hulunbuir League where farmers till their land using methods familiar to north Chinese farmers. The village was settled by the parents and grandparents of the farmers we met. The area was then wild land, marsh, and forest. Because it was poor for farming or herding, people settled here fairly late. Han Chinese came from impoverished regions across the line of stone, hoping to scratch some sort of living out of dry and sandy earth. The area was less attractive to Mongol herdsmen.

The earliest Han settled during the 1930s. There were about one hundred families by 1940, including those living nearby in what is now Genghis Khan town. Surrounded by a moat built with hired Chinese labor, Japanese also farmed nearby, until they left at the end of World War II. They employed Chinese migrants to farm and cut forest. Koreans, more numerous still, also formed villages where they still grow high quality rice. Although farmers settled the area at mid-century, only one-quarter of Tranquillity's present residents were born elsewhere, mostly in China's northeastern provinces. Fully one-third of resident migrants arrived before 1949, so they have had ample time to develop a strong sense of community, with traditions and a way of life adjusted to local conditions.

Tranquillity Under the Commune

It takes barely half an hour to walk the four kilometers between Tranquillity's three hamlets but because the dusty road winds about to avoid tilled ridges and rushing streams people have the sense that the hamlets are further apart than they really are. The perception obtained substance in 1958, when the three hamlets became separate commune teams. Tranquillity and two neighboring natural villages comprised Tranquillity brigade, one of 12 in Genghis Khan Commune. To avoid inequalities and power concentrations, each brigade included several hamlets of roughly similar size and resources. As elsewhere, the team became the basic unit of production and accounting within the commune.

The commune promised economies of scale that would overcome the limited land and meager family resources that put peasants at the mercy of a capricious and ungenerous nature. Collective organization consolidated tiny parcels of family land and redeemed the ridges between them. The commune managed land and labor in an overall fashion. Members worked a six to eight hour day, longer during busy periods, in return for labor points. Their value and number depended on the specific tasks people did and on the number of days they worked. A day of "heavy" male labor in the fields was worth 12 points, but a day of "heavy" carpentry brought 14 points.[2] Team management was in the hands of several cadres; the team foreman assigned tasks and points in terms of each worker's "ability, experience, and strength".

There were few sources of income apart from labor points earned. Most of the time, leaders discouraged family sidelines. Some people sold a few of the vegetables they grew in small family gardens (only two to three *fen* per person).[3] With the help of kinsmen who worked on the train, a few enterprising women transported home grown vegetables to a nearby mining town, but that was risky since it was illegal. People with special skills earned little more. The carpenter who hammered out commune wagons with homemade tools saw his higher wages delivered to brigade and team, and got work points instead.

Although life was simple and hard, the commune guaranteed families coarse grains of the region and oil, and deducted their value from family labor points. People often complained that some families, content to live on their grain allotments and on vegetables grown on private garden plots, put few hours and little energy into the collective fields. Because of that, others had to work harder to maintain output and work point value.[4] Indeed, many recall that there was so little motivation that team cadres had to press them to put in a good day's work. Even with hard work people could only hope to earn a point or two more than the day's standard, so there was little difference between what top and bottom earners ultimately brought home (see also Selden 1985:193-204).

While the commune, like the independent farm family before it, depended heavily on the labor of women, men, and children, commitment to the collective rarely matched that to the home economy. Output per laborer was so low that it was difficult simply to maintain production. The team urged people to put time and effort in common fields, but the collective consciousness that political campaigns tried to evoke proved hard to sustain.[5] Scale of operation, a serious problem in both pastoral and farming collectives, undermined their success (Butler 1985; Evans 1990; Nee 1985; Parish 1985; Unger 1985; Zweig 1985).

The main problem was low productivity and hence low work point value. Net income from farming, wages, and sidelines determined the value of a labor point. That value fluctuated over time, but was never high. When output began to fall so too did work point value, to a low of .04 RMB in 1980. Many families could not earn enough to pay for grain advances that year, and most ended up owing money. It was time for new economic arrangements.[6]

Division of Labor: Women and Men in the Commune

Although they no longer owned land or major implements, families were economic units whose heads received and managed the income that members earned, and family composition governed household income. Women, young people, and the elderly weeded, fertilized, harvested, and processed crops. But households with several men could earn the most because the brigade reserved the best paying jobs for them. High point tasks like plowing with a draft animal, piling straw for horses, or driving a horse cart, said to require special strength of arm and wrist, were not assigned to women.

But in order to make a decent living, all family members had to do something. If there were not enough men, a woman, a youngster, or even an older person could substitute. People say that women actually did more farming during the collective period than in earlier family farming.[7] In theory, women doing the same "heavy" jobs as men could earn as many work points, but in fact they normally earned two to three points less. The assumption, endorsed by women as well as men, was that women are "not strong enough" to do the heaviest work, and that even when they work in the fields women normally work "less well than men." Further, since the leadership defined women's work as "lighter," they gave them fewer points (Johnson 1983; Andors 1983). Finally, women put in shorter days because they had household tasks to do. The fact that they worked fewer hours at lower wages, and thus brought in less income than men, reinforced the traditional notion that men are "more valuable".

During the Great Leap Forward (1958-1960), the leadership relieved women of many domestic burdens in an unusual effort to draw them into the fields. For a brief (and unsuccessful) period of several months, even food preparation and child care were done in common. Although the extremes of those days were short lived, women continued their heavy field labor. One informant described the pressure upon women to work:

> Under the commune we had free grain distributions, we could gather fuel from the hillsides without charge, and we were paid to work. So, if our daughters-in-law hadn't worked in the fields we would have had grain to eat, but we wouldn't have earned very much, which is why we were anxious to see them go out to work. We needed their earnings. If we didn't accumulate enough work points during the year, we might not even have been able to pay for all the grain we ate, since the value of grain received from the team was

subtracted from the total number of work points our family earned. But there were some people who simply didn't care about this. They were willing to eat and owe. They wouldn't work hard and therefore couldn't pay their debts to the collective. This was a problem that caused trouble, but there was little anyone could do about it because we couldn't just allow people to starve.

Without women's farm work, households could not make ends meet, and the brigade could not maintain production. The amount of outside work women did depended on their age, on whether or not they were married, and on the ages of their children. Teenagers, too, learned to farm early and were usually competent by 15 or 16. Upon marriage, especially if a young couple partitioned to set its own household, the need for a woman's outside earnings was great. Young wives usually joined work teams.

For one or two months before childbirth, and during the first month after, women might remain at home. They normally returned to the fields after that. If several family members were earning work points they might stay home even longer but, by the time their infants were several months old, most resumed working in the fields. Although women did work in the fields, they did less then men. Women also had to care for children, wash and sew clothing, tend pigs and chickens, make fires, and prepare the family meals. For that reason, they left for work later than the men and returned earlier.

Women often found themselves torn between farming and domestic responsibilities. If they gave birth in fall or winter, they had to leave their children in the care of others at planting time. Those that delivered in spring would be needed in the fields during harvest. A mother-in-law or mother might be called upon to care for children, and thus to relieve a younger woman for work in the fields (brides often came from families living close by). Lacking such help, a young mother might place her toddler in a nursery run by some older women, a seasonal remnant of the Great Leap Forward. She might also leave her infant in the care of older siblings or even alone, constrained on the family sleeping platform (*kang*). The latter solution could have tragic consequences if her infant managed to fall from the two-foot high platform onto a brick floor. Because she often worked far from home, nursing was inconvenient. A mother could not take her infant to the fields. Having the baby brought whenever it cried to be fed, or returning often to nurse, was usually impractical. Since nearly all able bodied women went to the fields during busy periods, this was a common problem without easy solution.

Later, after her sons married, a woman might gradually reduce her work in the fields to care for her grandchildren and do lighter household work. In that way she released younger family members for work outside; her daughters-in-law replaced her in the fields. But even after they retired from full labor in the fields, older folks expected to take on light field tasks, especially during periods of high demand. They could plant potatoes, pull weeds, turn compost, and help process the harvest. The contribution was not without consequence, moreover, since it earned labor points (albeit half the number accorded younger workers).

Many of the essential characteristics of labor use under the collective -- the intensive use of all able workers, the minimal use of machines, and the general substitutability of labor -- are salient in our cultivating villages even today. The types and amounts of labor needed have changed in recent years, but these three features have endured.

Dissolution of the Commune

By 1979 the commune was in serious trouble because members were not willing to work for low wages. The value of the work point had by then fallen so low that many were in debt. Rumors of plans to replace the commune with a system of land use based on some form of small group only worsened morale. Many anticipated the change, and team cadres could not get people to work. Tranquillity's Party Secretary described the situation as follows:

> Something very peculiar occurred. Many men 40 and over simply stopped reporting for work. They were certainly too young to be retiring, but that's what they did nonetheless. We began to call them "younger generation old timers." They remained at home and found other ways to earn money. For example, some sold tobacco from their private garden plots. As a result, most of the field workers were young and inexperienced. They were not able to do the work well and, because the value of the work point was by then very low, no one saw any reason to work hard. Everyone could count on an annual food ration in grain, potatoes, beans, even if one didn't work. So we really had to change the commune system at that time.
>
> I remember that, before the family contract system, our brigade always had substantial grain losses due to theft. Because many people were not working, not earning work points, they stole grain. At the end of 1981 we lost nearly 50,000 kilograms of grain that way. Even before the present contract system was initiated, we tried other ways to encourage members to work. We tried offering free lunch to all willing to work, for example. But in the end we still had to move to some form of responsibility system.

The actual change did not take place in one step. First, in 1980, the brigade tried to raise work enthusiasm through a piecework system. Every day the team head and labor foreman announced the tasks that had to be done and how many work points each would be worth when completed.

Members then volunteered for work they preferred. They were paid by the task rather than by the hour, so if workers finished early, they could earn additional points doing other things. Although they could earn more points than before, point value was still low. For that reason there continued to be little enthusiasm for work. As one cadre put it, "There were many tasks for which it was hard to find workers because no one really wanted to work, and because those that did work did so without heart."

Next, smaller groups of families took over basic production, replacing the team. Each got land and machines, but not team buildings or animals. Tranquillity Brigade's three teams divided themselves into several groups of around 10 people. Each received land on contract, per capita. People chose relatives and best friends, taking into account the labor and abilities of their partners' households. But even such close bonds could not override family self interest. Group members argued about how to manage resources and divide earnings, and the disputes were particularly bitter precisely because they were between close relatives and friends.

Even grouping related people, then, did not eliminate problems of self interest. Evans (1990:159) points out that calculating the work of each family member had always been irksome for the household head since he was inclined to consider the product of his farm the result of his own skill and effort. But this new system invited awkward comparisons of work among closely related families as well as within them. Nearly everyone pressed for adoption of an individual family-based system because, as elsewhere in Inner Mongolia, members "couldn't get along" (Howard 1988:52). Toward the end of 1982, the brigade shifted to a new system in which collective land was contracted to individual households under long term contracts. This is called the "contract" (*chengbao*) system.

After years of collectivization, the family regained its role as the source of workers, manager of household income, and producer of much of what members consume, but with an important difference. Land is still publicly owned; it cannot be bought or sold. For that reason it cannot reconcentrate in fewer hands as in former times. Neither natural catastrophe, sloth, nor poor judgement can create a class of landless peasants that a smaller group of well off landlords can dominate. Families may sink into poverty, but they cannot resolve the problem by buying and selling land.

Under the contract system, a written agreement between household and team defines rights and obligations. Cultivators agree to sell a certain amount of grain to the government Grain Management Station at a state set price. In return, for a length of time, they have the right to manage their land and to dispose of the rest of their crop nearly as they choose. Cultivators also must deliver an agricultural tax, contribute to the team's accumulation and welfare funds, and do public labor.

Cadres recalled and then redivided the land, team equipment, and the sheep and work cows among the households of each team. The collective sold or contracted team buildings, water pumps, and other items of large equipment to individual farmers. Land was partly allotted by the number of laborers a family had, and partly by the number of family members.[8] It was classified into three grades, depending on quality and distance from the village. Every family ended up with land of each type, the plots determined by lot. Cadres tried to ensure that shares would be about the same; they took into account distance from roads and water, drainage, soil quality. Despite changes since then, the average holding per person has remained about the same, for Han households, just under 6 *mu* including garden plots. This is not a large amount of land. Although peasant holdings are much larger than farms inside the Great Wall, the growing season is short in Inner Mongolia, and no family can get rich on production alone.[9]

Around five percent of team land is kept in "reserve" for new household members. When people leave by death or marriage their land flows back to the reserve. The estimated reserve needed was based on an ideal annual rate of population growth of 10 per 1,000 persons. At that rate, team reserves should meet village needs for 10 years, but only if residents do not exceed family planning targets.

The team assessed animals; members drew lots and paid for them. The resources of different teams had diverged over the years. Since Tranquillity's second team had many animals, every household was able to get a few. This was not the case in the third team. Salaried workers -- cadres, elementary school teachers, medical staff, the electrician -- did not at first draw lots for land or animals. Their wages were expected to offset the larger shares of ordinary farmers. Each member of a cadre household received two *mu* of middle level, tax free land.[10] Because the real value of their wages shrunk over time, however, cadres received land like everyone else in subsequent distributions.

At the outset, the intention was to contract land out for at least 15 years to encourage farmers to improve it. But family division, population growth, and losses of land to natural causes created problems that led to two further land reallocations. Tranquillity's Party Secretary explained the reasons for these changes:

> The main reason for the first reallocation was widespread dissatisfaction over land quality. When the family responsibility system was first begun, people had only one concern -- to get their own land. They didn't give much thought at that time to the quality of the land they were getting. So, after four years, many of them found that some of their land classified as high grade was actually producing less than expected. They were not fallowing their land, some were not even paying close attention to proper rotation so, in time, their

land was yielding less and less. Some could not even meet their quotas. So there was considerable pressure to reallocate village land. It was therefore reclassified and reallocated under new, 15 year contracts.

After only two years, at the end of 1989, we had to carry out a second reallocation. The reason then was that the structure of many families had changed because of births, deaths, partitions, and marriages. We altered land allocation accordingly but, as a result of our adjustments, many families found themselves cultivating many small pieces of land -- sometimes as many as seven or eight plots in different places. They were hard to till. We needed to reconcentrate holdings. So once again we reclassified and redistributed village land.

When people joined households, they were entitled to land from reserves; when they left or died, their allocations were to be restored to the reserve. The result of this process was land fragmentation. Household heads know that fragmented land is hard to till, so they try to avoid it when they divide. Many carve out a single piece of second grade land for a departing son, instead of a small plot of each grade. That too creates inequalities.

There were many arguments. Some had attended their plots, applying lots of natural and chemical fertilizer. Their land was productive, so they were not eager for a land reallocation. But others had been lazy and had done little to improve their land. They very much wanted to see a redivision of village land. Those not in favor pointed out that the state had called for long term contracts, a recommendation that we were now disregarding. We village cadres could only weakly counter that, while we certainly did have to obey instructions from above, those instructions also required us to reform and improve the responsibility system. But we had a very hard time explaining this to villagers. And as a matter of fact we still do not have a new contract. Quite honestly, we are reluctant now to specify a duration because we have already had to change contract terms twice. We don't want to have to go back on what we agree to again. This time we will wait until higher authorities clarify matters so we can guarantee contract duration.

At present, the distance between those who are relatively wealthy and those who are relatively poor is growing. People who are less well off are anxious to acquire better land, but those who are better off are reluctant to see changes in land holding. To complicate matters, there have been floods during the last three years that washed away much land. And in winter, strong winds brought a lot of sand to the waters and to the land, driving quality down. So our land is constantly changing. Nature alters it constantly so, even if we were to make a long term contract now, there would inevitably be more problems down the road.

Of course, people with land that nature has damaged have a hard time coping. But some people will refuse to work hard whatever the length of contract. Nothing will keep them from spoiling their land. When they lack food, they borrow from the team. Relatives and friends lend them money for their taxes. They manage to pay their taxes and quotas each year, but they are clearly ruining their land. There really is nothing we can do about such people.

Cadres nonetheless do exert some control over productive resources and processes. In carrying out the three land distributions, for example, they balanced the quality and amount of land they gave different families. In one way, the redistributions may even have strengthened their power. Peasants know that tenure is tenuous, and this very awareness may bolster cadres' authority at the same time that it influences cropping decisions and land preservation (Oi 1989).

The redistributions contributed to widespread peasant insecurity. Farmers that had worked their land carefully and had used their resources well lost land they had struggled to improve. For that reason many are now reluctant to invest their time and resources in the land. Had the village kept to the long term contracts, as other areas have done, land might by now be considered *de facto* family property (see Potter and Potter 1989). But this is not the case in Tranquillity.

People of Tranquillity

The casual visitor sees little difference between Tranquillity and other north Chinese farming villages. In architecture, clothing, food, and work, few cultural markers signal departure from a familiar Chinese way of life. Because of their small numbers, and in response to the common demands of cultivation, Mongols and Manchus live interspersed with the Han majority, work at the same tasks, and cannot be told apart. People give little thought to differences of ethnicity. It is not because ethnic minorities lack political recognition or power that they have been assimilated. Indeed, the reverse is the case.[11] Yet, they know little of their own ethnic traditions; our survey found no one who could speak a language other than Chinese. Intermarriage is common (see also Ma 1990, Table 1).

Few villagers leave Tranquillity permanently. Our survey revealed only three people away doing temporary work or studying. While population growth and net in-migration place increasing pressure on local resources, pursuits other than farming offer only little relief. Moreover, there are few public institutions to serve this growing population. A small hostel for old folks without kin is a retreat of last resort. Only a few old people without surviving sons, daughters, or grandchildren find refuge there. Since Tranquillity is near town, however, the people can use town clinics and other facilities for a fee.[12]

Making a Living in Tranquillity

Each household is now thrown back on its own resources, no village wide meshing of labor exists. The family determines when and where to plant, how to enlarge its labor pool, and how to work with others. Each decides what to do with its resources, time, and labor. There are few machines apart from tractors. Cultivation still calls for a lot of human and animal energy.

It is not easy to earn a living by farming in China (Huang 1990:214-218). On the Inner Mongolian frontier it is especially difficult. Apart from constraints imposed by poor soils and a harsh climate, farmers have no money to buy fertilizers and other materials for planting, inputs are scarce, and there is a limited local market for their crops (Albert 1991). It is hard to travel on crowded trains to larger markets. Villagers are still basically subsistence peasants. They produce mainly to feed their families and meet state quotas, and only in small part for sale in the open market. The situation here differs from that along China's eastern coast, or further south, where there are substantial markets, and where peasants sometimes produce crops and sideline products entirely for cash.[13] But there are still other considerations that govern and constrain planting decisions.

The Land Barrier

The finite supply of land, the basic productive resource, most restricts making a living in Tranquillity. In commune days, under team management, the entire collective could absorb losses from natural disasters. They did not fall disproportionately on any one household. Further, there was considerable flexibility in the use of land and labor. The leaders could decide which were the best areas for a particular crop, and who would do what work. They could even consider growing crops like wheat, which benefit from economies of scale. But now the family makes the important decisions, and it does with more limited labor and smaller, more scattered plots of land. To protect against nature's caprices, every family tills plots in different places, trying to vary what and where it plants so that sudden floods or droughts will not affect all land. One household of 10 in our survey farmed 50 *mu* in nine separate plots. As a result, the timing of tasks varies.

Although many households have enough labor to farm more land, they cannot expand because all tillable land is now cultivated. The village actually loses some land each year to flooding, erosion, or construction. Some farmers plant hillside or sandy river bank, but they need a lot of labor to do that, rights are not secure, and returns are marginal. People are likely to invest little labor and capital in such land, and prefer crops (like sunflowers) that are hardy, need little work, and are not quota or tax crops. Or, a family may choose to rent a piece of reserve land, which is allocated by lottery each year. The contract is for one year, renewable if the village does not need the land.

In other areas of China, where there are more ways for rural people to make a living apart from cultivation, it is common for farmers to lend land to other (usually related) families, but that is rare here.[14] If people do borrow or rent a bit of land, there is little incentive to invest labor or capital, or to conserve the soil by carefully rotating crops. Given the difficulty and insecurity associated with these methods of increasing farm size, many villagers prefer nonfarm sidelines, although entrepreneurship and sideline enterprise are not as well developed here as in other areas of China.[15] In 1987, cultivation and small barnyard animals accounted for three-quarters of all production value in Tranquillity. Table 2.1 provides a breakdown of village income by source, with comparative data for Middle Village to which we will turn later in this chapter.

Since there is little land on which to pasture cows, horses, or sheep, few farmers invest in livestock other than draft animals.[16] These graze at the margins of production, along the edges of fields, in wild areas, on unused hillsides -- in places where they do not compete with humans for food. In winter, they feed on husks and stalks. Unable to enlarge their farms or raise livestock, and with limited possibilities for sidelines, farmers try to work the land they have harder and more carefully. They prepare and

TABLE 2.1 Income by Source, Location, and Percent: Han 1987

Source	Tranquillity (N=106)	Middle Village (N=132)
Cultivation	57	51
Large animals & their products	5	27
Other sidelines	19	6
Pigs, poultry & eggs	14	14
Remittances	1	--
Wages	4	2
Totals (RMB)	390,245	594,925

apply fertilizers. They diversify, adding high value crops to the extent small holdings and limited markets allow. Much thought must therefore be given to what to plant, where, and in what order.

Unless a farmer can apply generous amounts of fertilizer, more than is available, he must rotate crops. Plants with long roots, like sugar beets and soybeans, exhaust soil nutrients; farmers cannot repeatedly plant them without degrading the land. Here, inconsistent policy has affected cropping strategies, yields, and soil fertility. Despite interest in increasing production, many farmers are reluctant to prepare natural or chemical fertilizers, due to the repeated land reassignments in recent years. Some are willing to sacrifice soil conservation for short term profit.[17]

The Constraints of Quotas

Apart from the land and labor families have, contractual quotas also influence cropping decisions. Farmers must grow designated amounts of grain for sale to state procurement agencies and market crops to pay taxes and cover production costs. Each year, before spring planting, higher level authorities assign the local Grain Management Station an amount of grain to collect based on past performance. There is a basic quota and an above quota target. Targets pass down the line to the village, then to each "small group" (formerly team), and finally to the farm household (Oi 1989:172-81).

Villagers must fulfill their quotas and are urged to sell additional grain to the state as well. Farmers deliver the basic corn and soybean quotas in kind, for a set price. They may not replace one with the other but can meet above quota targets in either crop. Most farmers plant about two-thirds of their small holdings in these two crops. Corn and soybeans are the two most important crops in Tranquillity, and in Middle village as well (Table 2.2). If farmers choose not to plant so much grain, for instance to reserve more land for potatoes needed to supply a family noodle making business, then they must buy grain from others to meet their targets.

Quotas are based on long term productivity so people are not concerned that if they grow more, their quotas will increase. But to induce farmers to sell grain at below market prices, officials offer discounted fertilizer and diesel fuel. They promise cash advances on next year's harvest, chemical fertilizer, and diesel fuel, in return for grain delivered at above quota prices.[18] There are other public obligations that require production for sale, like the annual land tax, about 3 RMB per *mu*, and the annual contribution to a village accumulation fund. This "management fee", about 6.5 RMB per household, underwrites village expenses, including the salaries of village cadres.[19] Petty proprietors pay fees for sideline enterprises.

TABLE 2.2 Cultivated Land by Main Crops and Location: Han 1987

Main Crop	Tranquillity % Total Area	Middle Village % Total Area
Broad beans	1	4
Corn	40	31
Millet	9	1
Potatoes	15	9
Rice	--	6
Soybeans	27	27
Sugar beets	6	9
Wheat	--	11
Other	2	1
Totals (*mu*)	3,083	3,689

Farming, the Bottom Line

Tranquillity peasants have begun to depart from subsistence farming. Although cultivation still provides most income, sidelines add considerably. No longer outside the money economy, farmers need to sell something to meet growing production costs. They need cash to buy chemical fertilizers, insecticides, seed, feed, and fuel. They repair equipment, use veterinarians, and hire labor. They pay taxes and some give money to relatives. In Tranquillity recurrent production costs alone come to 845 RMB per household (1987), or 26 percent of the total value produced per household. Table 2.3 breaks down these expenses here and, for purposes of later comparison, for Middle Village as well. A quarter of village households have also bought tractors. People increasingly buy large items of farm equipment now that they have some cash and can find them in the market.

Although many families now own them, tractors cannot yet replace animals in cultivation. In the small and scattered plots, tractors can be unwieldy. Further, once corn has grown, the kind of machines farmers use here cannot pass over the plants. At that point tractor owners also use animals to build mounds.[20] And because fuel prices have risen dramatically, cows and horses are less costly to maintain.[21] For all these reasons, tractor owners increasingly reserve their machines for sideline activities.

TABLE 2.3 Expenses by Type, Location, and Percent: Han 1987

Type Expense	Tranquillity (N=106)	Middle Village (N=132)
Equipment repair	3	1
Feed	14	31
Fertilizer	23	19
Fuel	9	5
Insecticide	--	1
Labor	1	3
Remittances	3	2
Seed	10	7
Sidelines	--	--
Taxes	35	29
Veterinarian	2	3
Totals (RMB)	89,549	167,206

Farm improvement depends more on labor than capital. Few farmers buy gas or electric pumps; they apply water by hand, if at all. They do not have hot houses. Nor do they benefit much from other innovations. The government has encouraged farmers to lay sheets of plastic over their fields to promote early growth, for example. But farmers cannot afford either the plastic or the new seeds needed for the innovation.[22] Farmers still rely more on their own labor, on the power of animals, and on nature and local conditions for a good crop. Notwithstanding, grain yields have risen since the responsibility system began.[23]

Since they cannot afford to fallow small holdings, most farmers rotate carefully and all apply fertilizers. Indeed, which crops they grow, and on what fields, depend on fertilizer availability. But there are also limits to the amounts and types of fertilizer that farmers can apply. Most buy chemical fertilizers, but they are costly and the supply is short.[24] Although farmers would use more chemicals were they available, they would not rely on them. They claim that chemicals produce dramatic improvements over the short term, but that the effect is less impressive over the long haul. Further, excessive use of chemical fertilizers hardens the soil, so that it retains less water and is harder to plow. For all these reasons, farmers also make compost from earth, droppings, roots, ash from under the *kang*, and other natural products. But these natural fertilizers, too, are limited in supply because of the enormous amount of time and labor needed to prepare them, especially carrying earth home from nearby river banks to mix with manures. A good farmer uses both types of fertilizer.

Apart from meeting quotas and expenses, families also buy the new consumer goods that have appeared in recent years. They constitute a measure of status and respectability, as do expenditures for marriage, which have also risen rapidly in recent years. To raise cash for these purposes, too, villagers must sell some of what they produce. Apart from their dealings with state procurement agencies, however, farmers have limited access to an open market based on supply and demand. Nearby Genghis Khan is too small a market for garden products or handicrafts. Zhalantun City is only an hour further by train, but it is also small. No one commutes to work in Zhalantun, and villagers do not sell farm products there. Raising cash is therefore no easy matter.

Cash is Good, but Eating Is Better

Farmers also take risks when they grew cash crops for sale on the open market. Transportation and cold storage are poor, and many crops quickly spoil once harvested. Customers may initially be willing to pay a good price for watermelons and honeydews, but if too many farmers plant them, demand is quickly saturated and price plummets. Furthermore, not everyone has the labor, skill, experience, or equipment to grow them, and melons do not travel well. No sensible farmer would be foolish enough to risk replacing subsistence-quota crops with cash crops of this sort. Despite their desire for cash, then, villagers actually only sell a few products -- pigs, melons, potatoes, cabbages, green beans, and a few other vegetables and fruits -- on the open market, and only in small quantities.

Farmers rarely sell corn, soybeans, or barnyard animals to private brokers despite the slightly higher price they might get that way. For the government does not permit sale of corn or soybeans on the open market during the two months of harvest. Since few farmers have much storage space, they have little choice but to deliver their crops to the state collection station soon after harvest (see Oi 1986b). After decades during which the state disparaged private entrepreneurs, many farmers are also wary of private brokers. One farmer illustrated that attitude this way:

If you sell your pig to a private broker he may try to cheat you two ways. He may misrepresent your animal's weight. Or he may agree to a price, receive the animal, slaughter it, and then claim that the meat is defective and that the price must therefore be reduced. State agencies don't do such things.

Villagers consume roughly 25 percent of all value produced at home. Their diet mainly consists of grain and vegetables. Every family has a small garden, free of quota and land tax, in which it grows a variety of fruits and vegetables, principally for home use. Most protein comes from bean products. A couple of pigs, a dozen chickens, a few ducks and geese further enrich diet and income. Most people raise two pigs every year, one for home consumption the other for sale.[25] They slaughter one at Spring Festival and the meat usually lasts through April, after which they may buy small amounts of pork for special events. Farmers also raise chickens, mainly to sell their eggs.

Despite a desire and need for cash, then, farmers do not grow crops for sale on the open market unless they meet other requirements as well. They dare not invest their land, time, and effort in risky crops no matter how potentially profitable, if the investment might jeopardize subsistence and ability to fulfill public quotas. They grow little that they cannot eat, use, or sell in the near future, and they struggle to keep production costs down. To that end they continue to rely more on family labor than on costly machines and chemicals.

Farming Procedures

Given that farmers largely depend on a variety of crops grown using traditional, labor intensive methods, cultivation sets the assignment of all family work. The labor needed to grow most crops, and especially corn and soybeans, is discontinuous. There are seasonal peaks in demand -- during field preparation, planting, mound building, weeding and hoeing, and at harvest. During each spurt in demand, farmers growing a particular crop must all finish their work within a short period of time. On a farm of 30 to 40 *mu*, two adults can finish some tasks with ease, others with difficulty, and still others must recruit some help (by exchange or hiring). Let us follow one household of five as they work their 42 *mu* of land. Living here are the 40 year old family head, his wife, mother, and two unmarried daughters. Several other children live elsewhere.

Currently short on adult males, the family head fully uses the women in his household. As well, he and his brother each own a work horse for use in their fields. Here the family head describes how he deployed labor for all the tasks his family had to do last year, and also his cooperation with others. (After they finished each job on his land, they repeated the work on the land of his brother as the price for his brother's help).

Preparation and Planting. At the beginning of April, using a horse, I drew two long poles through our fields to uproot stubble left over from the last harvest. Some people bring it home for fuel, others leave it in the field for fertilizer. Working by myself, I uprooted the stubble on all my fields in two days and my second daughter (age 18) helped carry it home over the course of three or four days.

Next she and I loaded carts of compost stored in my courtyard, which I carted out to the fields. Together we loaded 10 carts each day, and I transported them all over a period of five days. During the last ten days of April, I spread it in the fields, which took about four days. With that done, I brought my horse to begin the work of plowing and field preparation. First I planted four *mu* of sugar beets. We made furrows, and on the mounds between made holes with a pick axe in which to place seeds. After planting, using our feet, we covered the holes with earth. Last time, it took my second daughter and me one day to finish this work.

I use a horse and plow to prepare my fields even though my first elder brother owns a tractor. Machines can save time but to really take advantage of their greater speed you have to have more labor than if you work with a draft animal alone. A horse pulls one plow, a tractor can pull two; but then you need one worker to drive the tractor, two to guide the plows, and two more to place the seeds. And it's hard to get diesel fuel. A horse is actually better if you intend, as we do, to plow shallow.

Next, with the help of my second elder brother, I prepared the fields for soybeans. We planted seeds in a line along the furrows, and made a second pass with the plow to cover the furrows. It took us four days to complete this work on 10 *mu*. Then it was time to plant corn. We do much the same for sugar beets except that, if the weather is very dry, we add a bit of water to each hole on the mound. Last time it took five or six days to plant 10 *mu* of corn with the help of second elder brother. Then we planted five *mu* of millet for fodder. My second elder brother and I finished that in a single day. One of us led the horse and plow to prepare long thin furrows while the other planted seeds. You need a second pass to cover the furrows.

Following millet we planted potatoes, a crop that requires a lot of labor. Everyone able to work in my family, and in that of my second elder brother, turned out to help including all the women. We usually work together to plant potatoes on my fields and his. First we cut potatoes into pieces (each of which must contain a bud), and carried them to the fields. We made holes with picks, and dropped a few pieces into each. We had to finish this quickly, before the potato pieces could dry out.

Next came hyacinth beans, then sunflowers. We planted the beans along the edges of our fields, in places where other crops are not grown. This is casual work that anyone with time can do. My daughter and I planted seven *mu* of sunflowers in five days. We planted them in holes, like potatoes.

About mid-July, I took a day to plant cabbages on half a *mu*. In addition to all this we planted vegetables in our garden -- seedlings for tobacco, eggplant, tomatoes, and peppers. We put them in at the beginning of April, and transplanted them at the beginning of June. It took about 30 days to plant everything.

Field Maintenance & Miscellaneous Work. From the last 10 days of May to the beginning of June we hoed to remove weeds, surplus seedlings, and to loosen the land. We normally spend from half a month to 20 days at that. I did most of the work with my second daughter. Then my brother and I plowed to build the mounds higher. Together the two of us can finish all my fields in two days. My wife helped to hoe a second time and to build the mounds again. That took another 10 days. Sometimes we can use my brother's tractor to build mounds, but only before the crops have grown too high. Once they have grown, we must use draft animals.

At the beginning of July it was time to prepare compost. I took my horse and cart to collect 20 carts of earth from the river nearby, which I brought home to mix with animal manures and then to store for later use. It took half a month to finish that. Then, my second elder brother and I collected over 20 carts of grass for winter fodder. By mid-August it was time to repair the house, to seal the leaks that develop in the roof each year, to patch the (mud) walls, and to remove ash from the sleeping platform.

Harvest. At the end of August I began to harvest my tobacco, and after September first, my sugar beets. Then, everyone in the family joins in one way or another. It took two people to harvest and carry in our sugar beets. When we cut off the leaves, even my old mother (79) helped. We worked all day and into the night, under lights. It took us five or six days to finish taking the leaves off, after which we promptly carried our beets to the collection station in town. We have to harvest, process, and deliver beets quickly, before they can freeze and before there is so much the market price falls.

Then it was time to harvest corn and, by the last ten days of September, millet and soybeans, although the order in which these crops are harvested can change. It took us over 20 days to harvest millet and soybeans last year. By then our vegetables had already been removed from the garden so we could pile the crop there to process. Corn is very troublesome to harvest. You have to pull off the cobs and husk them, then haul them home to dry in the courtyard. The women always help with this work, and we hire someone with a thresher to remove the kernels from the cobs.

Soybeans have to be cut from the plant, carted home, and piled in the courtyard. After the ground freezes we use stones to thresh them, as we do millet. Next we harvested potatoes. We plowed to uncover them and then picked them by hand. Again, everyone had to help. By the last 10 days of November, we had harvested and processed everything.

Crops should be harvested as quickly as possible, which is why there is such a great need for labor. For one thing, the days get shorter at that time of year. When crops are ripe they can fall over, and then it is hard to harvest them. And then frost can strike at any time from the first of October. Should snow come early, our crop would be ruined. So millet must be harvested before Mid-Autumn Festival. If we are late with the sugar beets, the evenings may be so cold that they freeze in the ground. Then it is hard to pull them up, to cut their leaves, and to remove the earth from them. When they thaw out, they lose sweetness and value. And if you leave any crop in the field too long there is always the concern that someone may steal it, although that is much less of a problem now than it was under the commune.

Winter Slack. Winter is our slack time, and the time to kill a pig to eat. That's when I gather weeds, leaves, and branches on the hillsides for winter fuel. Last year I carried three carts of the stuff home. I need a bit less than others because I get some coal through my sister in town.[26] Grazing the horses is my job. My wife takes care of our home, cares for the pigs, makes their food, and feeds them three times a day. She feeds the poultry, makes our food, sews clothes and shoes. She puts up our vegetables -- cabbage, cucumbers, potatoes, and radishes -- which we store in our floor cave. We eat these things during winter. All these domestic chores really keep her busy.

Division of Labor

Farm size, household labor, and choice of crops are related. Many tasks take several workers. Families with more or fewer men and women, or children and adults, allocate labor to meet the need differently but, for most purposes, household members suffice. There are certain jobs, however, that are considered "men's work."

The more central the crop, the greater its demand on family labor, the more likely men are to do the work. Here, farmers think of grain and vegetable cultivation as men's work. Potatoes, sugar beets, beans, and leafy vegetables are important sources of cash income, and men do most of the work growing them as well.[27] Women have little to do with horses and cows, but there are some tasks, like tending backyard gardens and smaller barnyard animals, that people consider women's work. And when families need more labor than men can provide, women farm alongside the men. In fact, women help at every stage of cultivation.

Men haul compost, but women help load the carts and spread it in the fields. It takes a man to guide the plow, but a woman may lead his horse. More men than women use the pick to make holes for seeds; but women plant, water, fertilize, and cover the holes with dirt. They rarely build mounds because that is done with horse and plow, but women hoe and weed. Sweet melons need a lot of labor, and growers rely on women to prune and spray insecticide weekly. Women also harvest, scrape the leaves and earth from sugar beets, thresh, dry, and mill. The farm family thus responds to labor need with considerable flexibility. Indeed, for most tasks women can replace men when necessary, and the elderly and very young may fill in as well.

Villagers occasionally mouth the old adage that "Boys are precious, girls useless." But because of the substitutability of labor, such utterances have little real substance in our farming villages. Daughters can help their parents even after they have married. In fact, several people claimed that married daughters are often more reliable than daughters-in-law. The restoration of family based production, and the development of sideline activity, should now enhance their value more than ever.

Young people of both sexes work from early on. Even children under 14 are called upon to help. Except on school holidays, they only do simple field tasks, however. By end of the school year, most of the heavy farm work has already been finished. In summer, they hoe, tend vegetables, help mill grain, work in the backyard garden, and help process the harvest. Youngsters draw water, do laundry, and handle other domestic chores. Parents short on labor may even be tempted to end schooling early. Teenagers certainly work hard; by 17 or 18, they have already learned the basic skills required. Boys and girls do much the same things at that age.

Farming can be too demanding for the elderly; an old couple would have a hard time plowing, building mounds, or collecting firewood on their own, for example. When they reach 65, therefore, most gradually retire, leaving all but the most pressing tasks to younger family members. They do not become idle even then. Old women can free younger ones for work outside the home by looking after grandchildren. Old people of both sexes lend a hand in the fields, and process harvested crops when labor is badly needed. They pull up potatoes and sugar beets, remove leaves and earth, thresh, tend the family vegetable garden, and do other light tasks.

Women of all ages farm. In addition, running the home is mainly their responsibility. The typical housewife spends at least two hours every other day just cooking food for the family pigs. She must pickle and salt large jars of vegetables, preserve eggs, dry vegetables and firewood. Women cook, clean, and sew clothing and bedding. Such household chores inevitably limit the time they can give to cultivation, which places the main burden for farming on men. Women certainly put shorter days in the fields than men. It is not easy for them to combine domestic and outside work, especially where they care for infants.

Because no woman can be in two places at the same time, it helps to have more than one in the household. It is more important to have two women than to have more than one man. Women can make up for a shortage of men in the fields, but it is hard to make up for a lack of women. As important as it is, the work of women is held in lower esteem than farming, which brings in the money. Men would not think of doing housework and have not been trained for it. Even old men are reluctant to do domestic work.

Housework belongs almost exclusively to women, but cultivation calls for the efforts of all family members, regardless of age or sex. A triple burden still weighs heavily on women, therefore; they manage the home, the children, and contribute to farming as well. But the substitutability of labor characteristic of farming also makes it possible for farmers to improve their incomes. Because they can use family labor flexibly, farmers can undertake sidelines of various sorts without greatly cutting into their farm work.

Combining Tasks

A variety of sidelines have emerged since 1978. They add more to income in Tranquillity than in the other sites studied. Farmers make and transport gravel, collect and sift sand for construction, process grain, make potato noodles and bean curd, tend small flocks of sheep, fish, and manage small grocery stores. Sidelines, like farming, are part market and part subsistence oriented. Peasant entrepreneurs supply most of their own inputs, and cannot afford purchased materials, capital, or labor (Szelenyi 1988). These are essentially subsistence sideliners rather than specialists.

Villagers coordinate sidelines with farming in many ways. They take advantage of labor free during slack periods, use local raw materials, and depend upon a local clientele. Sidelines also profit from the substitutability of labor that farming allows. Women spend more time in the fields when family sidelines call for the labor of men. When men cannot be replaced in the fields, then women can take up the slack in the family store or mill.

Many households thus haul sand and gravel to buyers in Genghis Khan, who in turn ship by rail to Zhalantun. But people do such work only when they are not busy in the fields, and especially during the winter slack. Sand is also easier to sift when it is cold. Although sifting sand, making gravel, and hauling are heavy "men's work," women commonly lend a hand when there are not enough men. Sidelines thus further increase the burdens of women. But they can also mean a considerable improvement in income, especially for successful farmers; the families with most income from sidelines are also those likely to have more substantial farming income. In many cases successful and profitable farming provides the tractors that make working with sand and gravel most rewarding.

Even when profitable, sidelines do not replace farming. Villagers prefer investments that are multifunctional, and that have some relevance to farming. A family that hauls sand also uses its tractor to farm. Likewise, millers rarely specialize in a single product; they use their equipment to mill both sorghum and millet, and also to hull and process corn into edible kernels and husks for pig feed. Some also make bean curd. In addition to milling grain, they may also make noodles. Noodle making can be quite profitable, but it requires a modest investment in machinery, special skills, and a lot of labor. It is a combination that few families have.

Noodle making, like sifting sand or making gravel, is a seasonal undertaking that largely depends on family labor. The miller uses potatoes from his own fields along with those grown by neighbors. He begins work in early August, when farmers harvest potatoes, and continues making noodles until the end of October when the weather becomes too cold to dry them outside. The work overlaps somewhat with farming, but noodle making is usually profitable enough to justify hiring some workers to augment family labor.

Convenience stores provide yet another way to supplement farm income. Several villagers have converted rooms into small shops where neighbors buy noodles, wine, beer, cigarettes, school supplies, cakes, and other snacks. It is one of the simplest sidelines to start because it requires minimal initial capital. Stock and worth gradually increase. In fact capital is less crucial than having enough family members to run store, home, and farm. Again, the flexibility of farming is an advantage. A woman, teenager, an old person, even a teacher can run a shop full or part-time. Shops are also geared to farming. Customers buy on credit and repay after harvest. Store owners repay wholesalers when they themselves are paid. During busy times, villagers buy wine and snacks for their workers. Inventory and demand thus reflect the agricultural cycle.

In other regions of China, people have been abandoning farming for full time rural sidelines, or to process industrial products. This has not occurred here.[28] As profitable as noodle making may be, and some millers earn more making them than from cultivation, it makes no sense to give up farming. It makes even less sense for people who sift sand or make gravel. All sidelines here depend too closely on local inputs, and most respond to a limited village demand.

Nor have villagers been inclined to give up farming for jobs.[29] People would surely welcome part-time work, especially during slack periods. But full-time jobs are few and competitive with farming. They would have to be very secure and profitable to be attractive. Even local teachers, cadres, and technicians, all of whom earn regular wages, do not depend exclusively on their jobs. All farm for their food, but they have a special need to enlist help during the busiest agricultural seasons. Although all villagers would like to supplement their income through sidelines and wages, then, farming continues to be the mainstay in Tranquillity.

Middle Village

Middle Village has a mixed, pastoral-cultivating economy. People mainly farm but have also begun to raise dairy cows in sheds. They thus bridge cultivation and pastoralism, and their way of life prompts us to explore how they raise cows and work the crops at the same time. What impact does the combination have on their family lives? Here, too, the concept of labor substitutability will be of use.

The Setting

Middle Village was settled late. Two-fifths of all present residents were migrants; only seven percent came before 1949. They were fleeing famines of the "three year disaster" which followed the Great Leap Forward or the Cultural Revolution's chaos. Mainly from the rural areas of neighboring Liaoning and Heilongjiang provinces, they came to make their livings as they had before, by farming. Even today most township residents (81 percent) have rural registration; everyone in our sample farms.

Middle Village, in Daur township, is further than Tranquillity from a train station and from Zhalantun, the closest city. We studied three natural villages that, together, form Middle Village. They are less than two kilometers apart and seven kilometers from the township center. When the Japanese invaded China in 1931, they brought families of Daur nationality from Heilongjiang to live and work here. The area was then mainly wild land, with a small area of poor pasture. The Daur settled and converted some pasture to cultivation. In 1933, Daur became a township.

Population size and composition have changed from a majority of Daur to only a few.[30] In 1988 there were 676 people in our study sites, nearly all of them Han. Manchus, Mongols, Daur, and Koreans each constituted only one percent of our research population. While Han are now the majority, the township head, one of two deputy heads, and the Party Secretary are Daur; a second deputy head is Mongol. Only the deputy Party Secretary is Han. Nominally, then, minority people still have a presence here. Like those in Tranquillity, however, Daur's ethnic minorities are today much like their Han neighbors in culture and language. No Han and very few minority residents can speak a language other than Chinese.[31]

Making a Living in Middle Village

As in Tranquility, it is hard to improve living standards through farming. The main difference has to do with how families add to their farm income.

Nonagricultural sidelines offer less promise because it is harder to get to a major urban center. The local government has therefore encouraged dairying. Villagers have too little pasture to support large herds, but there is enough to graze some cows. Mostly they raise dairy cows in sheds, buying fodder from other places. Dairying was added to a more traditional cultivating regime. Here, too, farming still determines income and the division of labor, and through them, other social and cultural features of Middle Village.

Land and Animal Resources. When the shift to family responsibility took place here in 1982, land was partially allocated by the number of workers in a family, and in part by the number of household members.[32] The average holding then was also between five and six *mu* per person. The contract term was 15 years. There, too, the community set up a reserve to adjust for changes in population. In practice, families with newborns, or members added by marriage, wait for an allocation, since most reserve land is rented out on three year contracts.[33]

People mainly plant crops (principally soybeans and corn) to meet subsistence needs and contract quotas. Here, too, they use about a quarter of what they produce. But Middle Village farmers will not grow anything that needs a continuous input of labor, that might compete with more lucrative dairying. Cultivating grain demands periodic labor and grain farmers still have time to raise a few head of dairy cows. Moreover, farmers can feed corn stalks to their livestock. Vegetables and potatoes would take more labor and would find no ready market. Farmers therefore give less land to them here (see Table 2.1).

In 1987, cultivation provided about the same proportion of income as in Tranquillity (see Table 2.2). But dairying displaces other sidelines in Middle Village, and contributes a larger part of overall income than do sidelines in Tranquillity. Sales of milk alone account for 21 percent of farm income. But dairying is only recent; under the commune farming had been the mainstay of local economy. People started to raise cows in small numbers only in 1979 when they were distributed to households on an experimental basis. The commune also had some cows. They were managed poorly, however, and there were considerable losses. The number of milk cows in Daur township rose from 195 in 1979, to 900 head by 1982, and up further to 1,250 by 1987. Nearly every household had cows by 1987. The average number per dairying household was only four, however, and not all of them yielded milk. The number of cows continues to rise.

To support the growing number of animals, pasture must be improved. Farmers are not allowed to convert existing pasture into farm land now, and 800 *mu* of cultivated land have been slated for restoration to pasture. Large areas have already been reseeded. Nonetheless, scarce pasture holds down herd sizes. Because families cannot raise many animals, they try instead to increase milk yields by improving animal stock through artificial insemination. Over 80 percent of the cows are now of higher yielding variety, and milk production has increased. The township produced only 160 tons of milk in 1979, but by 1987 production reached 985 tons. Production was high enough by 1985 to start a regular milk collection station.

Combining Tasks. Dairying, like cultivation, uses much family labor. Eighteen percent of all households have six or more dairy cows. It takes both women and men to farm and also care for family herds. About one-third of all working age villagers do so.

Farm expenses reflect the needs of both cultivation and dairying (see Table 2.3). Villagers spend a lot on fodder and feed supplements because of the shortage of pasture. They also pay some wages to cowherds. The mean production cost per Han household here in 1987 was 1,267 RMB, much higher than Tranquillity's 845 RMB. Feed and supplements came to fully one-third of this amount. Although costs have risen rapidly in recent years, dairying is still worthwhile, and there are few other ways to improve upon farm income. Only 10 percent of Han households earned wages in 1987, and wages paid out were a small fraction of production costs.[34]

A few families earn extra money providing services, or process or make things with local products. Some gather medicinal herbs, mill grain, make bean curd cakes, grow mushrooms, make soy sauce, cut hair, or chop wood, for example. But families that raise cows cannot afford to put time into such sidelines, and they are also restrained by the lack of markets.

Division of Labor. Women and men share field and garden work more equally than in Tranquillity. While other sidelines make use of free labor during slacks in the cultivating cycle, dairying calls for a continuous, additional input of labor. Dairymen milk, feed, and water the animals, and clean their stalls every day, even during busy farming periods. Women replace men more often than in Tranquillity to relieve them for work with the family cows. One woman can handle the milking, domestic chores, and also help in the fields, although she has to work hard to do it all.

Nearly a third of all working age Han tend dairy cows. To some extent, small herds keep in check the problem of doing very different sorts of work. Farmers also hire cowboys to graze some of their cows on nearby pastures during the daytime, and feed the rest in sheds. Villagers grow some of the fodder they need and buy the rest. Thus there is no need to travel far, nor do they spend much time away cutting hay for their animals. Because animals and stalls are close by and women labor in the fields and in dairying, people here can raise cows and attend to their fields as well.

Because of the heavy demand on labor farming makes, Middle Villagers blur the labor division by sex, in pastoral work and in farming. In theory, women are responsible for milking while men maintain the sheds, graze the animals in summer, and feed and water them in winter. But women also farm and men often help with the milking. When men are busy in the fields, women help in the sheds.[35]

Although teenagers and young adults of both sexes help with farming and cows, dairying requires maturity. Inattention, carelessness, and mistakes can be costly and irreversible, which is why young people tend animals less than adults. Still, even they can substitute for adults for some purposes. Girls can help with milking, and all teenagers can help clean sheds. They contribute to pastoral work indirectly, by helping with farming to relieve adults for work with the family cows.

Older folks, those 65 and over, still farm, although they do less than people in their middle years. Experience can be more important than strength, however, so older men can relieve younger families members for more arduous field work by tending cows. Nearly half the elderly men in Middle Village tend cows; some even help with milking. They do more work with animals than teenagers.

In both farming villages, then, the proximity of homes and places of work, together with the discontinuous nature of farming, make it possible for women and men to stand in for each other. This is how Tranquillity villagers can undertake sidelines to supplement their limited income from cultivation, and Middle villagers combine farming with dairying.

Summary

Inner Mongolian farmers have little control over the timing of work. Nature dictates that. They prepare fields, plant, and later harvest their crops at much the same time on many small plots. The season is short and they must finish before the frost. During busy periods everyone is busy, and reliance on people and draft animals, not machines, makes work slow. This makes great demands on family labor during peak times, but creates a surplus at others. When busy, families use all labor, male and female, old and young. Since they till fields close to home, domestic chores do not keep women from helping. Between peaks of labor demand, all family members can turn to sidelines. The boundary between women's and men's work is less well defined than in the pastoral sites we visit in later chapters.

Because farming is not especially profitable, and not expandable, alternatives are attractive. Flexible use of labor makes them possible. Sidelines in Tranquillity and dairying in Middle Village thus add to farm income. But limited capital, lack of convenient and sizeable markets, poor communications and transportation, and scarce natural resources conspire to limit the profitability of most sidelines. This stands in the way of a more elaborate diversification like that found in the coastal and southern farming regions of China.

Notes

1.   Clifford Geertz (1970). Owen Lattimore anticipated the problem inherent in Geertz's linkage between upland and extensive cultivation:

> Wittfogel, surveying the relevant material, makes the point that there have been considerable misconceptions, especially among Western observers and students, regarding a supposedly more intensive Southern agriculture and more extensive Northern agriculture. There are undoubtedly differences in the degree of intensiveness as between the rice paddies of the South and mid-China and the millet and wheat and beans of the North. In kind, however, they are not different. The agricultural economy of the North is as intensive as the social organization of the Chinese can make it. . . .In the North, as in the South, the determining consideration is the farming of the best land, the concentration of the most people on the most productive land, and multiple cropping in order to keep the land and the people busy (Lattimore 1962:36-37).

2.   Other examples of points earned per day of work in 1979 are: storekeepers 10 points per day; shepherds 11 points; workers that fed penned animals 11 points; horse drivers 14 points; spring plowing and spreading seed, 14 points.

3.   Under the collectives, private plots were reassigned often causing problems for those who put labor and resources into their land, only to lose it to another family or to the collective fields (Oi 1989:138). This redistribution problem continues in Tranquillity today.

4.   The grain ration (*kouliang*) consisted of a basic grain ration and a work point component. The state guaranteed each peasant a basic grain ration, which they had to pay for or go into debt. The second component included grain and cash. Since the number of people (*kou*, literally mouths) in a household determined the basic distribution, hardworking peasants with many work points but few mouths might receive less than those who did less work but had more children (Oi 1989:33-40).

5.   The problem was common to Chinese communities generally. In a recent study of rural development in the Yangzi delta, Huang summarized it as follows:

> My best evidence is qualitative: the fact that all peasants interviewed on the subject agree that there had been much loitering work under the collectives, that people tend to finish their work much more quickly under the family-responsibility system, and that once finished, people will go off to do other things, including resting and "playing." Pressed for a quantitative scale of the

differences in work efficiency between the two kinds of work organization, most say that for normal farm work outside of the busy periods, the same jobs now take only two-thirds as much time as in the old days (Huang 1990:220).

6.   Between 1958 and 1960 work point value peaked at 0.3 RMB. An increase in population during the 1960s lowered its value. In 1966, one point was worth about 0.2 RMB, but by 1977 work point value dropped to under 0.1 RMB and kept going down.

Huang (1990:199-200) argues that the collective could better tolerate lower marginal returns to labor than a capitalist enterprise which hired workers. The goal was universal employment rather than simply increased labor output. This encouraged a dependence on labor rather than capital investment, but it also contributed to a drop in consumption.

7.   In a recent study of rural development in the Yangzi Delta, for example, Huang observed that the new system,

dramatically changed things for peasant women. . . .In both North China and the Yangzi delta, women had served mainly as auxiliary farm labor, to be drawn on to differing degrees depending on need. Even in the Yangzi delta, where farm production was comparatively more familized, women were far from being involved full time in agriculture month in and month out. The coming of the collective workpoint system brought women fully into production and remunerated them according to their labor (although payment was made in practice to the head of the household) (Huang 1990:201).

8.   During the first allocation, 20 percent of team land was divided in terms of the number of family laborers (three *mu* of land for each). The rest was divided according to number of family members, over four *mu* for each person. Men were considered full, and women only half labor. During subsequent allocations land was distributed only by number of family members, regardless of age or sex. The distribution was similar elsewhere in Inner Mongolia (Howard 1988:55).

9.   The mean per capita area reported by Potter and Potter (1989:108) for the Guangdong commune they studied, excluding the town population, was 1.3 *mu*. However, the growing season is much longer in China's southeastern provinces, and multiple cropping is possible.

10.   This piece of land is called *kouliang* (see endnote 4 above). At present the term refers to tax and quota free land which supplies household grain.

11.   In all of the sites we visited, key government positions at the local level were in the hands of minority people. Here, the *zhen* Head is Ewenke; a Deputy Head is Korean. A second Deputy Head is Han, the Party Secretary and the Vice Party Secretary are both Han.

12.   For a general discussion of the low level of social services at the village level today, see Feuchtwang (1987).

13.   As Pat Howard notes:

Although Yunnan and Inner Mongolia are both border regions inhabited by ethnic minorities, there is a world of difference between the monsoon climate and tropical forests and gardens of Xishuangbanna and farming on the arid Inner Mongolian plateau where dry winds and sand from the Gobi Desert blast and dehydrate the land and its crops almost daily. In this environment can be found some of the worst poverty in China. . . .Production is relatively undiversified -- mostly millet, wheat, oats, potatoes, sunflowers, sugar beets, and soy beans. Vegetables are grown on land near city and town markets where peasant incomes are consequently much higher. But for peasants located far from urban markets, the prospects for development of lucrative sidelines are much more limited. The consequent relative poverty of these areas is quite visible (1988:55).

14. The borrower usually gives a small payment in kind for use of the land and pays the required taxes and quotas (Howard 1988). The situation is different elsewhere. In Shanxi (1983), for example, only one-third of peasant households remained engaged in diversified farming. Another third specialized in industrial or sideline production, or services, and the rest were in specialized commodity production, and they cultivated 58 percent of responsibility land, supplying grain for most of the other households (Croll 1987b:113).

15. For example, Huang (1990:218,355) found that industry and sidelines together provided 79 percent of total production value in Huayang (1983) and sixty-four percent in China (1986).

16. Forty-three percent of all Han households in Tranquillity owned at least one draft animal, with a mean of 2.7 for owning households. Only four percent had six or more cows.

17. One farmer described rotation procedures and their relationship to tenure security as follows:

In summer I no longer have to work in the fields, my three sons plant my 50 *mu* without too much difficulty. This year we planted 10 *mu* in corn, 5 in potatoes, 20 in soybeans, 5 in sugar beets, and 3 *mu* of sweet melons. We didn't plant millet because we sold our horses last year. When we had horses we needed millet straw for winter and early spring fodder. The other reason we didn't plant millet is that, when the brigade reallocated farm land at the end of last year, we received nearly 50 *mu*, but we couldn't be sure what the previous cultivators had grown on particular plots. If I planted millet in the wrong sequence my yields would drop off sharply.

This is a question of crop rotation. You cannot plant the same crop on the same field repeatedly, you must rotate with other crops. If you plant soybeans one year, then you should plant corn or millet the next. If you plant millet, then you should plant potatoes or corn the next year. If potatoes, then next you should plant corn. If you put in sugar beets, then next year choose either millet or corn. Corn can always be planted, even after itself. But if you plant yellow beans twice, production may decline 50 to 70 percent the second time. That's yet another reason why I didn't plant millet this time.

18. Farmers sell corn and soybeans mainly to state procurement agencies. In 1989, they delivered 32 percent of Tranquillity's corn-soybean yield to the state, of which 44 percent was sold at the lower price. In 1989, to meet their basic quotas, farmers delivered an average of 10.77 kg of soybeans and 8.25 kg of corn at quota prices for each *mu* of land they cultivated. Millet, sugar beets, and various beans are sold to state procurement agencies, closer to market prices. Figures for Middle Village (1987) show that those prices exceeded both the controlled and the above quota prices offered by the state, by one-quarter or more. The same is probably true for Tranquillity.

19. The team remits most of the management fee to the village (brigade), retaining only 2 RMB per household. The fee subsumes a number of separate levies; a "public relations fee" which underwrites official entertainment, a fee of .05 RMB per *mu* for running the village old age home, and 0.1 RMB per *mu* as subsidy for retired soldiers. In addition to these assessments, every family must provide three days of "compulsory public labor", or 3 RMB per day per household member, regardless of age or sex. The obligation should be assigned according to the number of "laborers" a family has, but local cadres claim that "it is really difficult to decide who is and who is not labor."

20. Fully 73 percent of all households without tractors also own at least one draft animal, the average is two. A substantial proportion (20 percent) have neither a tractor nor a draft animal. They borrow animals or machines, trading fuel tickets for help with their crops. Even farmers with tractors usually own a draft animal.

21. The distribution system for gasoline and diesel fuel is the same as for chemical fertilizer. Extra rations are available at the negotiated price, the amount varies and depends on both objective criteria, such as the amount of work one has contracted, and subjective criteria relating to position and connections.

22. Some farmers did use these sheets as part of a 1987 government financed experiment. When the experiment was over, however, few could afford to repeat it on their own.

23. The mean grain yield in *jin* per *mu* rose from 340 in 1985, to 602 in 1988. Increased use of chemical fertilizers and tractors contributed to this rise.

24. Although farmers in the Yangzi delta can easily buy fertilizer and other inputs (cf. Huang 1990), they are less available here. Oi (1986a) argues that, because of insufficient fertilizer, fuel, and other supplies, peasants still depend on cadre discretion for distribution.

25. Seventy-one percent of Han households owned a pig. The mean per household was 1.8 in 1987, or 2.5 per household raising pigs.

26. Urban registered households can get coal in this area, rural ones cannot.

27. We constructed a detailed list of tasks for each major crop and activity and asked people to rate every household member as "doing a lot", "doing some", "doing a little", or "doing none" of the work involved. We draw upon that survey here, and upon what we learned during regular interviews. Our account thus relies on their observations rather than our own.

28. See Potter and Potter (1989:321-323), Howard (1988:77-96), and Huang (1990:288-291). Oi (1989:190-191) found that as sidelines and enterprises developed, a land surplus emerged because a significant proportion of the population left farming. Some areas even invite outsiders to contract farmland to

run as a family firms (*jiating nongchang*). While Hinton (1990) is highly critical of this trend away from agriculture, Huang (1990:214-218) contends that farming has actually become the "nonprofitable" sideline in the Yangzi area. The trend is not universal, however. As in our area, Croll (1987b:113-4) reports fewer specialized households in inland China than in the coastal regions.

29. Only 14 percent of Tranquillity households reported earning wages in 1987, but 70 percent reported income from sidelines.

30. In 1949, Daur township had a population of 3,962, of which 59 percent were Daur, 34 percent Han, and the remainder Ewenke, Mongol or Korean. By 1966, the population had grown to 4,375, with Han comprising 61 percent. By 1985, it reached 11,032, and Han were then 81 percent of the population while Daur and Mongols constituted only 12 and 4 percent respectively.

31. Of 11 male and 14 minority females in our sample, only one man and three women reported that they could speak a minority language "at least a little," but all spoke Chinese fluently.

32. Number of family members determined the distribution of roughly 70 percent of the land, although there was variation from brigade to brigade.

33. The tax on such land is higher than normal. The regular *chengbaofei* (contract tax) here is 10 RMB per *mu*. For land contracted from reserve on a short term basis assessments range from 15-20 RMB.

34. Although Han families spent only three percent of all production costs on wages, fully 42 percent did pay some wages, mainly to cowboys for pasturing cows daily. The mean paid was only 102 RMB, however.

35. Over two-fifths of the working age people that reported tending dairy cows were women. Nearly half of all women watered cows, and two-thirds milked them.

3

Chinese Farmers: Economy and Society

Cultivation is still the bedrock of domestic economy in Tranquillity and Middle Village. Farmers have always had to work long, hard hours during certain phases of the cultivation cycle but, with return to a family based system, people work even harder at new combinations of tasks. Many want to take on additional family projects, apart from farming, to improve their income. The way families deploy their labor thus affects standards of living and economic differentiation within the community. As some farmers start sidelines to escape the constraints of land, their new uses of labor also echo in their family lives. In this chapter we look at how the shift to family responsibility and associated changes in use of family labor affect economy, family structure, and features of community in the two farming villages.

Responsibility and Socioeconomic Differentiation

Farmers report that income improved with the responsibility system. Motivation increased because people not only decide for themselves what they will do with their land and labor, but also how they will spend what they make. Working harder, they have increased yields, investments, and incomes. People insist that despite problems associated with the shift to family management, more families were poor and in debt before. Even those currently in difficulty agree that life is better now.

While income has undoubtedly risen, we cannot easily use local data to compare the changes in our farming villages. Government survey quality and procedure vary from place to place, and the data upon which the figures are based can be faulty.[1] Nonetheless, they are often the only ones available, and we at least get a sense of relative change from them. These show that farmers in both villages are better off. Table 3.1 says that, adjusted for inflation, net income per person in Tranquillity rose about 30 percent in five years.[2] The figure for 1987 is close to that in our survey for that year, 594 RMB per capita for Han.[3] Income rose in Daur township

64

TABLE 3.1 Income Improvement in Tranquillity Village, 1985-1989

Year	Net Income per Person (RMB)	Adjusted Net Income per Person (RMB)
1985	423	423
1986	475	500
1987	560	552
1988	600	553
1989	800	---

Source: Data for Tranquillity were provided by the local government. To compensate for inflation we adjust Tranquillity's income by the "rural cost of living index" for Inner Mongolia in 1985 (*Source: Statistical Abstracts of China* for 1986 through 1989).

as well, although the improvement started before the shift to family responsibility, from the time dairying was introduced. Income took an upward spurt more recently, as more Middle Village families bought dairy cows.[4] Our own survey found higher per capital net income than in Tranquillity, 712 RMB per capita compared to only 594 RMB (Han).

As Table 3.2 shows, there is no difference between communities in average area cultivated, or in land distribution. It is because dairying adds so much to farm income that Middle Villagers do better. In Daur the proportion of family income accounted for by dairying rose from only three percent in 1978 to 30 percent by 1985. In Middle Village cows contributed 25 percent of income in 1987, an average of 1,099 RMB per household. In Tranquillity other sidelines provided only 19 percent of income, an average of only 705 RMB per household.

Income Distribution

Income has generally risen, but have some people become poor even as others prospered? A 1989 survey exploring income distribution in a sample of Hulunbuir League villages found that this was not the case. Only seven percent of rural households were below a "poverty line" officially defined as 200 RMB per person.[5] In contrast, 31 percent of the households were "wealthy," earning over 800 RMB per person (*Hulunbuir Bao*, May 29, 1990).

TABLE 3.2 Land Cultivated by Location: Han 1987

Area (mu)	Tranquillity (%)	Middle Village (%)
None	0.9	1.5
1-29	61.3	64.4
30-69	34.9	32.6
70 and over	2.8	1.5
Mean per person (mu)	5.9	5.6
No. households	106	132

Hulunbuir villagers earn little because the League is remote, with poor communications; commerce, manufacture, and services are all undeveloped. The League study found that the poor have little land and family labor, low capital investment, low educational levels, and high dependency ratios; few take up nonagricultural sidelines. The wealthy farmed an average area 70 percent larger, and enjoyed twice the fixed assets of production. Every poor worker supported two dependents; the wealthy supported only 1.8.[6] Poor families earned only five percent of their income from nonagricultural sources, the wealthy eight percent.

As Table 3.3 shows, the same proportion of households were "poor" in our two farming villages in 1987. Although there were a few truly poor households in each, we did not find great poverty or striking inequality (see also Nee 1989). Further, we must be careful when we define poverty by income alone. Families can experience a loss during any one year due to some unusual expense -- a marriage, purchase of a tractor, equipment repair. And informants commonly exaggerate expenses but underestimate income.

While there can be little doubt that income has risen, is it equitably distributed? And what are current living standards like? Middle Village income was about average for the League; in Tranquillity it was below. The proportion of wealthy families was higher than in the League, but lower in Tranquillity. The income spread (Gini) was much the same in the two villages, however. Without reliable data over time, we cannot precisely describe trends. Still, villagers perceive that the new climate has increased income disparity. They know that some people work harder and use their resources more imaginatively than others, and they see families diverging. What then are the factors responsible for differences within communities?

TABLE 3.3 Per Capita Income by Location: Han 1987

Income (RMB)	Tranquillity (%)	Middle Village (%)
200 or less	6.7	6.8
201-400	25.7	18.2
401-600	26.7	23.5
601-800	21.9	15.2
801-1000	7.6	16.7
1001-1200	3.8	6.8
1201-1400	4.8	5.3
1401+	2.9	7.6
Gini	.34	.32
No. households	105	132

Land and Income

Land is still the single most important resource upon which people depend. In both communities together, the "wealthy" farmed areas 40 percent larger than the "poor".[7] And simple regressions indicate that, in each community, families with the most land and crop earnings enjoyed highest overall incomes. Although Tranquillity's cultivated area has declined slightly in recent years, mainly because of flood erosion, overall production has risen.[8] The mean grain yield increased over time from 340 jin per mu in 1985, to 602 jin in 1988, mainly due to greater use of chemical fertilizers. Families with tractors also earn more than average. But not every family can afford a tractor; it is mainly the wealthier ones, those with more land, that buy them.[9] They then use their machines for sidelines as well as farming, and it is those sidelines that so greatly expand household income.

Using the official definition of poverty, of 200 RMB or less per person, there were only seven poor households in Tranquillity and nine in Middle Village. Ten out of the total 16 tilled smaller than average holdings. Only one was landless, and that was the one with an income loss in 1987. Nine now have more members than average but have not been able to increase their farm holdings or to develop sidelines sufficient to match their growth in size.

Other Sources of Income

People earn extra money selling pigs and chickens and by sidelines of various sorts. Families with sidelines in Tranquillity and those that raise dairy cows in Middle Village certainly earn more. Dairying is recent and, as one Tranquillity farmer told us, family sidelines, too, have only recently achieved sufficient respectability to become an important source of income:

> It's hard to find other ways to make money here, so people want to have their own land and to be able to decide what they will do and when they will do it. They can decide how to manage their land and how they might earn money doing other things, sidelines. Before the responsibility system, every family had a private garden plot of two to three *fen*. We could sell vegetables we grew there to make some extra money. But after the responsibility system was started, many new sidelines appeared -- collecting and sifting sand for construction, making gravel, transporting sand and gravel, cutting grass for animals, working at construction, manufacturing potato noodles, running small stores, and the like. All of this work is managed by individual families, the team has nothing to do with it.

Seventy percent of Tranquillity villagers have some sort of nonagricultural sideline.[10] They are more common there than in any of the other three locations we studied. For those that have them, sidelines add an average of 1,009 RMB to income. They contribute substantially to income differences in Tranquillity; 31 percent of the wealthy households' income came from sidelines in 1987, compared to only 10 percent for the poor.[11] Similarly in Middle Village, dairying furnished 29 percent of wealthy family income, but only seven percent in poor households.

Few earn wages in either village, and they do not make a significant contribution to income disparity.[12] The few families that depend on wages tend to be without other sources of income; simple regressions show that the more wages households earn, the less land they cultivate. Whereas sidelines complement farming, starting and stopping in rhythm with peaks and slacks, salaried work is less flexible. People with jobs cannot easily manage farms, and those that have land in Tranquillity often lend it out. Salaried workers also have little time for sidelines. However, in Middle Village a few people manage to hold regular jobs and farm. Some even raise a few dairy cows. We will find this combination of small scale dairying and salaried work more common in one of the pastoral sites we discuss in later chapters.

Education and Income

All children complete elementary school now. It is no longer the privilege of a few that it was in pre-Communist days. In Table 3.4, which combines Tranquillity and Middle Village, we see that the education of girls has especially improved. Yet education is still modest. Children and teenagers have a part to play in farming, dairying, and sidelines. While fewer than five percent of boys and girls 10 to 19 have had no formal schooling, therefore, most go no further than primary school. Around half those 15 to 19 have only a primary school education. Some attend lower middle school; few go further.

Farmers can put literacy to practical use by reading technical books and magazines on agriculture and sidelines. They can thus learn the newest ways to grow crops like sweet melon, or to raise large flocks of poultry. But beyond elementary school, education has little to offer youngsters destined to replace their parents. We find little in our data to suggest a relationship between education and income. People 16 to 64 had 5.1 years of schooling in wealthy families and only 4.4 years in poor ones, but the difference is not statistically significant (our numbers are quite small). If we compare only household heads, who make most crucial economic decisions, we again find no significant difference between poor and wealthy. The weight of the evidence is that, for people who remain in the village, there is little relationship between education attained and income.

It is no surprise that few parents see much use for education beyond elementary or middle school. Nonetheless, a few do arrange up to post-middle school education for their children. Hoping that the extra schooling may provide a way out of the community to an easier life, they are willing

TABLE 3.4 Education in Tranquillity and Middle Villages by Sex and Age: Han

Age	Males		Females	
	No.	Mean Years	No.	Mean Years
10-14	58	3.9	75	3.9
15-19	84	5.9	74	5.8
20-39	196	6.3	184	4.5
40-59	90	5.7	78	2.1
60+	51	1.2	38	0.3

to use "back door" methods to access the better schools in nearby cities. To fully realize the advantages of such education, however, the children must find a way to remain in the city, to somehow acquire urban household registration, and that is still hard to arrange.[13]

Dependency, Family Size, and Income

When land was redistributed, the team assigned some to each person. Larger families therefore received more. Even now there is a significant relationship between household size and income in the two farming villages. Better off families are generally larger; they also have fewer dependents. In poor households each worker supports 1.7 persons, compared to only 1.5 in wealthy ones.[14] But the income advantage of the wealthy households is not simply because they are larger, work bigger farms, and therefore have more income from crops. More important, families with more workers are able to improve farm income by sidelines (in Tranquillity), or raising milk cows (in Middle Village).[15] Because women and men can assume each other's farm tasks, even newly partitioned households can start a sideline. The larger families do so more easily and profitably, however, because they generally also have more land and farm income, as well as more workers.

We found that overall income is significantly related to household size, to land area, and to income from several sources: from crops, sale of smaller barnyard animals, wages, and from dairying or other non-farm sidelines. But multiple regression found that some of these variables contributed more to income differences than others. In brief, sidelines and cultivation added most to the income differences between households in Tranquillity, although wages, and income from sales of draft animals, and from smaller barnyard animals also had a significant effect. In Middle Village, dairying was most important, followed by cultivation and then sidelines.[16] In short, farming is the basis of livelihood in both communities, but households with supplementary economic activities enjoy the highest incomes (see also Huang 1990).

This finding has serious long term implications for economic stratification. Under the collective, families generally did better as they matured, as workers were added. They lost their advantage when family division reduced manpower and brought families back to the starting point of development. In that way family evolution tended to equalize incomes. Families still partition and divide land, yet something has changed. Now, the wealthy are more likely to work sidelines (in Tranquillity), and to invest most heavily in dairying (in Middle Village). They can thus maintain, even increase, their edge over others (Selden 1985). If villagers had to rely entirely upon cultivation, the income differences among households would likely be much narrower.

As it is, they are widening. The current view that modernization calls for a freeing of individual initiative has replaced older egalitarian notions at the foundation of collectives. The slogan "everyone eating out of the same big pot" has given way to "some will get rich sooner," which legitimizes the increase in earnings of some households. Still, in this society that has worked hard to root out extremes of wealth and misery, even a modest increase in inequality causes concern. However, since people here have not gotten poorer, their concern has not turned to outrage. While differences between households' earnings may have widened, most have seen their living standard get better.

Responsibility, Private Enterprise, and Labor

With family responsibility farmers, particularly those with family sidelines or dairy cows, have heavier workloads. They cannot easily reduce their problem through mechanization, which saves on human power at the expense of capital. Here, labor is cheap and capital scarce. More, the small scale of farming, and of most sidelines, makes it hard to replace human or animal power with machines. So villagers still rely as much as they can on their own labor and on draft animals.

The few large, expensive farm implements and draft animals formerly owned by teams are now the property of individual families. Since not every family owns a draft animal or tractor, people share and exchange labor, tools, animals, and expensive equipment when necessary.[17] We find no sign yet of joint ownership (see Howard 1988:97-143). Indeed, Tranquillity families prefer independence, as elsewhere in China.[18] The reluctance to formalize long term arrangements with other households may stand in the way of potentially fruitful larger scale undertakings.

Instead of depending on others, most try to increase the number of workers in their households, and to use them better. Still, few families can muster all the workers they need for some cultivating and sideline tasks and during periods of peak labor demand. They must look to close blood kin, in-laws, or friends. Partitioned brothers, in-laws, and married daughters return to help out. Farmers prefer to base cooperation on kinship ties rather than on pragmatic business considerations. Because there is no solid legal framework protecting property, the elements of capitalism -- land, capital, and even labor -- cannot be secure. Policy changes can threaten rights to property at any time, as they have in the past. Kinship, with all its ambiguities, still promises greater trust than other relationships (Landa and Salaff 1987).

Viewing traditional peasant society as a natural economy, Evans (1990:146-147) argues that collectivization bridled the flexible use of peasant household labor and the natural cooperation of families. He describes the logic of traditional cooperation and labor exchange as rough reciprocity, a delicately tuned social mechanism between equals. Evans argues that, by bringing together people not considered equals, the collective cut across and undermined the natural groupings so important in traditional production. And so it is not surprising that Tranquillity farmers limit the exchanges they strike outside the family. One described the problem as follows:

At present few farmers are eager to cooperate with others. Even working with close relatives is a problem. It's very difficult to figure out how to be fair when you divide profits. Worse, close friends and relatives can't easily discuss matters of money. So it's really hard to decide how to evaluate the different contributions made. Some of us do cooperate on a short term basis. During spring, for example, a family with a horse may try to help another horse owning family because it's better to pull one plow with two animals. But we rarely continue such short term cooperation or extend it to other activities.

Households that regularly lack hands because a member formerly registered in the village has permanently left, may return part of its land to the community reserve. Or, if the residence change is short term, they may temporarily lend some land to close kin. They are less likely to hire workers. When they do, they usually hire from nearby villages, from among families that have too little land or that are growing crops on a different cycle. Within the community, farmers are all growing much the same crops, so everyone is hard pressed at about the same time.

Changes in Living Standard

As incomes rise, more people buy consumer goods and services, and there are many more things to buy now. Forty-six percent of all Han households (villages combined) own at least one TV.[19] As Table 3.5 shows, Middle villagers are especially likely to own the more expensive household goods.

Table 3.6 breaks down living expenses in each village during 1987. Alone, these costs came to 76 percent of gross household income in Tranquillity. Thanks to dairying, Middle villagers fared slightly better. There they amounted to only 60 percent of gross income. If we consider other regular costs as well, then net income per person was only 594 RMB in Tranquillity, and 712 in Middle Village. Even if some people overstate expenses and downplay income, family budgets clearly allow little room for

TABLE 3.5 Consumer Durables by Location and Percent Households Owning at Least One: Han 1988

Item	Tranquillity (%)	Middle Village (%)
Bicycle	85	81
Clock	68	75
Clothes washer	4	11
Sewing machine	57	65
Sofa	8	18
Tape recorder	11	18
TV	35	56
Radio	42	51
Watch	42	51
No. households	106	133

emergencies, let alone for savings or investment. Some also have debts to pay, although people do not speak easily about such matters.

And many costs are rising. Families pay more to bring their children up, to feed, dress, educate, and marry them off. At the same time, children spend more time in school, delaying and reducing the economic contribution they make. Further, many major expenses once underwritten by the collective, like education and medical care, are now the family's burden.

The cost of housing, too, has been rising. The type of home people live in is one indication of their status and wealth. In Tranquillity families build houses of mud. Thanks to dairying, many Middle Village homes are newer and of more substantial construction.[20] Of all homes constructed since 1976 in the two farming sites combined, 62 percent were built after the responsibility system began. People are building more and spending more. From 1976 through 1981, they spent an average of 837 RMB for a new home; thereafter the average was 1,935 RMB.[21]

In the past, people could build anywhere within the residential area of the village. There was no limit on size, and permission was not required to start. Because of growing pressure on residential land, cadres now require builders to apply for permission to build, and pay a sizable fee. Building lots are limited to four hundred square meters, including garden space.

TABLE 3.6 Living Costs in Tranquillity and Middle Villages: Han 1987*

Cost Item	Tranquillity		Middle Village	
	Mean per Household	(%)	Mean per Household	(%)
Durables	84	3	88	3
Education	66	2	55	2
Food	1,358	49	1,492	55
Housing	196	7	309	11
Medical	294	10	201	7
Nondurables	300	11	281	10
Other Social	169	6	134	5
Ritual	334	12	182	7
Totals	2,780	100	2,719	100

*"Living costs" include amounts paid for purchased items and the value of food produced calculated in local market prices. "Food" includes meat, grain, supplements, dairy products, tobacco, tea, and liquor consumed. "Other social" costs include transportation and miscellaneous cultural-social expenses. The proportional contribution of all items to overall living costs did not differ significantly between cultivating sites.

And gardens are now barely large enough to grow vegetables for the family to eat.[22]

The Cost of Marriage

Marriage is no longer the simple matter it was during more spartan years of Chinese communism. Cadres now tolerate greater ritual display, and villagers, wealthier than before, spend much more. Parents prepare long in advance, diverting a great deal of energy and value from other possible uses. Kin and neighbors have come to expect lavish feasts. Bridewealth given by the groom's side, and dowry by the bride's, not only endow a new marriage but also measure social position. For that reason parents parade a dowry throughout a village, even if its destination is a groom's family next door.

We asked villagers to recall budgets for past marriages. It is not a simple matter to obtain such estimates, however, because people forget, and because the value of things has changed. Nonetheless, the estimates show a dramatic increase in the cost of marriage since 1979, especially after the shift to a privatized economy. Comparing Han marriage expenses in both villages for 1960-1978 with those in 1979-1988, we find a substantial increase for both groom and bride.

Getting children married is probably the heaviest burden any family must bear. Marriage has traditionally been much more costly for the groom. Nearly all men married during 1960-1978 spent something; the mean was 844 RMB. During 1979-1988, the amount doubled to 1,684 RMB.[23] We may consider 3,000 RMB or more spent on the groom's side to be costly by local standards since it represents more than a year's income. Nonetheless, households spending that much rose from one to 16 percent from 1960 to 1988.[24] The proportion spending less than 1,000 RMB declined from 65 to only 23 percent.

The costs of marrying daughters have also increased. Only half the families that married off daughters during the first period reported expenditures. But as income improved during the second period, 75 percent had expenses to report, a significant increase. The amounts increased as well. If we define "costly" marriages on the bride's side as 500 RMB or over, then the proportion of such marriages rose from 6 percent during the first period, to 17 percent during the second. Parents spent a mean of 201 RMB during the first period, but 329 RMB in the second.

The money mainly went for dowries and small family feasts. The absolute value of dowries was never large. Rarely was it large enough to determine a woman's marital prospects or to assure voice in her husband's family. By not coming empty handed, however, a bride did get more status and leverage in her husband's family.

Some scholars view bridewealth as repayment for the lost services of daughters, a loss undoubtedly more keenly felt when women's work outside the home contributes a lot to the domestic economy. Such is the case in these villages, where women toil in fields, work sidelines, or raise cows. Since a bride lives with her husband's family at marriage, his people profit most from her adult labor. Villagers find it reasonable, therefore, that the groom's parents should compensate her parents for the energy and money they spent raising her. Village cadres have long discouraged such transactions, pejoratively labelling them "feudal." Yet, nearly a quarter of all grooms marrying in 1960-1978, and again in 1979-1988, paid bridewealth. Even those with little income often did so.[25]

Parents take some time to save even the smaller sums needed to marry daughters off. Ability to marry daughters properly is another indication of rising income and improved station in life. Many people also believe that it is only appropriate that some family property flow to daughters in the form of dowries, since daughters have helped produce family assets. Still, some families were content to receive compensation for their daughter's labor without giving dowry in return. Bridewealth without dowry was significantly more common than dowry without bridewealth during both periods. The net flow of wealth to the bride's parents reflects the special importance of women's labor.

After marriage there are still other expenses. At some point in its development every family divides, and people save money for partitioning sons. The task has become greater in recent years because sons partition earlier. People have to work harder to achieve ever rising standards. No one would want to reverse these changes, but they do lead people to rethink older notions about marriage, family division, and family reproduction.

Patterns of Marriage

To take best advantage of the new, privatized economy, families need enough labor. They build the family work force through marriage. Under the collective, a daughter-in-law not only shared domestic work, she also handed over the value of work points she earned in collective fields. Under the new system women make an even greater and more varied contribution, so families are still keen to bring in daughters-in-law early. And as before, people evaluate prospective daughters-in-law by how they will fit into the family work force.

Finding Brides

What then does one look for in a mate for a son or daughter? Villagers prefer partners similar in education. In 86 percent of marriages (both sites combined), husbands had as much or only a few more years of formal education.[26] As well, people with urban registration prefer to see children marry others with similar registration. To marry someone with rural registration would not upgrade the registration of the rural partner. For their part, rural folk may worry that a city girl cannot farm. Ethnic groups may intermarry, however. Not only are the minorities' language, custom, behavior, and economy like the Han's, they are so few that they only provide a small pool of eligible mates. For that reason, minority women are significantly more likely to intermarry than Han. Of 31 minority women in our Tranquillity survey, 68 percent took Han husbands; only 13 percent of 109 Han women married minority men.[27]

Villagers often choose local girls, which also eases bringing them into the household work force. Communities in this area usually contain families of many different surnames, so although Han dislike marrying within the same descent group, they can still find mates locally. Further, Han Chinese on this frontier have long had special reason to look close for marriage partners. From the outset, Han were surrounded by people culturally quite different from themselves, with whom relationships were not always friendly. The basic contest was not between Han of different agnatic or regional origin, but between Han and others. That encouraged alliance building within the community, and marriage was an important means to that end.[28]

Community endogamous marriage has been most common in Tranquillity.[29] Han settled earlier there, displacing or sinicizing the few minority peoples they found, so the pool of eligible Han spouses has been larger. More Middle villagers are migrants. Many of the earlier ones were either married before they came or sent for spouses from their home region after arrival. They still wished to maintain ties to their home province.[30]

Marriage Age

The burden of farm work is so heavy that the elderly cannot do without the help of a strong son or son-in-law and at least one younger woman. Thus, to ensure their own eventual replacement, parents bear sons and provide them with wives as early as possible. Daughters-in-law replace departing daughters, and family reproduction begins early. Croll (1983:12) notes that during the collective people could not hire workers, so marriage was the main way to add household labor. The new economy has only increased the amount, variety, and importance of women's work. Because their economic and reproductive contributions are important, parents remain eager to see children marry early.

But the government has had a different agenda. To slow population growth, it has pressed people to delay marriage (Tien 1991). The Marriage Law of the People's Republic of China (1950) set legal marriage at 20 for men and 18 for women. During the 1970s, the state urged even later marriage (25 for men and 23 for women) and used administrative delays to bring that about. The revised Marriage Law (1980) raised the legal ages to 22 for men and 20 for women but, at the same time, cadres relaxed administrative restraints that had earlier promoted late marriage. As a result, people married closer to the legal ages (Coale 1987; Hardee-Cleaveland & Banister 1988:269-70). The dissolution of the commune also undermined the ability of cadres to delay marriage. At the same time, privatization increased household labor needs, thus encouraging earlier marriage.

From 1950 through 1988, the mean age at marriage for men in Tranquillity and Middle Village combined was 22.3; women married at 20.1.[31] Although they have to confront disapproving cadres, many couples still marry under the legal age. Thus, 15 percent of the men and 18 percent of women married since 1950 wed below the legal ages established in 1950. When the thresholds were raised in 1980, actual marriage age changed little.[32] People time marriage as much to suit their needs as to follow the law, and they truly need to bring daughters-in-law in early as extra workers. In villages elsewhere in China, the average age of marriage has even declined in recent years (Banister 1987:152-165; Potter and Potter 1989:238).

Family and Kinship

Before collectivization, when families controlled the means of production, each person depended on the family head. People preferred "stem" families (parents and a married son), which ensure care for the elderly. They also supply more workers for the recurrent peaks in labor need characteristic of farming, and especially unirrigated farming. In some areas of China, families invested capital and personnel beyond farming: in crafts, small businesses, or in salaried employment. As Cohen has pointed out, such multi-enterprise family investment often delayed partition. This sometimes resulted in "joint" families consisting of married brothers and their parents (Cohen 1976).[33] By remaining together, married brothers could save on labor and capital, and move both from enterprise to enterprise. When the households that comprised the complex family lived apart, they could best avoid the strife that so often forced the family to divide. Unusual technological considerations might also inhibit family division (Cohen 1976, Pasternak 1983). But in these farming villages there has been little nonfarm investment and no special technological reasons to delay family division.

The joint family was usually fragile and short-lived. Strife among women eventually triggered division. Conflicts flowed from the nature of property relations. Following Chinese custom, property passed from father to sons. The practice underlay conflicts between mother and daughter-in-law and between sisters-in-law, all of whom depended on men for access to the family estate. A woman tried to exert some control first through her husband, and then through her sons. But the sons' wives also sought some control through their husbands, trying to defend the interests of their own nuclear units against similar ones within the larger family (see M. Wolf 1972). If there were several married sons, their wives, in competition with each other as well as with their mother-in-law, put so much pressure on the family that it eventually divided.

The dynamics changed with collectivization, when income came mainly from work points earned. As Evans notes, the cooperative system "clearly advertises the relative contributions of each member of the family and therefore can loosen or undermine the bonds of dependency and the sources of authority within the peasant family" (1990:129). In effect, when individuals became wage earners, family heads lost much of the economic control they had, along with their ability to diversify family investments. There was also a change in inheritance, and any transition to ownership in common is likely to weaken the control of family heads.

As a result of these changes, the family was easier to divide. A couple could more readily establish independence, and might even increase income if partition left them with fewer dependents to support. Even then, someone had to care for the elderly and infirm, those who earned few work points. Stem families were therefore still common under the collective. But married brothers rarely remained long in the same family because there was little reason to do so.

The stem family still suits the way people work their farms. Young couples benefit because there may be two males to handle men's work.[34] It is even more useful to have more than one woman, since it is hard for one person to combine farming and domestic work. Each family's burden has increased, while farming has remained labor intensive. Under the circumstances, even aging parents can help. By sharing domestic work, they relieve younger family members for work in the fields or at sidelines, and they can help during periods of peak demand. So long as families remain together, then, they can depend less on others.

The elderly also benefit, of course. Today, with family limitation and rising life expectancy, the proportion of older dependents to supporters increases. But rural workers still do not enjoy the security of pensions, and indeed, social services have shrunk since the collective was disbanded (Feuchtwang 1987). By living together with married children, aging people can gradually transfer their burdens to younger workers and at the same time get their help.

Stresses invariably build, however, eventually to the point where the family can no longer contain them. Since land is now apportioned on a per capita basis, the family head cannot keep sons from leaving by threatening to deny them land. Even new brides can anticipate an eventual allocation of community land. By apportioning the most important means of production to individuals rather than families, then, the new system assures a certain independence and facilitates family division. In the course of time, all but one son normally leaves to set up independent households.

After partition or out-marriage, parents cannot use economic controls to command the support and help of children living independently. Practical and moral considerations encourage their continued help, however.

Villagers would still consider children unfilial were they to abandon their parents after family division, and public morality still has great force. When they finance costly marriages, moreover, parents create powerful obligations that children cannot easily ignore. Although parents can no longer use control over productive resources to compel support, these other ties still bind. Thus, 21 percent of all Han households in the two villages supported kin.[35]

When family division does occur, it usually results in a stem family and one or more independent conjugal units. At any point in time, therefore, we find mostly nuclear families in the community. Average household size in the two villages combined was 4.9 persons in 1987, the mean for rural China generally (*Zhongguo Tongji* 1989: 726, 742).[36] However, households may be similar in size yet differ in composition.

In both communities people still prefer patrilocal to neolocal marriage. Three-quarters of women married after 1948 lived with their husband's parents at marriage. Neolocal marriages are even less common now than under the collectives. Their percentage dropped significantly from 29 in the period 1955-1982 to only 11 percent of all marriages during 1983-1988. Sons rarely move out when they marry; departures normally occur some time later.[37] Stem families are therefore common. Now, 30 percent of all households in these communities are stem, 37 percent of the population live in stem families, and nearly everyone has done so.[38]

The diversification of family enterprises in recent years has also encouraged stem families by putting a premium on keeping women as well as men under one roof. The new tolerance of family investment and economic diversification could eventually produce more joint families as well if, for example, the combination of family sidelines were to call even more for the labor of several adults of the same sex. At present, however, stem families can handle most non-farm work.

Few families are very large and complex, but neither are there many very simple ones. Only three percent of all families consist of couples or individuals living alone.[39] Very rarely do the elderly live alone. Because they cannot farm on their own, those that do usually make their living from some easier to handle sideline. One elderly Tranquillity villager makes a modest living gathering and selling traditional medicinal herbs, for example. Another runs a small local cafe. An elderly Middle Village couple earns a meager living from a pair of dairy cows. But people do not think independent living is ideal for the aging.

For all families, independence can only be temporary. At some point everyone must cooperate with others. Family composition is constantly changing, so every household can expect to have too little or too much labor at times. Indeed, most find it necessary to reach out for help during periods of peak labor demand. They exchange labor and share equipment with people on whom they feel they can rely. They turn first to close agnatic kin, to brothers and sons. They are more likely to live close by than married daughters and sisters. But even relatives by marriage may exchange labor since they, too, are often nearby. The bond between parents and daughters, or between brothers and sisters, tenuous and unsung in tradition, can be important nonetheless. Here daughters are not "lost" to their natal families at marriage; the bond with parents usually continues to be strong.[40] As our case studies will show, when called upon for help, married daughters and their husbands sometimes lend labor, equipment, and money.

Farming and Family Reproduction

In addition to early marriage, villagers have long favored having many children to ensure that some will survive. The problem was especially pressing in pre-Communist days when there were high rates of infant mortality. But even under collectives there were many advantages and few disadvantages to having numerous children. Raising them was not too costly, since medical care, education, and other services were subsidized. By guaranteeing food to poor families, even those in debt, the distribution system underwrote fertility (Nee 1985). Marrying children off, particularly under austere socialist policies, cost little, and all family members could do some sort of farm work. In recent years, state policy and changed economic conditions discourage many children.

Pre-Family Planning Fertility

Pre-family planning conditions favored reproduction; ever married Han women 40 and over in the two farming villages have a mean parity of 6.4. Early marriage gave a timely reproductive start. On average, women bore their first child at 20. The nature of work also raised fertility levels through the impact on nursing. The duration and frequency of breast feeding is one of the most important proximate determinants of fertility.[41]

Women were aware that prolonged and frequent nursing inhibits conception. In fact many told us that nursing used to be their way to control child spacing and childbearing. Some intentionally prolonged nursing to delay conception, and thus to protect recently born infants. But even when mothers wanted to nurse often and long, they were not always in a position to do so because of the work they did. Mothers that regularly left home to work in family fields were often not present to nurse their infants. This could have made women more fecund (Van Esterik and

Greiner 1981). As well, frequent infant deaths might have resulted in shorter birth intervals and higher fertility.

Responses to Family Planning

In recent years, Tranquillity and Middle villagers have changed their reproductive behavior. There are both anti- and pro-natalist pressures on peasant families. While infant and child mortality have declined, farming continues to reward above replacement fertility. However, since the early 1980s, the state's systematic attempts to limit childbearing to one or two children and the increasing cost of raising children has worked against bearing many offspring.

In 1978, family planning became a basic national policy. In 1979 the government announced its "one child" policy, with inducements and sanctions to reduce the number of births rapidly to one child per couple. In 1982-1983, there was almost mandatory IUD insertion for women with one child, abortions for unauthorized pregnancies, and sterilization for couples with two or more children. Implementation of the family limitation program was especially strict in 1983. Then, because of resistance to the strict family limitation efforts of 1982-1983, the program was softened (Croll 1983; Wasserstrom 1984).

The people of Inner Mongolia have not escaped national efforts to delay and limit reproduction. Far as it is from Beijing, the will of the state has found its way to Inner Mongolia. But by comparison to interior China, cadres have not strictly enforced family planning.[42] Tranquillity began tentative efforts at family planning early, in 1976, when women under 40 with two children were offered free sterilization. Cadres did not penalize those that did not accept the operation. Women that did were rewarded with 15 days of work points, as well as wheat and soybean oil supplements. Cadres told us that "many" women agreed to the procedure because "they were already overburdened with children and didn't want any more." In 1983 the program took a more serious turn. Then, women under 40 with two children were "required," by incentives and penalties, to undergo sterilization. Women accepting the procedure received 50 RMB; reluctant mothers got fined 200 RMB per year until they complied.

Now, cadres schedule births to meet birth quotas assigned the village from above. Families with unauthorized first births can be fined and may have to wait for an allocation of the child's land. The parents must reapply yearly for permission to have the child already born. In the course of time, authorization will normally be granted and land then allocated. Fines paid, however, will not be refunded.

Having given birth to their first child, a couple may sign a "One Child Certificate." They gain certain advantages. There will be no fee when the child enters elementary school and, through age 14, the child enjoys free medical care. Should the parents later find themselves in financial trouble and be unable to support themselves, the village will try to provide relief. In addition, the child gets a double portion of land, half of which is tax and quota free. Finally, certificate holders receive 30 RMB per year as an award. Should a "One Child Family" later have a second, however, they must return the extra portion of land and all awards. Cadres will press them to submit to sterilization and they would have to pay a double penalty for their unauthorized birth.

But cadres do not compel couples to sign "One Child Certificates." They permit minority parents to have a second child "if they so desire." There are restrictions even here, however. Minority parents must wait at least four years between their first and second births. Tranquillity parents of any nationality having a second child before this may have to endure a fine of 100-200 RMB a year until the end of the fourth year. Only then do cadres give the child land. They reportedly fine parents even more if they have an unauthorized second birth, give no land for that child, and press hard for sterilization. The exact amount of the fine (from 500-1,000 RMB) depends on the offenders' "attitude." If the parents openly admit their error, offer to pay a penalty, and on their own submit to sterilization, then the penalty might be less.

Officially, Han may bear a second child only if the first is female, or if the parents are without siblings. These exceptions reflect the special role males play supporting parents. If their first child is male, a second birth is technically prohibited and a fine levied. Should a couple insist and have a third child, the village leadership will withdraw land allocation for one person. Tranquillity cadres insist that land may in time be given for an unauthorized second birth but never for a third, even after the parents have paid their fines.

In Middle Village as well, family planning efforts tightened up only in 1983. From that time, penalties were imposed -- for birth of a third child reportedly 50 RMB per year, 80 RMB for a fourth, and 100 RMB for a fifth. Third and higher order births were not listed in the household registers, so land was not given them. These are stated policies. But aware of the increasing need local people have for labor and their continued concern for care in old age, cadres largely let slide the formal regulations for the first two children.

Parents in both farming sites resist formal and informal pressures to limit childbearing. We were not able to get data on fines and penalties cadres assess or rewards they delivered. But villagers stressed that formal regulations restricting birth of first and second children did not bear on them or their neighbors heavily or uniformly. There is an unspoken expectation that the community wants two children, which local officials appear to respect. In practice, even Han face few real obstacles to bearing a second child, especially if they first bear a daughter. Few cadres are eager to enforce regulations on the books very strictly. Third children are a different matter. Cadres greatly increase pressure on parents to undergo sterilization after a second birth, even on minority couples. It is our impression, however, that the sanctions are not heavy.

Where couples cannot afford to pay assessed penalties, cadres may take furniture, animals, TVs, homes, or other personal property. Judging from what we learned, however, they have never actually done so. Even fines seem to be uncommon. Few of the villagers we spoke with could actually name someone that had paid one. And everyone assured us that with the higher standard of living achieved since privatization most couples would pay heavy fines to have a second child and to avoid sterilization after its birth.

We have highlighted how the responsibility system has thrown families back on their own resources and intensified family labor needs. We have also noted that with community supports diminished bearing children and caring for the aged is even more a family responsibility. By themselves, these changes would have encouraged parents to have more children. But more children survive now; the crude death rate in Hulunbuir dropped from 10.8 per thousand population in 1964 to only 3.7 in 1984 (*Hulunbuir* 1986: 45). Without doubt, the general decline has been mirrored in lower infant and child mortality, so parents can now count on raising the children they bear. While the cost of raising them has been going up, however, their contribution to the domestic economy has declined.

Indeed, the family planning program is probably tapping antinatalist inclinations long present. Had they been free to do so, younger women might have placed brakes on childbearing much earlier. Even some older women, who in former times pressed for many children, now lament the energy they devoted to raising them. They voice the hope that their daughters and daughters-in-law will not repeat the mistake. Present government policy, propaganda, and enforcement have empowered them to do just that. Young women can now make some reproductive decisions that were not theirs to make in the past. More than family planning regulations and pressures have brought about the precipitous decline in third or higher parities.

On balance, people do limit their childbearing. There were 112 births in the two sites from 1980 to 1988, when stricter family planning policies were imposed. Of these, 44 percent were second parity, 24 percent third, and 15 percent were fourth parity or above. Clearly, many women have second and even higher parity births. But comparison with the preceding decade, 1969 to 1979, shows that villagers are changing their family building patterns. Of 141 births during that earlier period, 17 percent were parity two, 13 percent third children, and as many as 61 percent fourth or higher.[43] Villagers had fewer children during the more recent period, but they did not meet state guidelines for at most two children.

Even young couples remain determined to have at least two children: 41 percent of all ever married women 15-29 have already had a second, while 20 percent have had a third or later birth. For women 30-39, 26 percent have had a second child, and fully 73 percent a higher parity birth.[44] With rising income, parents can pay the fines and penalties for these higher parities. They do not delay second births the recommended four years. Nine percent of second births to women 30-34 and only five percent to those 15-29 came after a four year wait.

Official guidelines strongly recommend having only one child, tolerate two, and level penalties for the third. To ensure that they will have enough workers and providers, families want more. Parents worry most that the family planning program will not allow them to have sons. If couples are to have only two children, the regulatory norm here, it is important that they have at least one son. But, as in other areas of China, most want daughters as well (see Whyte and Gu 1987; Pasternak 1985).[45]

In reality girls, too, are precious. They cost relatively little to raise and marry off, and they are helpful even after marriage. Strong bonds endure after marriage. Daughters often continue to live nearby, visit frequently, and help when needed. Their mothers may baby-sit when the younger woman's labor is needed elsewhere. The trend to fewer children may increase the value of daughters simply because the aging will have fewer sons upon which to rely. Despite the old adage that "boys are precious, girls useless," many couples still want a daughter.

A recent Daur township report claims that almost all Han and over half of minority women of reproductive age are using some method to limit family size. Half the Han have been sterilized, although they do not prefer this procedure. Apart from the irreversible loss of reproductive capacity it entails, people believe that sterilization reduces resistance to stress. A woman will be particularly vulnerable to illness during the long Inner Mongolian winters. Male sterilization is also problematic for it drains away energy and power. Tranquillity's Women's Federation provides free birth control pills and other contraceptives. Women with two births must either be sterilized or use an IUD (14 percent use an IUD).[46] Town physicians visit Middle Village three times a year to Xray IUD users, to ensure that the devices are in place. Although there is effective limitation of births now, parents still desire more than one or two children. Early patrilocal marriage, a preference for stem families, and the resistance to strict family limitation not only continue older themes, but suit new conditions well.

Summary

Because of the way families farm, the labor intensive methods they use, the peaks in labor demand, and their non-farming undertakings, families have to mobilize more workers than under the commune. They must also use the labor they have efficiently. More liberal attitudes toward private enterprise offer new ways to escape land hunger and improve income. The new economy has at once raised the standard of living and widened economic differences, but without creating new poverty. The family responsibility system rewards hard work. Yields increased and, along with them, income. Non-farming sidelines have especially improved living standards. But to take up the new sidelines that make the domestic economy more variegated and productive farmers need still more labor. The family farm therefore makes full use of the flexible division of labor that cultivation allows. And to assure best use of family workers, and support of the aging, families marry early, prefer extended families, and resist a "one child family" model. In the end, farmers here still embrace the traditional stem family, and extol values associated with a more traditional Chinese way of life. In the next two chapters we trace some of the economic and family structure changes we have been describing in a few of the farm families we met.

Notes

1. As Howard (1988:59) noted when trying to collect budgets, "Many families do not keep very exact records of income and expenses either because they are not that concerned or they simply do not have the necessary reading, writing, and accounting skills." In some cases, local cadres gave us figures that seem casually arrived at and lower than those we calculated. It is significant, then, that they considered our figures reasonable.

2. Oi (1989:157-58) also finds that peasant incomes increased substantially since 1978. She reports that average rural income in China, adjusted for inflation, reached 400 RMB by late 1985. The overall rate of increase from 1980-1985 was 14 percent annually. Tranquillity is thus in line with interior China.

3. We defined gross income as the value of all production from cultivation, animals, sidelines, and wages as well as remittances and pensions. It includes production consumed. We estimated the worth of consumed value according to market prices in each area. Expenses include all production costs -- fuel, equipment repair, fertilizer, labor, insecticides, feeds, veterinarian costs, seed, taxes, and sideline expenses. Net income is the difference between income and expenditures.

4. Official figures found that unadjusted per person income in the township increased from 132 RMB in 1978, to 150 RMB in 1981, and up to 341 RMB in 1982.

5.   The regional Statistics Bureau found that 7.8 percent of peasant households in the region's rural areas had an income below 200 *yuan* in 1988. The average per capita net income was 126 *yuan* in 1978, 389 in 1987, and 500 in 1988. ("Inner Mongolia Statistical Communique for 1988," Huhehote *Neimenggu Ribao*, 10 March, 1989, p. 2, in FBIS-CHI-89-070, 13 April, 1989, p. 49; "Inner Mongolia 10-Year Economic Progress Viewed," Huhehote *Neimungu Ribao*, 30 December, 1988, p. 1, in FBIS-CHI-89-017, 27 January, 1989, p. 60).

6.   A worker here is defined as any person 16 to 64.

7.   The difference was significant; the poor cultivated 21.5 *mu* compared to 30.1 by the wealthy.

8.   Village records trace an overall decline in cultivated area from 3,645 *mu* in 1985 to 3,524 *mu* in 1989.

9.   There are significant differences between Tranquillity Han households that do and do not own tractors:

Item	With Tractors	Without Tractors
Mean cultivated area (*mu*)	40.2	25.3
Mean cultivation income (RMB)	2,746	1,872
Mean sideline income (RMB)	1,904	334

10.   We distinguish four sources of income: from barnyard animals (pigs and poultry), pastoral activity (tending cows, horses, and sheep), cultivation, and noncultivating sidelines. Sidelines commonly involve some sort of product processing.

11.   Four of Tranquillity's seven poor households had neither sideline income nor wages. Most of Middle Village's poor had very small herds; five only had a couple of cows, a sixth had only three. By village standards only these six were really poor. Further, eight of Middle Village's nine poor households had a bad year; in 1987 none of their cows produced milk, and four families also had large veterinarian bills.

12.   Only 14 percent of Tranquillity's Han households reported wages in 1987, with a mean (per earning household) of 1,046 RMB. Even fewer Middle Village Han households (10 percent) had wages, with an average of 1,012 RMB.

13.   Cadres still control the registration process, which remains a source of their continued power (Feuchtwang 1987).

14.   We note, however, that while the direction is consistent with the Hulunbuir findings, the number of poor households here is small and the difference is not statistically significant.

15.   For both villages together regression shows a significant correlation between income and size of farm, but household size is related to income only where there are sidelines (in Tranquillity), or where households raise dairy cows (Middle Village).

16. Beta weights show how much change in income is produced by a standardized change in each independent variable when the others are controlled (Blalock 1972: 453). The Beta scores below are all significant, p=.0000. Area cultivated and family size are not included because, when the other independent variables are controlled, their effects alone are not significant. In short, differences of income depend less on family size than on what families do with the people they have. It should also be noted that while income from sale of draft animals contributed significantly to income in Tranquillity, very few households sold them:

Income Source	Middle Village (Beta)	Tranquillity (Beta)
Barnyard animals	.17882	.24510
Cultivation	.47058	.60889
Large animals	.51058	.23734
Other sidelines	.35392	.62557
Wages	.21056	.21266
Multiple R	.99760	.99187
R squared	.99521	.98381
Adjusted R square	.99502	.98300

17. Huang (1990:218) also highlights the heavy emphasis given to human labor. He tells us that,

The family unit . . . has two distinct organizational advantages over the collective: it is particularly amenable to a two-tiered remuneration structure, usually stratified by gender between the man and the woman; it is also particularly amenable to the use of unremunerated spare-time labor. It is therefore a lower-cost form of labor organization for small-scale sideline production [and] for spare-time farming than the collective.

18. In Yunnan province, Unger and Xiong similarly observe that,

For a quarter century under the collectives, the peasants of these villages had cooperated in owning and working the land together as a group. Yet today, families are decidedly reluctant to jointly own or manage any agricultural enterprises whatsoever, even with a close friend or relative (Unger and Xiong 1990:14-15).

19. This is substantially higher than the 17 percent for rural China generally in 1986 (*Zhongguo Tongji* 1987:825).

20.   In Tranquillity 93 percent of the homes are of mud, in Middle Village only 53 percent, the rest are built of stone and brick.

21.   Middle Villagers spent more on new housing during both periods. During the first, their average was 1,039 RMB, compared to 592 RMB in Tranquillity. During the second period, it was 2,238 RMB compared to 1,474 RMB in Tranquillity. The difference is in the same direction for both periods, but statistically significant only for the first.

22.   Gardens now average .5-1.0 *mu*. Older homes have more space and larger gardens; 820 square meters, with a garden large enough to grow a bit of produce for sale, is common.

23.   Informants were better able to estimate overall expenses than the cost of particular items, like bridewealth, dowry, feast. There is no significant difference in the costs of marriage between Tranquillity and Middle Village for either period.

24.   The largest expenditure reported for a son's marriage was 5,100 RMB.

25.   It was the custom for the bride's family to spend most of the bridewealth received on her dowry. They might even add to it from their own resources. Some anthropologists refer to marital transactions of this sort as "indirect dowry" since the bridewealth given constitutes the basis of dowry received.

26.   The better educated men averaged only 2.7 years more education than their wives. In 14 percent of marriages the wife had more education, and in those cases the mean difference was 2.4 years.

27.   We have data on only four non-Han marriages in Middle Village, where the number of minority people is very small: three of them married Han men, while only three out of 140 Han women married a minority husband. For comparable survey data on intermarriage in rural Inner Mongolian, see Ma (1990).

28.   High proportions of community endogamous marriages, under similar frontier conditions, have been described for Taiwan (Pasternak 1972).

29.   We collected detailed histories for 111 Tranquillity marriages.   In 35 percent of the cases, both spouses were originally Tranquillity residents. Fifty-four percent of the grooms grew up in Tranquillity and, of their number, 65 percent married Tranquillity girls, while another 13 percent found partners elsewhere within the *zhen*.

30.   Of all Middle Village marriages, only 13 percent joined Middle villagers. Of 141 married men surveyed, only 31 percent were raised in the community. Even so, 41 percent of them wed village girls, and another 7 percent found spouses elsewhere within the township.

31.   In Tranquillity, the ages were 22.2 for men and 20.4 for women, and in Middle Village, 22.5 for men and 19.6 for women. We combine the two communities for this analysis because marriage ages do not differ significantly.

32.   If we look separately at those who married under the first marriage law and after its revision, we find that from 1950 to 1980 men married at 22.4 and women at 20. During the period 1981-1988, males married at 22.1, and females at 20.2.

33.   The dynamics of family evolution have been ably described elsewhere, so we need only summarize the circumstances that lead to family division here (Cohen 1976; Freedman 1958; Pasternak 1983; Wolf & Huang 1980).

34.   Stem families were not only larger (6.0 persons compared to 4.5 in nuclear families) in our two cultivating sites, they also contained significantly more workers -- 4.6 persons 15 and over, compared to 2.9 in nuclear families.

35.   For those in our two sites reporting them, the mean remittance was 111 RMB during 1987.

36.   The means were 5.0 and 4.8 in Tranquillity and Middle Village respectively, not a significant difference.

37.   Croll (1981:146) similarly observes that, for Jiang Village, conjugal households are set up not at the time of marriage, but rather coincide with household division. They are rarely established before birth of the third child or the marriage of a second son.

38.   Twenty-nine percent of households in Tranquillity and 30 percent in Middle Village were stem households. The distribution of forms among the minorities in the two sites was not significantly different.

39.   There are only six such households, ten persons in all, seven of whom are aged 60 or over.

40.   Thirty-one percent of women with living parents in our Tranquillity fertility survey saw their parents daily, fully 73 percent saw them at least once a month. In Middle Village 33 percent visited their parents daily, and 63 percent monthly. In neither village did women report never seeing their parents. See Gallin (1960); Judd (1989).

41.   Numerous studies confirm that lactation prolongs postpartum amenorrhea, providing some protection against pregnancy. Studies from underdeveloped nations suggest that duration of lactational amenorrhea is shorter for women who introduce supplements earlier (Bongaarts 1983; El-Manawi and Foda 1971; Perez, et al 1972; Prema and Ravindranath 1982; Simpson-Hebert and Hoffman 1981). For China see Chung (1979).

42.   The data for these paragraphs comes from discussions with Tranquillity's Party Secretary, and with the family planning cadre.

43.   The proportions fourth and higher parity are significantly different between periods.

44.   Ninety-six percent of the oldest women 40 and over had three or more children.

45.   That people do want daughters is shown by the many couples who opt to have a second even if their first child is male. Of 41 Tranquillity and Middle Village women with second borns in our fertility surveys, 61 percent had their second child after birth of a son.

46.   Compare Potter and Potter (1989:235) who, in southeastern China, found a low proportion sterilized and high number using IUDs in 1979.

4

People of Tranquillity

The fortunes of Tranquillity folk rise and fall with the number of workers their families can muster. The crops they can grow and the sidelines they can start depend as well on capital, and initiative, and also on government policy. In this chapter and the next, we look at several families in different stages of development and with different economic capacities. The cases illustrate how farmers manage their livelihoods, adjusting what they do to the labor, land, and capital resources they have. These are family portraits constructed from longer conversations to convey variations in family lives and decisions.

We begin with a family blessed with ample labor. The head and his wife, able workers in their own right, live with their married son. By remaining together this family has enough labor to farm well, and even to branch out into a profitable sideline. Su Guoqing, the household head, leads us through the farming cycle. He tells us what must be done and how he manages to get it all done. He also teaches us something about marriage and about relations within and between farm families.

The Sus: A Strong Family

The Sus have lived in Tranquillity for many years, and have done well. After a period of hardship, through effort and diligence, they achieved respect and security in the village. Guoqing, like his brothers living separately, enjoys a reputation as a person who can "get things done." There are many able workers in his household. They till more land and have greater sideline income than most. In 1987 family net income was 5,873 RMB, twice the village average. Cultivation alone came to 2,417 RMB, also above average.

The Sus earn a good living by local standards. They live simply, but comfortably, in a roomy, fenced compound set back from the road. Guoqing's courtyard faces that of his elder brother. A small river flows lazily nearby. When water is high, ducks swim slowly by, and village children row on it. When water is low, nothing passes the muddy shore. The walls of their house, in good repair, are of earth and brick, and the roofing is of thatch. Guoqing built this house over two decades ago, and it is still quite solid by village standards.

In basic design, his house is like most others in Tranquillity. There are two main sleeping rooms off the kitchen, with a large sleeping platform (*kang*) in each. The simple kitchen contains two stoves, a hand operated water pump, and a covered pit beneath the floor where vegetables put up for winter are stored. Through flues, warm air is funneled from the kitchen stoves into the coldest walls of the bedrooms and under the beds. That is the sole source of heat during the bitter Inner Mongolian winter. In summer, the house is cool and comfortable. Even by local standards furnishings and possessions are simple. In every room a single bulb provides light. There is a radio, two wardrobes, and a couple of bicycles, but no TV. He prefers to spend what money he earns on things that will expand income. For him, the tractor to start his sideline came first.

Su Guoqing and his wife are both now 54. They have six daughters and two sons. Three of their children , their eldest son (23) and two daughters (18 and 17), were still living at home when we first visited in 1988. By the time of our second visit two years later the son had married. The new couple then lived in one of the compound's two bedrooms, displacing the girls who now shared the other sleeping platform with their parents.

Getting Started and Building Up

Guoqing's father brought his family here from Jilin province to escape poverty. When they arrived, however, they found conditions only slightly better.

> We came here about 1942. I must have been only four or five at the time. I still remember the years of massive floods that finally brought us here. We were trying to escape hunger. So my parents, two brothers, two sisters, my grandfather, and myself came here. But when we arrived, we found a rough frontier. There were only 13 or 14 Han families -- mostly people named Tang, Gao, and Bu. We came here because my mother's parents, and two uncles on her father's side, were already settled here. They offered to help us. Two of her married sisters were also here at the time. In fact all of them were related to us through my mother. At first we all shared one room in the compound of my mother's two older brothers. They were then still living together in a joint family. They worked common land, put their money in one pot, and their wives took turns cooking. The compound was crowded even without us.

Mother's first elder brother already had four children, her second brother had three.

Trouble followed us from Jilin, and found us again soon after we arrived in Tranquillity. During our second year here my mother contracted *ke shan*, a disease that was common then.[1] She vomited, fainted, and that was it. It was a frightening illness. She became ill at daybreak, and by the time the sun had risen fully she was dead! Soon after, my grandfather died of typhoid fever. One of my younger sisters then died of measles. The three of them died within a single year! And soon after that, both of mother's sisters followed her to the grave, again the result of *ke shan*. So we had escaped starvation in Jilin only to find living conditions hard here too. Illness was commonplace, and death familiar.

The family had always raised some animals, perhaps because they had little land to begin with. For three generations, they had tended draft animals for others. In addition they had pigs and ducks. Guoqing believes that their knowledge of animals gradually earned them respect in the community. Still, those earliest years were hard and prosperity came slowly. Poverty still stood in the way when it came time for Guoqing to marry. His parents delayed the marriage he so much desired because they felt they could not afford it, allowing it finally only because they badly needed more female labor.

Grandfather raised pigs, and father herded livestock for others. So, when the cooperative was started our situation improved greatly. Father then earned a good living as cowherd, tending collective draft animals. That was specialized work which brought in a lot of work points, and Father could work even when the weather was bad and the crops poor. From the time I was eight, I looked after other people's pigs. Each family had at least 10 in those days, so I could earn quite a bit. My older brother became a cowherd in a nearby village, but my younger brother and sister were still too small to work. They just played all day.

By that time there were schools even in remote rural areas like this, so I was able to go to one even while adding to family income. There weren't many Han around here. Hoping, Lianggongchang, and Tranquillity hamlets were still a single village then, with a common primary school. I graduated in its very first class, in 1953. After that I became a full time worker.

Eventually I was drawn to one of old Wang's daughters. Like us, they were from Jilin, the same county but a different commune. This was not an arranged thing, we met on our own and fell in love. I married even before my older brother, which is not so common here. But marriage didn't come easily. We very much wanted to marry, but our parents on both sides opposed it. Hers were not happy to see her marry into a poorer family. Mine, too, were concerned that our "gates" were not equivalent, and also that my elder brother had not yet married. They worried about integrating a daughter-in-law from a better off family, and about how much they'd have to pay for the marriage. But we kept pressing and, after about two years, in the spring of 1954, we finally married. We were both 19. Because both families had put up so much resistance, the time between our meeting and marriage was quite long by village standards. My elder brother married the next winter.

What finally opened the way for marriage was the fact that Guoqing's parents were getting older, they really needed someone to help with women's work. That is what finally shifted the balance in favor of the marriage. But because they had so little money, they kept the marriage simple. The Sus asked for no dowry and, apart from clothing, spent only 50 RMB on the marriage itself. The marriage of Guoqing's elder brother married was also very simple.

My elder brother is 58 this year. He, too, married a Tranquillity girl, a woman from team two. Her family, like us, were Liaoning migrants. They also came to avoid famine, following an older male cousin. My elder brother has three sons and a daughter. Party Secretary Su is his oldest son. His second son works in a grain station in Zhalantun City, the third lives here, farms, and has a small neighborhood shop. His married daughter also still lives in Tranquillity.

I have a younger brother here as well. In 1957, he married a woman from nearby Hoping, from yet another family of Liaoning migrants. Someone in her hamlet introduced them. His marriage was fancier than ours; he pressed for more furniture and bedding. There were suitcases, wardrobes, books, a bike, and even a sewing machine. The family spent 900 RMB just for the wedding feast! We killed a pig and invited lots of guests for the banquet. But by that time we were doing better, you see, so his marriage could finally give our family "face." Moreover, by that time it had become fashionable for people to do such things when they marry. My youngest sister married last, in 1958.

As time passed, our compound became increasingly crowded, until it was no longer possible for all of us to continue living together. When my younger brother's eldest son married, there was no room for him so he moved to his wife's hamlet. We don't consider that a true matrilocal marriage, however. He just found a house in their village. He didn't actually join her family or give any of his children her surname. He only moved there because there was more housing space in Hoping hamlet. My younger brother's daughter also married a Hoping man, and she lives there now as well.

Although the brothers have now divided into separate families, their relationship continues to be close. They cooperate in many ways, helping in time of need without carefully measuring the balance between that which is given and that received.

One of my nephews, the one with the convenience store, has fallen on hard times. He was already short on labor, having only two unmarried daughters. But worse, he is now in hospital with a serious heart ailment. Before he fell ill, he was already doing most of the field work himself. Now there is no one left in his family to do men's work. So the burden has shifted to his daughters, and we brothers and cousins naturally have to pitch in more than before.

The Sus respond to need and distress, but also take pride in each other's accomplishments. Guoqing was particularly pleased to talk about his nephew, Party Secretary Su, a much respected figure in the village. A "new style cadre," this nephew had advanced by virtue of his education, his evident leadership ability, and his modern agrarian skills rather than simply by his political adroitness.

He is the eldest son of my eldest brother. He graduated high school in Genghis Khan town, then returned to Tranquillity. After a short time, because villagers looked up to him, he was elected village head. Later, he got the chance to study veterinary medicine in Zhalantun, which was quite an honor. He graduated after a year and a half and once again returned to Tranquillity. He was our veterinarian, and also headed the village militia before becoming Party Secretary.

Family Division

As the family grew, the forces driving members apart eventually overwhelmed the advantages of living and working as one. A major adjustment was called for to ensure continued cooperation. The brothers Su would have to come apart in order to remain together.

Because it involves a fracturing of the most basic and essential social unit, family division, even under the best of circumstances, creates an uncertain atmosphere. It inevitably raises questions about the moral character of members, and especially about the filial piety of sons. Men should appear unswerving in their devotion to the larger family. They therefore pass blame for elevating the interests of conjugal units over those of the larger family to convenient agents -- women. Outsiders to begin with, women are seen as having a narrower, more emotional, vision of family. They can make it impossible for even the most filial of sons to remain together.

Our first house was built way back in 1953. Ten of us were living in only three rooms, it was really too crowded. We three brothers worked the land with our father, the women did housework in turn. Each took charge of all the domestic work in three-day turns. And when it was not their turn they helped in the fields. There was nothing spontaneous about the arrangement, it was all very systematic. But now there were so many of us that we argued a lot. So, in 1958, we decided to divide. At that time I already had two kids, my elder brother had one. We didn't raise the issue ourselves. Father brought it up.

Their father told them that, while he felt it was time for the family to partition, he could not afford to build a new house for each of his sons. The two elder ones would have to borrow or rent homes. He and his wife would live on with their youngest son, who would care for them in their older years. What contribution the older sons might also make to their parents was left open at that time.

So our family dwelling became home for my younger brother and parents. My elder brother eventually built a new house for his family just beside Father's courtyard. When I saw his new home, I said, "Well, I should build my own house as well." I really envied it, so I borrowed 320 RMB and built one of my own with the help of friends and neighbors. Over 30 people came to work on it. It took only half a month, and we moved in.

But my elder brother didn't immediately live in his new house when he partitioned. He didn't want to wait for it to be finished. Even before, he moved into a thatch hut. He did that because he was angry at how Father had handled our family division. He felt that, as eldest son, he had done a lot for all of us over the years. He had contributed the most. And all that time we had gotten along pretty well. Why then was Father being so partial, giving everything to our younger brother! He was really distressed, and our wives started to quarrel about what Father had done.

We didn't know exactly how much Father had saved up, but one thing was certain. By tending animals, Father would be able to fend for himself better than we. We elder brothers certainly couldn't hope to do as well. It would be very hard for us to make a go of it on our own. So we didn't talk about family division until the women began to quarrel. They inflamed the situation and, eventually, when we could bear their arguments no longer, we divided.

For five years thereafter, we didn't talk to each other. When we passed on the road, we simply walked on without speaking. Our children still got along, they had no problem at all. Then, one winter day in 1963, my younger brother went to the river bank to cut trees for fuel. It was a bitterly cold and icy day. He cut one and was carrying it home when he slipped on the ice and fell. As he did, he struck his head and became unconscious. He might have frozen to death there had my eldest son not seen what had happened. Luckily, the boy just happened to be walking nearby and saw everything. So, he came running home and called me. He said, "Second Uncle fell on the ice, he's bleeding and unconscious."

I thought, even though our relations are pretty bad, he's still my brother. It's my obligation to help him. So I ran and called my elder brother. Together we rushed over and saw that the situation was really serious. We carried him home, and then immediately to the hospital. We remained with him there until he got better. He was very moved by that. It turned our relationship around.

Father still lives with him, but now we all get along well. We even send little presents to Father at New Year's and on other festivals. But we don't send money because he has made it clear that he doesn't want that. My father retired from work completely only in 1980. He is now 83! His eyesight is poor but his health is still quite good.

Relationships Beyond the Family

Despite the difficulties the brothers have had with each other, Guoqing still feels that he can count most on his brothers and sons. They often work together and share equipment. Relationships that flow from common descent are traditionally more useful than those established by marriage. In part this is because they share the property that passes in the male line. It also results from the traditional, patrilocal pattern of marriage which physically groups patrilineally related males. Sons and brothers are more likely than affines to live nearby. Nonetheless, Guoqing also maintains close ties with kin by marriage, particularly with his sons-in-law. While daughters join their husbands when they marry, they frequently live nearby here, often in the same village. These relationships, too, can be instrumental in Tranquillity.

In fact, it is important to maintain and reaffirm periodically ties with people outside the immediate family -- with classmates and workmates as well as distant patrilineal kin and relatives by marriage. Guoqing often pointed with pride to the people he could turn to in need. He spoke of distant kinsmen still in Jilin with whom he continued to maintain some contact. Despite the long time since his family left there for a new life on the Inner Mongolian frontier, he is still informed about relatives left behind, and particularly about those well placed. He also maintained close ties with his wife's relatives here.

Her relatives, too, are farmers. We have close relations with them. I sometimes exchange labor with my parents-in-law. In fact, we help each other in many ways. For example, when her family divided I had to help out because they argued, just the way we did. If you expect problems during family division you may want to ask some neutral person, perhaps the village head or Party Secretary to help. It's always a good idea to choose some respected person, someone with authority, to mediate. But people most commonly invite a relative to observe and make suggestions when they have a family division. We prefer to do it that way because family division is so very sensitive a matter, it can generate vicious gossip. Family division is embarrassing, so we certainly want to play it down. If you invite brigade cadres to participate, people might well conclude that the problems are larger than they really are. So, for that reason, we prefer to ask kin by marriage to help work things out.

Marrying Daughters

Family partition was the end of one phase of family life and the start of another. From that time, Guoqing found himself in a very different role. He and his wife then had to build a new family with their own resources. Their interests and obligations now shifted fully to their own conjugal family. No longer the son, Guoqing had become the father.

With four daughters and two sons, it soon became Guoqing's task to prepare for their marriages. As his father had done before him, he began taking steps to ensure family continuity and support for his wife and himself in old age. Guoqing's account of his children's marriages conveys a sense of what marriage entailed, and especially of its rising cost. As is the custom here, his daughters all wed young -- two at 21, the others at 19. They also married cheaply. Their dowries were modest, as were the ceremonies. Making a proper marriage for a daughter is certainly an important parental obligation, but it is not nearly so heavy a burden as the marriage of a son.

My eldest daughter (born 1955) only attended school for two years. She became a worker in team fields for several years after that, until 1976, when she married a man from our team. They're the same age. They met working in the fields. Here boys and girls often marry people they already know. They may have met at a meeting of the local militia or Youth League, for example.

But people who meet on their own that way very often run into family opposition, usually for economic reasons. They want to marry, but one side may be in economic difficulty, not able to afford it. The other side will be reluctant to forge a bond of marriage with a family in such distress. You wouldn't want to see your daughter marry into a family that couldn't even provide a proper wedding, would you? There may also be opposition because of some question of character -- some suspicion about the personality of the future mate or about the situation in his family. Since they are local people, we know more about them.

There may be some reservations but these days, once youngsters have made up their minds to marry, their parents really can't prevent it. Their objections usually end a few years after the marriage and, certainly, once the couple has had children. Parents usually come around then. My own opinion is that free choice in marriage is a good thing, so long as your daughter has a person of good character in mind. In that case there shouldn't be any reason to be against the marriage.

But I did oppose the marriage of my own eldest daughter because the guy had a reputation for getting into fist fights. He was often rude to people. Everyone said he had a bad temperament, and many villagers warned that he wasn't a good kid. Well, I managed to delay the marriage for two years but eventually they got married anyway. I have to admit that, despite my apprehensions, it didn't turn out too badly in the end.

She had to have a dowry, of course. She wanted a mirror and a sewing machine. She paid for them herself, but I used my contacts to help find them. One of my schoolmates, a cadre here, helped a lot. Things like that were not easy to find at that time. My wife and I gave them 50 RMB, and bought a cover for their sewing machine.

The marriage of my second daughter was also a simple affair. She finished elementary school and then, like her elder sister, went to work in collective fields. Two years later (in 1978) she married a man in nearby Dongdesheng village. She has two children now, a son and younger daughter. When she married we just gave them a set of new coverlets. She bought herself a sewing machine although, again, I helped find it.

It's usual practice here to carry the bride to her husband's home on the day of her wedding. My eldest daughter made the trip in a cow cart. We took a round about route through the village because her husband's home was very near. It would have been silly to go directly there. She would have had to get down from the cart right after getting into it! Besides, no one would have seen that a marriage was taking place. So we led the cart around the whole village before dropping her off at her new home.

After they married, they farmed here for a number of years. In 1986, they moved to an experimental cooperative in Yakeshi. They arranged that through one of her husband's connections. There they got a large piece of land to plant as they saw fit. I went all the way there to help them build a new house, which we finished in 16 days. Although they live in Yakeshi now, they have not yet formally changed their household registration. So I still work their land here. They will formally change their household registration later, if everything works out there as they hope.

By the time my third daughter was born (in 1961), we already had two daughters and a son. After graduating lower middle school she too married a Tranquillity villager, someone she had met on her own. I had no objection at all to that marriage. Our fourth daughter also married a farmer, a boy introduced through my wife's kin in a nearby village.

At the time our third and fourth daughters married, our living conditions were still pretty poor. And since we had already financed the marriages of three children, we didn't have much to spend on another marriage. So both of them married early, but at very little expense. We just gave our third daughter 50 RMB and two sets of clothing. Our fourth daughter bought herself a watch, although I did help her find it. You see, in those days it was still hard to find watches and sewing machines, especially valued brands. I used my connections to locate those things for her.

The Sus gave more attention to the education of their sons and invested more heavily in their marriages as well. This was not from any lack of affection for their daughters. In fact the Sus still have close relations with their married daughters, who often visit and help when called on. The greater investment in sons reflects, instead, a simple reality. The future of the family and the well being of Guoqing and his wife in their later years are in the hands of their sons.

Both sons went to high school. But Guoqing made it clear to his daughters that their education beyond primary school was of less value than their full help. None went to high school, although the youngest two did attend school longer than the oldest. Their labor was by then less needed.

My second daughter went to school for eight years. She was really bright and could have gone further, but I didn't allow it. The way I see it, today's world isn't a safe place. It made us uneasy to have a young girl going back and forth to Genghis town each day just to go to high school. And in winter it would already have turned dark by the time she started for home.

It's true, of course, that had she gone to high school in Genghis, she wouldn't necessarily have had to come home each night. The principal, my former classmate, actually offered to let her stay in his home. But she didn't seem entirely easy about that plan. So when she said, "I'm embarrassed to trouble people that way," I just quickly said, "Then don't go." The same thing happened with my youngest daughter, and she didn't go past junior high either.

The response of Guoqing's second daughter was predictable. Good breeding and feminine modesty would dictate that she express some reluctance to the idea of living in the home of her father's old schoolmate. Regardless of her real feelings, any other expressed response would have been inappropriate. It was perhaps somewhat less predictable that her father would leap upon her words the way he did. Both girls quickly realized the futility of any further conversation and gave up further study. Both remained at home to help their parents farm and await marriage.

Marrying Sons

Guoqing did not extend his views on the limited value of education to men. He himself had more formal education than most of his peers, and his sons went to school longer than most as well. In fact he is convinced that education can be a real asset for boys, that it may provide a profitable way out of farming. To his mind, farming has always been a dead end, now and in the future. So besides providing a sound education for his sons, Guoqing has mobilized every connection and made every effort to find regular jobs for his sons. There can be little doubt that the greater attention Guoqing has given his sons has also required substantially more investment than he made in raising his daughters.

While my eldest son (born 1959) was still in high school, I found a place for him in the People's Liberation Army through "back door" connections. He passed the necessary physical examination, but they sent him back home anyway when they discovered that he had not graduated high school. We were very disappointed because, had he gotten into the army, he would have had a good chance at a city job and urban registration at the end of his tour of duty. But we didn't give up. We still hoped to find some way for him to get out of farming. Well, we needed an elementary level teacher here at that time. My son took and passed the necessary exam and became a teacher in the locally run (*min ban*) school.

He and his wife met on their own. She is also a Tranquillity villager, and a teacher here too. When he raised the matter of marriage with her I readily agreed to it. Like him she was no ordinary farm girl. She had gone to teacher's school in Zhalantun City. After a three month course there she returned to Tranquillity to teach. Then, three years later, she took a special teacher upgrading course for a year or so more. She managed to get into that program because, being Mongol, she fell under a special quota. When she finished, they reclassified her as a "state teacher," which meant that she could then change her household registration from rural to urban. Now my son is trying hard to find a way to change his as well.

They knew each other for about four years before they actually married. For this place, that was a very long time. They had to wait that long because she was two years older than he. My son was 16 when they met, below the legal age for marriage. Of course, many people urged an early marriage anyway. "Why wait," they asked, "since they have already met and get along well, what difference does it make?" But we were reluctant to break the law. Nonetheless, when they finally did marry (in 1979), he was just 20.

I thought highly of that girl from the beginning. She showed good sense. During their long engagement, for example, they could have seen each other often had they chosen to. They didn't because, according to our custom, we would have had to give her a small gift of money or clothing with each of her visits. She didn't want us to have to spend money like that, so she chose to come only at Spring Festival and on other major holidays. On those occasions we would go to fetch her, give her some sort of gift, and then bring her back home the same evening. Then she'd return the next day to pay her respects and give us a small gift.

She was always very considerate that way. Even though she made it a point to come infrequently, it was as though they were already married. In fact, when she did visit she usually addressed us as "mama" and "papa," the way daughters-in-law do. It went along like that for four years, until they married. And then we only gave a token bridewealth.

You have to understand that, even before they married, our two families already had cooperative relations. Her father and I already had a deep friendship. We had worked together in the commune and had gotten along very well then. Even now we often exchange labor. He borrows my tractor, and I his ox. So the bridewealth I gave was more a symbolic offering, intended only to deepen our ties. We didn't think of it as an economic transaction, like buying something.

Even the way we gave it shows that it was only a token gift. I said to him, "I'm just lending you this 300 RMB. We earn more than you, so we can afford it. Pay it back whenever you like." But once they were married I said to him, "You know, you really don't have to repay what I lent you. After all you raised her and sent her to us to be our daughter-in-law. Raising a daughter is not an easy thing to do!"

Guoqing's accounts of family weddings reveal the increasing burden that marriage imposes. His descriptions also tell us something about the sort of help that these central events require.

Before a wedding, it's customary that the two sets of parents meet to discuss final arrangements. The couple is also there, as are their brothers and sisters. We have to fix a marriage date. Usually we prefer a "red letter day," like a Saturday or Sunday.[2] It's up to the groom's parents to speak first. We say something like, "Our son and your daughter clearly get along very well, and everyone knows it. Shouldn't we therefore decide a marriage date?" Then there is usually a gentle give and take on that issue. Of course everything is done subtly, not directly. Everyone present is free to offer a suggestion.

The actual wedding of my son took four days. With the help of friends and neighbors, we butchered a 380 catty pig on the first day. On the second day, a lot of friends, neighbors, and relatives came to help us set tables for the wedding feast. We also got ready all the cooking utensils we would need. On the third day, the bride and her family arrived. We instructed the new couple to worship heaven and earth, and then to bow before us, the groom's parents. Finally they bowed to each other. There was no elaborate ritual other than that. Here we just bow three times and that's it.

The ceremonies were simple, but the cost wasn't. Even in 1979, a son's wedding was expensive. My courtyard wasn't big enough to hold all the guests. We had to set some tables up in my brother's courtyard nearby as well to seat them all. Altogether we set 52 tables (each table seats eight guests). On each we served 20 different dishes at a cost of nearly 40 RMB per table. We killed a lot of chickens and caught 70 catties of fish in the river just for the event. The wedding feast alone cost us somewhere between 1,500 and 3,000 RMB! But that wasn't the end of it. On the fourth day, we had to feast all the friends, neighbors, and relatives that had helped prepare the wedding feast, serve the food, and clean up afterward. Also all the people who had gone to fetch the bride. We feasted 10 tables just for that.

And then there were all the gifts needed to start the new couple off. We gave them a set of cooking and kitchen ware, a full length wardrobe, a chest of drawers, sofa and chairs, a tea table, a pair of leather suitcases, seven suits of new clothing, and four sets of bedding. These things cost us about 1,900 RMB. And of course there was the bridewealth.

When Guoqing's aspirations for his children came to fruition, when it appeared that a way had finally opened for their sortie from Tranquillity, he apparently had some second thoughts. An opportunity did arise, but it would require the departure of his eldest son and daughter-in-law. He worried about what the loss of their labor on the farm would mean. For that reason, too, he urged them to delay until he could bring in a second daughter-in-law.

They only lived with us for a year after they married. Then they partitioned to be on their own (in 1980). By then they already had a child. Even earlier, my daughter-in-law was invited to take a more prestigious position at the school in Genghis Khan town. It was a good opportunity, but I was against it. For one thing, I felt that it wasn't entirely safe for a young woman to travel back and forth along the road each day. And it really would not have been convenient for them to live apart from us either. So I proposed that they wait until my second son could marry. In the meanwhile, they could stay here and help me. I felt certain that another opportunity would present itself later. So she turned the job down.

Beneath all the praise Guoqing had for his daughter-in-law, there lurked just a hint of displeasure. There were moments when he flashed resentment at the departure of his son and daughter-in-law. We also find in his conversation a reminder of the obligations marriage creates.

When salaried people marry, they usually take full responsibility for building a home of their own. But in this situation, even though both of them were salaried, I helped out. I used my contacts to help them locate building materials, and at a good price! I got them some of the wood they needed. Although most of the cost was theirs, I still think of their new house as partly mine. During the year they lived here with me, I fed them. They never gave me anything. I said to them, "Don't bother giving me any of what you earn, save it to build your home." And as a matter of fact, even had they insisted on giving me money, I would only have put it aside to return when they were ready to build their home.

So I supported them all that time. And keep in mind too that, although I didn't spend much on their house, I did spend a lot on their marriage. When they married, my son was earning 400 RMB a year, his wife even more. She made over 1,000 RMB a year then because of her higher qualifications. So, do you think it was really all that hard for them to build their own home? I

don't think so. They were able to do it quite easily, especially since I made
it possible for them to save for it. They really didn't have a problem getting
the money together on their own, even in the short period of one year, and in
the end they built themselves a solid two room home of earth and brick.

This couple was in position to secure much coveted urban household
registration for themselves, with all its privileges. Guoqing's daughter-in-
law had in fact already achieved it by virtue of her advanced education.
She could have found a job in town or city had she so chosen, but she
elected instead to remain in the village with her husband. They determined
to find some way to change his registration as well. That would not be a
simple matter, however. Marriage with an urban registered person does not
automatically convey such registration to the rural partner.

They would have to use "back door" connections to get urban registration.
A lot would depend on Guoqing's daughter-in-law, since she knew more
people in a position to help. But the Sus tapped whatever human resources
they could as well. As a result of all these efforts, they eventually managed
to attain urban registration for the young husband. The couple can now
find urban jobs and move out of the village, but have not yet done so. For
the present, they continue to live and teach in the village and help Guoqing
on the farm, until his second son can take that responsibility over fully.

Marriage brings added labor and at the same time creates obligations
that serve to assure the loyalty of sons. It also creates or reaffirms
important bonds between families. Therefore marriage cannot be a matter
of individual preferences alone. Even when young people meet on their
own, their parents invariably enter into complex negotiations. The process
usually results in positive, useful ties, but the negotiations can also become
hidden shoals upon which potential relations founder. Even after marriage,
the mutual aid that proximity allows can easily be outweighed by family
disharmonies. Such was the case when Guoqing's second son married. It
started out well, but ended up poorly.

They, too, met on their own, and Guoqing had no objection to this "free"
marriage, because he already had a good working relationship with the girl's
father. Their wedding would provide a fine occasion for cementing ties, for
converting friendship into kinship. Guoqing made good use of it by inviting
many acquaintances and spending a lot. The problems arose only later, as
family life unfolded.

Guoqing spent much more getting his second son married. This marriage
came after family fortunes had improved and at a time of rising expectations. Things had been quite different when his first son married. Then
Guoqing had little to spend, and his first son and his son's wife had both
been teachers, the sort of people everyone expected to disapprove of
elaborate weddings. Educated people, like cadres, usually observe state

policy recommendations closely. Further, they both had good incomes of their own so they needed his financial help less. But there was yet another reason to spend more on the marriage of his second son. Guoqing hoped this boy would remain with him, to support him in his old age. He did, in fact, spend more. There was even an engagement ceremony, something he had not given for his first son.

When my second son graduated high school in Genghis Khan (in 1980), he worked here on the farm with me. He was 22 when he married, a bit young, but we were anxious to see him bring in a wife and get his family started. She was also a villager, they'd met in the local militia. Because our families had always gotten along well, no one opposed this marriage. So they became engaged after a year, and married after three. Marrying this son was more expensive than the marriage of my first. Most of the added cost was for the engagement and in the marriage gifts. I gave her family 300 RMB as bridewealth, and bought her two suits of clothing and two pairs of shoes. The whole engagement must have cost us about 1,500 RMB! But it's good to have a proper engagement, it's a way to publicly announce an impending marriage. And, after an engagement we no longer have to worry so much about idle gossip in the community. The couple can relate in a more open way.

Actually we parents on both sides already knew what was going on before we had any formal negotiation. We notice they are often together, that they seem to get along. They are clearly interested in each other. But since they haven't said anything, we can't easily raise the issue ourselves. Still, at some point it did become my job to talk about it, because I'm ultimately responsible for seeing to it that we bring in a daughter-in-law. Of course, I still have to arrange a proper "go-between," someone both sides would respect, to help us handle the sensitive negotiations. Some people ask the village head or Party Secretary to help with the negotiations, for example.

We prepared 15 tables for our engagement feast. Her relatives started to arrive as early as 7:30 in the morning and continued to come until about 9:00. Each time one arrived at the gate, we all lined up to welcome them, to offer them cigarettes, candy, and tea. The children in our family went over to be introduced to their new kin. We told them what kinship terms they should henceforth use, and they respectfully offered cigarettes to each of their new relatives. The children of their family did the same for us. Our future daughter-in-law formally addressed us as "mama" and "papa," and we gave her a "red envelope" containing 100 RMB. Our son went over to his future in-laws and did the same; they gave him 50 RMB.

Together we discussed the gifts that we would give the bride. We wrote two lists on red paper, and both household heads and a witness signed them. Each family kept a copy. It's very important to be clear about what the groom's side has agreed to. Should the marriage fail, they might be called upon to return gifts given. Then came the engagement feast. In every village there is someone who knows how to prepare such a feast. It's a job that calls for experience. Normally the person is a friend or neighbor, someone quite willing to help for nothing. But we usually give a token gift of about 50 RMB anyway. During the feast, as is customary, the couple toasted each guest in turn, and were toasted by them in return. The hosts and guests toasted each other as well. After the meal, we all drank tea and chatted.

All this cost a lot, but our expenses were actually only just beginning. Before the wedding, we bought them a large wardrobe, a TV (which was to became the family TV here), a quilt storage box, items of clothing, and four sets of bedding. Altogether we must have spent about 3,200 RMB to equip the new couple! On top of that we prepared 47 tables for the wedding feast, each with 20 dishes. There were over 300 wedding guests. Once again we had to use my brother's courtyard to seat them all. The wedding feast alone cost us something like 1,500 RMB!

By Guoqing's calculation, wedding costs reached a total of about 4,700 RMB, offset to some extent by the "red envelopes" relatives and guests gave. We do not know exactly how much was collected from those envelopes, nor was Guoqing very clear about whether monies received were delivered to the new couple or retained by him to reduce his expenditures. But he was clear on one point, that expenditures exceeded the value of gifts received. Indeed, the costs were staggering considering that they amounted to four-fifths of all family income in 1987.

Hopes & Hidden Menaces

The stem family produced by marriage operated out of a common budget that Guoqing himself controlled. It was an arrangement that would serve him well, so long as it endured. But despite his heavy investment in the marriage of his second son and his anticipation of good and useful relations with her family, relations soon soured within the Su family. By the time of our second visit, the household was already coming apart. Guoqing and his wife were anxious for grandchildren. Trouble surfaced over that issue. The young couple did have a son shortly after marriage, but he died at birth. His death was a heavy blow to Guoqing and his wife, and Guoqing's wife blamed the loss on her daughter-in-law. According to neighbors, when she was about to deliver, the Sus called the village midwife. But the expectant mother, without medication and inexperienced, was in such pain that she would not let anyone near. Her mother-in-law blamed the loss of her grandchild on her daughter-in-law's inability to endure discomfort and hardship. Both women have resented each other since. At the time of our second visit, resentment had festered into a major crisis.

Here old folks like us usually live with one of their sons. I expect my second son to stay with me now that he has married, and they have no desire to move out. Everything works fine. When they earn some money outside they give it to me, and when they need something I give them the money to buy it. For example, when they say, "I need to buy some clothing," I say, "If I give you so much, will that do?" If they say, "Okay," fine, I give it to them. But if they tell me it's not enough, then I add a bit more. We have no real problems about money.

But, to tell the truth, we do have problems of a different sort. To my wife's mind, the loss of our grandchild proved that our daughter-in-law wasn't a good country girl. The two have been uneasy around each other from the time of that tragedy, but they didn't let it really come out in the open until recently, during an argument over some small matter. The next thing I knew my daughter-in-law wanted a divorce.

The Village Secretary subsequently told us that the girl actually came to request a divorce, but that he had refused to write the necessary document of permission. He felt it was too rash to demand a divorce just because of some small argument, so he insisted on a delay and tried to reconcile the couple. He temporized, pointing out that they were both from the same village, from neighboring families.

Think about it! If you go through with this divorce you will still live here and your families will still be here. Think of how difficult it will be for everyone whenever you meet in the street. If one of you had married in from outside, that would have been a different matter. I would be more willing to write a letter of permission for you in that case.

Although the couple did not divorce, Guoqing's daughter-in-law did not immediately return but went instead to stay with her own parents. A week later his son, remorseful that he had not come to his wife's defense during the crisis, went to fetch her back. He went to see her bearing a gift of sunflower seeds, and persuaded her that things would return to normal if she would return. She did return, but things were not the same as before. The issue of divorce was not raised again but family relations had permanently soured.

By the time of our second visit, the only solution anyone could think of was a second family division. All Guoqing's hopes for a happy, tranquil old age were unraveling. They still lived in one house, but already had separate stoves and ate apart. For the present they still worked their fields together. People usually time their family divisions to occur just after harvest, after crops grown with common labor have been brought in. When the next harvest is in, then, the Sus will formally divide everything, including the harvest itself.

Making a Living the Collective Way

The Sus had not fared well under the commune. With many dependent children, but few adults, they had little income. Even with hard work they found it impossible to climb out of debt. Guoqing attributes their dramatic change for the better to the family responsibility system, and to the fact that their children have now become working adults. As we trace the development of his family economy from simple beginnings to relative affluence by village standards, we see how he used his land, labor, capital, and relationships. We also get an insider's view of collective life.

I was a committee member, an ordinary team cadre. I've never been a brigade level cadre. I also worked in the collective fields. For a time I was the only laborer in my family, until my eldest daughter dropped out of school and started to earn work points, too. But she only worked a couple of years, and then married out. Her labor was replaced by that of my second daughter, but soon she too married out. Then my third daughter worked a couple of years, and my fourth only for one year. So, because we had so little labor, our living conditions were pretty bad. We were worst off when the kids were very young, and I was the only work point earner in the family. Then we often had to borrow from the collective just to keep going, and we were always in debt at year's end.

Under the collective you passed work to me and I passed it back to you. No one wanted to work the common fields. Still, I was willing to work hard. Just to pay our debts, I worked the land by day during the summer months and also grazed animals along the river banks at night. I earned 10 points during the day and another 15 at night. So, by killing myself, I managed to bring in about 25 points a day, which was the highest per person income in the brigade at that time. It was truly gruelling!

By working like that, I managed to earn more points than anyone else. In my best year I earned 9,800 points! You know, no one else earned as much at that time. That same year I thought I would finally be able to pay off all my debts. But because the value of the work point was only .05 RMB, I actually ended up still owing 90 RMB. And that certainly wasn't the worst time for me. I once owed as much as 380 RMB! That was a lot of money at that time. Money then was really worth something, several times what it's worth today.

The only other way I could hope to repay my debts was by selling two or three pigs every year. But still I couldn't climb out of debt. Despite all my efforts, I ended up with very little. Year after year, I borrowed to stay afloat. But to tell the truth, I had no reason to be ashamed. Nearly 70 percent of commune families were in debt like me. Everything changed with the family contract system. Then, the more workers you had in your family and the harder you worked, the more you could earn.

Do you know, the village government is still trying to get us to repay debts from that earlier time! Sure they can get their way, since they control the land. Luckily, we're now better able to pay off those debts. I still owe 180 RMB from that time, plus interest, a total of 380 RMB. How does it happen that I owe so much? I paid 180 RMB to join the collective. When the new system began, they returned our original investment. Well, being poor, I went and immediately spent that money. Then, quite suddenly, the local government announced that it wanted the money back as payment on our debts. But I had already spent it. So if you include interest, I still owe them 380 RMB.

Do you know why I haven't paid this debt off? I could have last year because I earned a lot of money hauling sand. But the director of the unit that buys our sand claimed he had no cash to pay us, he could only give us IOUs. So I went to the cadres and said, "I didn't earn cash this year, but I do have these chits. Can I give them to you to pay my debts?" They said, "That won't do, chits aren't money. You can't use them to pay debts." So in the end, I didn't pay what I owe.

Responsibility & New Possibilities

Su Guoqing was one of the first farmers here to buy a tractor. It took some effort, but it also opened economic doors for him. He draws on his now abundant family labor to collect and haul construction sand. With his tractor they can take up one of Tranquillity's most profitable family sidelines.

When collective lands were divided up, the Su family had six people. The family received 36 *mu* of land. Now, in addition to the 20 *mu* of his four family members, he works the land of his eldest daughter and her husband who left. Guoqing can continue to work their land until they permanently change their household registration. He agreed to give them 25 RMB for each *mu* he cultivates, but instead he gives them 500 *jin* of corn and millet. They grow rice where they are, so they are pleased to receive coarser grains.

My eldest son now tills his three *mu* of *kouliang* land very easily on his own. He can hold his teaching job and manage that much land without my help. As a matter of fact, he usually comes to help me when I am short of labor. Sometimes he helps me plow, but I don't need his help to build my mounds. He's a hard worker; he teaches during the day, and corrects homework at night. He's very busy but he nonetheless manages to find the time to help me when I need it. His wife also comes to help us do one thing or another.

After the brigade disbanded, I drew a work horse in the animal lottery. It was a two year old, worth about 450 RMB. Later she had three colts. I used her for four or five years, and then sold them all. I got it into my head that a tractor would be better than a horse. Why? Like people, horses often get sick, and that means vet bills. It means money and effort. Tractors never get sick, and when they do break down you just bring them to town and have them repaired, that's it.

At that time, the possibility that I might also use this machine to haul sand and gravel still wasn't in my mind. I only thought of farming. So, I sold all my horses for 2,000 RMB (four years ago), and bought a second hand tractor for 4,700 RMB, with a cart thrown in. By my estimate, the machine still had many good years left, perhaps three-quarters of its use time. Relatives lent me 1,700 RMB, interest free, which I put together with my own savings of 1,000 RMB, and the 2,000 RMB I had earned selling my horses. I was able to repay everything I owed at the end of that year, just from my harvest.

Well, I soon found that the tractor was indeed much faster at certain jobs than a horse. Another advantage was that the tractor could draw up to four plows at time. In fact there is one farmer here who actually does that. A horse can draw only one plow at a time, and it certainly can't match a tractor when it comes to hauling sand. I often also use mine to help my older brother haul things, his machine is old and often breaks down. And when friends or neighbors have similar problems, or need the work of a tractor, I help them as well. In the course of a normal year I may devote about 15 days to helping others this way. I never get paid, but I know they'll help me when I need it.

But my tractor also turned out to have certain disadvantages. For one thing it really tires me out! Also, these days our plots are so scattered that it's not always so convenient to use. I have a small piece of land near my neighbor's field which my tractor can't get at. But a horse turns easily in that plot, without doing damage to the field ridges or to my neighbor's field. Moreover, when the corn is high and we want to built our mounds, you can't do it with a tractor. You have to use an animal for that. Most tractor owners here don't raise draft animals so, when their corn is high, they borrow one or have a friend with a horse do the work. And then there is the problem of fuel, it's really expensive.

Having begun with too few workers, Guoqing's family now has an abundance of labor with few dependents. Guoqing normally works his land with the help of his own family members, his married son, daughter-in-law, and his two unmarried daughters. The family grows vegetables in their backyard garden and they raise chickens and pigs. For most tasks family labor is sufficient, but for some they must still call upon others -- especially on brothers, sons, daughters, and sons-in-law.

To harvest our corn we have to use a special tractor because ours can't handle the job when the corn is so high. We hire one from a neighboring village and pay 10 RMB an hour. The work moves fast, we harvest about 2,500 kg in an hour. You need a lot of labor, so several households usually work together, six or seven workers exchange labor. Last year, we called upon four other households to work with us. In addition to my younger son and me, our team included my older and younger brothers, and a neighbor. We often work together other times as well.

The recent reallocations of village land distress Guoqing. This is a farmer who is very attentive to proper crop rotation, to what he plants and in what order. He is also quite willing to invest the labor and capital necessary to improve yields. But, in his view, the uncertainties generated by recent land reallocations have undermined all that.

> After the last land division, I had trouble deciding how to rotate crops on all my fields. You have to know what the former cultivator grew on any particular plot, and over several seasons, before you can properly decide what you should plant next. But on many of the fields newly allocated to us, it wasn't all that clear. I have a feeling our harvest this year will suffer because of that. My nephew (Party Secretary Su, an excellent farmer) grew six rows of soybeans on land that had belonged to others. He needed to grow soybeans but, as it turned out, the field had recently been planted in them. He didn't realize that when he planted them, however. Recently he called me to take a look. He said, "You see, it has hardly sprouted." Well, that only shows that you can't put in soybeans twice like that.
>
> We also need to know what fertilizers have been used. I applied lots of fertilizer to my potato crop this time, so I think I my harvest will be good. You know, my biggest problem now is getting enough chemical fertilizer. There simply isn't enough to go around. I use more compost on my land. I need from 70 to 80 cartloads of the stuff. But, even with all my family helping, we can only collect and process 20 cartloads by ourselves. So, while we would like to use more fertilizer and compost, we really can't.
>
> So, I rotate fertilizers, one year to this field, next year to that. Clearly that's not the best solution, the result will surely be some drop in yield if you do that. Since I can't get more chemical fertilizer, all I can do is to try to collect and process more compost. But there are also good reasons not to take the trouble. It may be good for the land but, given recent history, I could end up working for someone else's benefit. They have already reallocated land twice. What's to stop them from doing it again? Each time they do that, the labor and effort you have invested collecting and processing compost becomes a gift to someone else! I could well end up with some lazy person's land. If they leave things as they are next year, I may start increasing my application of compost again. But if there is another change, forget it!
>
> Apart from our fields, we also plant two *mu* of garden. In 1989, we grew cucumber, hot pepper, and eggplant there. Tending the family garden is something I usually do myself, my younger son doesn't have anything to do with it. These days young people think it's beneath them to garden. It's for older folks and women. In fact they don't even know how. But they certainly do know how to eat what we grow! As soon as the cucumbers are ripe they gobble them up! I work in the fields during the daytime and tend the family garden in the evening. I grow more than we can eat ourselves there, and the rest I sell.

The brothers Su all enjoy reputations as good farmers, interested in new, modern techniques. They are willing to experiment, and other villagers watch them closely. Their family fortunes have improved, because the new system rewards hard work, skill, and commitment. When Guoqing reinvested some of his income in a tractor, he began hauling sand as a sideline. Many Tranquillity families, even those with less income and savings, might try promising techniques and crops, but lack of credit and other problems too often stand in the way.

Three years ago, our town head went to a demonstration in Zhalantun City organized by the Committee on Technology and Science. They had planted an experimental plot of corn under special plastic sheeting that holds in heat and moisture. The corn had an early start, and grew with fewer weeds. The technique produced a very fine yield. When he returned, our Town Head proposed that nearby Dengda village try it out. They wanted no part of the experiment, even though sheeting was free. But my nephew, our village head, was willing to give it a try. So the village allocated 370 *mu* for the experiment, and we covered it with plastic.

Of course, that sort of thing requires lots of labor. One person couldn't possibly do it alone, so we helped each other. The project was an enormous success. We had super yields three years in a row! Everyone was impressed, and local officials publicly congratulated my nephew. Even the Committee on Technology and Science in Zhalantun praised him. In fact it was all that praise that led to his promotion from village head to Party Secretary here.

But despite the experiment's success we no longer use plastic sheeting here. You see, once the experiment was over, the authorities told us that we were on our own. Originally they had given us the plastic sheeting. Once it was clear what it could do, everyone naturally wanted to get their hands on some. But then they would no longer provide it. They wouldn't even let us pay for it later, after the harvest. They claimed they couldn't afford to meet the demand. But plastic sheeting costs too much for us to buy on our own.

And farmers were well aware that, had they actually managed to come up with the necessary funds themselves, and had something then gone wrong and their crop failed, they would really have been in deep trouble. Since they are close to subsistence producers, farmers here cannot afford to risk the little they have. The scarcity of materials, their cost, and limited access to credit all prevent experimentation. It is not that farmers are not willing to farm more efficiently, but because of these obstacles, they turn to non-farm sidelines like collecting, sifting, and transporting construction sand instead. Success there, too, requires some capital, an adequate supply of family labor and its judicious use.

You know, there's quite a lot of sand here. In fact outsiders joke about sand being our "local product"! Legend has it that there was an unusually heavy rain long ago that produced a great flood. Nearby mountains were eroded, washed away by the waters, and sand was carried here and deposited. It is said that the whole place then was just sand. Then came strong winds that deposited earth over the sand, and that is how it came to be the way it is now.

Naturally, all this sand doesn't help our crops, but we can make money selling it to construction agencies. We collect and sift it, and I use my tractor to haul it for others as well as for myself. It's profitable work but hard. We all work at it -- my son, my daughters, and myself. Working together during the summer months, we can dig, sift, and haul six cartloads of sand in a single day. In winter we haul 11 a day. We do better in winter, because you can drive right over empty fields and frozen rivers. When the ground is frozen the sand is also less moist and therefore easier to sift. We earn nearly 3,000 RMB a year just from sand!

Now that my daughters are grown, they can really help me haul sand, in addition to working in our fields. And when they finish family work, they occasionally work for others. Recently they went to Hoping village to help with hoeing, for example. They worked 10 days for 10 RMB per person day. If they are away that long, they sleep in the home of their employer. Of course they're not alone, we wouldn't allow that. Even if they don't know their host, they always go in the company of villagers that do.

As profitable as preparing and hauling sand can be, cultivation remains the basis of village economy and takes precedence. People still think of themselves as farmers, whatever other sidelines they may do. It is in land that they place their greatest confidence. In the end, the land will feed them even if sidelines fail. For that reason, people normally undertake only sidelines that do not compete with cultivation.

Sifting and hauling sand doesn't interfere with our farming, and it doesn't damage our farmland. We only collect sand along the river banks. It is forbidden to take it from cultivable fields. And we only work at it during our slack periods, so it doesn't take labor from the fields either. Because we have a tractor we can finish all our planting in 15 to 20 days. Then we have a 20 day slack, and that's when my younger son and I go to the river to dig and sift sand. My daughters help too, digging and sifting, but only we men do the hauling. We collect sand for about 20 days but stop when it's time to build our mounds. So we work with sand for a time in summer, and again after we have harvested and milled our grain. Then we have time to work with sand until the New Year.

By combining his sideline with farming, Guoqing does well. He could do better still were he able to get all the fertilizer and plastic sheeting he would like. But under present constraints, most of his added income continues to flow from his sideline. So his best strategy now is a balance, working his sideline and farming in turn and using all the labor he can muster within his family.

But to do really well at this sideline, having workers is not enough. Many families have enough men and women to dig and sift sand, but only those with tractors can haul it. Land, labor, and tractor ownership are thus related. Families that own tractors are generally larger, and also have more land than those that do not. They have more land because they are larger. If they use their land and labor well, and are prepared to live frugally they can save the money to buy a tractor, as Guoqing did. With labor, land, and tractor in place, this money making sideline requires that a family rationally allocate the labor it has. Women can play an important role in collecting sand, so it would be folly to confine their contribution to the homestead. It is only by making fullest use of all labor, even that of youngsters, that a family can meet the challenge of cultivation and at the same time take best advantage of new possibilities for increasing income.

Notes

1.   Black fever (leishmaniasis) is spread by sand flies. Eliminated from much of Asia a decade ago, it has recently resurfaced in the Indian province of Bihar. The disease begins with a high fever and leads to enlargement of the liver, and to anemia. If untreated it is fatal.

2.   The Chinese desk calendar prints Saturday and Sunday in red ink, thus "red letter day."

5

More Farm Households: Weak Labor

Families without enough workers have a hard time staying afloat. In this chapter we visit two such families. In one, a husband's death shifts the balance against his young widow for some time, until her children are grown. In the other, success finding work for children outside the community leaves an elderly couple alone. Ironically, that family's accomplishment threatens to become its own undoing.

The Hes: The Fragility of Widowhood

She was only 40 when cancer claimed him in 1987, beginning what seemed to her at the time, a free fall. They had not been doing badly until then. They had a TV, a tape recorder, a radio, two bicycles, and several watches. They were living simply, but comfortably, in a three bedroom mud and brick dwelling, built in 1978. But from the moment of her husband's passing, life changed dramatically for this mother of five. Suddenly, she found herself with a farm and children, but no man to help her. An enormous effort would be required simply to hold ground. A woman in her vulnerable position has to lean on all relationships to get the labor she needs. She would have to depend on the generosity of others until her sons were old enough to do the work of men. The best she could hope for in the meanwhile would be to tread water, to feed her children and herself.

Family Background

He Taili and her husband were born in adjacent brigades. Like many Tranquillity villagers, their parents were Liaoning migrants whose relatives smoothed the way for them. A brother and two sisters still live nearby. Her husband has four younger brothers and a sister in the village. So Taili has many relatives in Tranquillity, on her husband's side as well as on her own. Because her husband was an eldest son, and the family had no other woman besides his mother to share women's chores, his parents were anxious to see him marry early. Taili found him attractive but had reservations. She could anticipate heavy responsibilities given that his siblings were all still young. Young women are often reluctant to marry eldest sons for such reasons. What she could not foresee, however, was that virtually all the domestic work would soon fall to her because her mother-in-law would bear yet another daughter.

> I was only 18 when I married. He was a year older. My maternal uncle introduced us. Both families were poor and in debt to the collective, so there was no dowry or bridewealth. My parents-in-law only gave me a couple of new quilts and a suit of clothes. They didn't buy any furniture for us, but did invite over 200 guests to the wedding banquet.
>
> There were lots of people in his family -- his father and paternal grandfather, his mother, and his younger brothers and sisters. But there weren't any adult females, so I had to do most of the work. To make matters worse, my mother-in-law gave birth to yet another daughter not long after we married! She was still tied down by that infant when, half a year later, our own daughter was born.

Taili worked in collective fields until her daughter was born, although her earnings were delivered not to her but to her father-in-law as family head. Then for a time after her infant was born, Taili stopped working in the fields. She remained at home and did the housework. She cooked, prepared food for the pigs and cleaned their stys.

Her in-laws had been eager to receive her, but they placed so heavy a burden on her from the start that tensions built quickly. By neighbors' accounts, Taili dutifully met all expectations. But she was not happy, and when she looks back on that time now she is filled with resentment. She had joined a family with many dependents and few workers. They depended too heavily on her labor and on that of her husband just to keep going. Her work points were especially needed because her husband had no way to increase his earnings by working harder. As a cadre in Tranquility brigade, he did not work in the fields. Eventually he did rise to Party Secretary but, during the early years, his earnings were limited.

Although Taili knew that she and her husband would eventually leave to set up a family of their own, that thought provided little consolation. In the meanwhile, they were working for others, sharing the rewards of their labor with many unproductive family members. It took three years to persuade her husband to divide from his parents. Once her husband was convinced, there was no way his parents could prevent it. In former times, when the family head still managed family land, he could use his control to discourage a son from leaving. But, now that livelihood came from work points and collective distributions, family division was easier. From the moment of partition, a young couple could reserve their energies for themselves.

> I had absolutely no control over what we earned. When we bought something to eat, we had to share it, so that in the end we actually had very little. I never had money to buy new clothing, and his parents didn't buy them for me either. So I decided we would be better off partitioning. Besides, it was very hard work with all of us living together. There were real tensions between my mother-in-law and me, and I wasn't the only one that had trouble getting along with her. After we left, my brothers-in-law married and their wives also partitioned because of her difficult personality.
>
> She was against our leaving. Naturally, she thought it would be better if I remained with them and continued to do most of the work. But we got little out of our hard work. My in-laws gave us nothing except a share of their debts! I pressed hard because I believed that if we didn't partition then, we might never have been able to do so. Once I had many young children of my own, it would have been much harder. I would be tied down then, unable to earn work points. It was already hard enough to think of going it alone with just one child. And to make matters worse, we had to borrow money to build a house to live in after family division. Had we divided later that, too, would have been harder if I was caring for more children.

Although villagers expect that one son in every family will remain to care for aging parents, custom does not dictate which son will play that role. Sometimes parents rotate living with different sons. Even after a decision has been taken, adjustments may follow, as was the case here. When Taili and her husband left, his youngest brother remained behind to care for their parents. When Taili's mother-in-law died in 1983, the lad was still unmarried. The family sorely needed someone to do women's work then.

> Because of that, his third son took his family and moved back to live with them. It didn't last. A month later, that son also died. His wife soon remarried and moved out. So, once again Father-in-Law and his fifth son found themselves alone, and again there was no one to do women's work. Fifth son eventually married (in 1984), but then my father-in-law decided to move in with us. He preferred me to that daughter-in-law. According to our custom it's a daughter-in-law's job to care for her husband's parents. But if she's very lazy then parents won't be eager to live with her. So my husband's father decided he preferred to live with us.

Independent Life During the Collective Era

As the price of independence, Taili had to work even harder. Besides having to manage all the housework on her own, she also had to work in collective fields. More than before, they would need whatever work points she could earn. But whatever they earned now would be theirs alone.

When we partitioned, they gave us nothing because they opposed it. We nonetheless managed to support ourselves and, eventually, our five children. My husband went to his office every morning, and I went to the fields. If I didn't work, we couldn't have survived. Our kids were too young to work, they just went to school. Certainly we could not have lived on my husband's salary alone. Brigade cadres' salaries were a kind of average of team salaries. In the end his was quite low, so I had to earn work points whenever I could.

I worked nearly every day during the three busy periods -- in spring, summer, and in autumn. I knew how to farm and could earn 600 points a year for what I did. If a women was as good as a man she might earn as much as 12 work points a day doing the same work for which a man earned 14 points. There was no way a woman could earn that much, no matter how hard she worked. The only possible reward for extra hard work was that, at the end of the year, a woman might be awarded a couple of days' worth of work points for each month she had worked.

But it was my idea to separate and live apart from my parents-in-law, so I was prepared to work longer and harder than usual, even harder than other woman in our brigade. I tried to find work outside the busy farming periods. Sometimes I worked at crop maintenance, or earned points watching the fields to keep animals from destroying the growing plants. I managed to find about two months of work doing such things.

In addition to my work outside, I did nearly all the housework myself. My husband could only help early in the morning, or in the afternoon after he returned from work. I sewed all our clothing and made our shoes. That was no small task, and it had to be done in a short time. I had to finish all of it before Autumn. So, during those early years, life was hard.

It was still difficult after the family responsibility system began. We got less land than others because my husband was a cadre, earning a salary. We had seven members in our family then, and we only received a bit over two *mu* of middle grade land for each of us. And when lots were drawn for animals and tools, we couldn't join in. My husband's salary was to be the basis of our income. I also raised three pigs.

Luckily, we received land like others later on, when the land was redistributed again. By then, it was clear that salaries were not keeping up with the improvements in farm income. So they assigned us land of all three grades out of reserve. Then my father-in-law came to live with us, and he added his land portion. He didn't work in the fields anymore, but just remained at home and grew tobacco in the garden. During that period, we lived together and put our money together.

We drew lots with the other farmers and got an ox. A few years later we bought another and then, each year, they calved. We sold some of them but held on to the good ones. When my husband died (1987), we had five. I sold one for 500 RMB soon after he died, but I won't sell any this year because the remaining four are really fine work animals. I'll keep them and use them to farm.

Balancing Childbearing and Production

Taili had three sons and two daughters. She had her first while still living with her parents-in-law. Because there were others in the family that earned work points, she was able to remain at home to nurse her infant. Her later children, all born after she and her husband partitioned, could not enjoy the same attention. She could no longer afford to remain at home with them; independence required that she cut corners.

I nursed all my children. When my first was born I didn't have to work in the fields. I remained at home and took care of my baby. I was there all the time and could nurse whenever it cried. But after family division, I had to work outside and there was no one to help me take care of my children. I couldn't always be there to nurse when they cried. My eldest daughter was born in January, my youngest son in December. Those were not busy times, so I was home most of the time. But the other three were all born in July, not long before the harvest, the busiest time of the year. So soon after they were born I had to work. We couldn't have eaten otherwise. They were only a few months old, but I had to leave them home alone. The older ones took care of the younger ones.

Pregnancy never kept me from working, either. It never occurred to me that I should stay home because of it. I did all the housework myself as well. My kids were still too young to help and there was no one else to do it. There was no choice, I had to start cooking and carrying water again one week after delivery. And I had to go back to the fields just as soon as I was able. In those years I worked so hard, even when I should have been taking it easier, that now I am prone to illness. Whenever I do hard work, my legs hurt and swell.

Childbearing really took a lot out of me. Frankly, I would have preferred even then to have had fewer children, and actually tried to. When the brigade urged us to use contraceptives (1974), my husband and I began to use condoms. I didn't even suspect that I was already pregnant! When I discovered it, I wanted to have an abortion. But by then the baby was already too far along. Then, after my last child, I started to use an IUD. When the brigade pressed women to be sterilized (1976), my health wasn't good so I didn't have the procedure, but continued to use an IUD. Still, I already had five kids. Raising most of them without a husband has not been easy.

After her husband's death, and while her children were in school, Taili did nearly everything herself. She learned to plow, something women rarely do. Taili was willing to endure hardship in order to make it possible for her children to go to school as far as they could. Her eldest son and daughter only completed elementary school, but Taili assured us that it was their choice to stop there, she would have supported them further. Her other children attended school longer than most, but for that reason could help little. Her second son, youngest son, and eldest daughter all finished junior high school.

Although she sorely needed male labor, Taili would not stand in the way if her children could find a way out of farming. Even before her husband's death they had sent their eldest son to live in town with her sister, hoping that somehow he might be able to get an urban job. And after her husband died, and despite her urgent need for help, she allowed him to remain in town and follow that route.

Death's Complicating of Life

The death of Taili's husband's threw her life into disarray and confronted her with even harsher realities than during her earlier struggles. She had to face despair and, in the process, Taili learned to see life, herself, and the people around her, in a different way.

When my husband got cancer (in 1986), doctors at the hospital in Zhalantun said they couldn't do anything for him, so we went all the way to Harbin in search of one that could. But he died a year later. My eldest son and daughter both married within a week of each other, while he was still in hospital. They hurried to do so, so that their father might witness the events. He could then die at least knowing that the family would carry on. It was expensive, but we really wanted him to know it before he passed away. To make their marriages possible, I had to borrow 1,200 RMB from the *zhen* government, and I borrowed from others as well. I've already paid back all those debts from my farm profits. I would never let my children pay them off.

When our eldest son married, we gave them two oxen and 4,000 RMB to buy what they wanted. We held the wedding feast in Genghis town because that's where my son's household registration was, with my sister's family. We invited more than 10 tables of guests, which cost us 200 RMB. We used vegetables we grew ourselves, and killed a pig. Since I already owned my own shop then, I didn't have to buy cigarettes or wine, just wheat and rice. The gifts we received came to 400 RMB, all of which I gave my son. When my daughters married I also provided for them, but less. We gave my eldest 1,000 RMB, which she used to buy a TV, a tape recorder, some new clothes, and a washing stand. At that time that was a substantial dowry.

Both her eldest children soon moved out, as did her second daughter, who married in 1988. Within a short period, Taili had endured the cost of two marriages, the loss of her husband, and departure of three family workers -- her three adult children. Now she found herself head of a household of three -- herself and two young boys, neither of whom were able to do a man's work. Her situation looked precarious, and friends and relatives worried about her.

Technically, the land allocated for my husband should have reverted to community reserve. But because of my husband's work as a cadre and my difficult position as a young widow, the brigade offered to let me continue to use it. I didn't take them up on the offer because, with the only man in our family gone, I simply didn't have the labor to farm that much. When he died, my father-in-law left too. By then he was too old to do much, and I could no longer care for him properly. So he went to live with his third son and took his land allocation with him. Even though we had less land than before, my remaining children were still too young to do very much, and I couldn't do it all alone. Nor could I have paid the taxes on any more land. If I had tried to farm more, I might well have ended up even deeper in debt. In fact, even without my husband's portion, I had trouble.

So, during the first year, my son-in-law and eldest son planted most of my land. They paid the management fee, tax, and quotas and kept the harvest. They left me only a few *mu*, enough to feed myself. I planted them myself and kept the entire harvest. I didn't need to meet taxes or quotas on those fields. In that way, they helped me through one year. By then my two younger sons were able to help more in the fields, so we took our land back.

During that time life was really hard. I had to do so many things myself, and I was unwilling to hire help. For one thing I didn't have the money to pay for labor. Furthermore, I was now a widow, which meant that I would have to be careful not to lean too heavily on others. I couldn't always ask others to help me. I had to learn to endure bitterness on my own.

Trying Another Way: Sidelines

Although Taili and her husband mainly farmed for a living, she had long been keen on doing something on her own. As soon as villagers were allowed to, she opened a small neighborhood store. After her husband died, her store came to be very important because it added income without much increasing her labor needs.

For a year or two I grew and sold vegetables to get the capital I needed for my shop. I planted green beans and other things for sale. Each day I rose at 4 AM, biked into town with a load of vegetables to sell. I earned as much as 20 RMB a day doing that. By 6 I was back cooking breakfast. Working hard that way I managed to save what I needed to get my store going. When I had saved 200 RMB (in 1984), I paid 20 RMB for a business license and bought my first stock. At first, I only sold noodles and wine and then, as my income grew, I gradually expanded my stock. I didn't have to invest any more, I simply poured my store earnings back into stock. Now it's worth 2,000 RMB!

Taili ran her store in rhythm with farming. She raised her capital from agriculture, sold on credit, and was paid by her customers after the harvest. Her neighbors tried to patronize her store, and she managed to improve her own sense of self confidence through this venture. But the way has not always been smooth. Indeed, Taili soon found that she would have to cultivate a harder disposition if she was to avoid being abused and taken advantage of.

My store is on the roadside, so people are always coming in and out to buy things, even in winter. My busiest times are during the busy farming periods. That's when people ask others to help in the fields. They have to buy wine and cigarettes for them. I'm also busy after school vacation, when kids have to buy notebooks and pencils for school.

I extend credit to my regular customers. Because they're all neighbors, I never consider that they won't pay me after harvest. However, because I sell on credit, I don't have lots of money on hand, which means that I can only buy what I can quickly turn over. I can't afford to build reserves or to buy potentially profitable things that sell slowly. Still, I sell many more items now than when I first started. Since my customers buy on credit, I buy what I need on credit too. I decide what will find a market, and buy from four or five wholesalers who trust me.

What I earn in my shop isn't all profit, I have to pay taxes and a management fee. And because I sell and buy on credit there are always outstanding debts. Right now I owe 400-500 RMB. My customers still owe me 900 RMB, so I don't much worry about it. They will pay after the harvest, and then I will pay off my own debts.

I know my wholesalers quite well. They take special care of me because I'm a widow, and because my husband was a respected Party Secretary here. His former colleagues also help me whenever they can. When he died they gave me a 100 RMB support subsidy. Since then brigade cadres have made it a point to buy from me what they need to entertain guests, and in that way, too, they look after me. There are four other stores like mine in the brigade, but they usually buy from me.

Here it's the husband that normally represents the family when dealing with others. Now I have to do it. The children are too young to deal with adults on an equal footing so there's no choice. Because my husband's death made it necessary for me to play a man's role, I had to become much tougher than before.

For example, sometimes young people came to my shop and tried to give me too little money. I had to show that I wasn't intimidated. It wasn't my nature to begin with, but my temperament had to change whether I liked it or not. During the years since my husband's death there have been no big problems, but there were times when people wanted to be high handed with me. I've learned to handle that.

A widow like me, living alone in a store, is vulnerable in many ways. I don't have an exact time to open or close my shop. I work whenever someone comes to buy, even at night. I sleep here in my store at night. So, when someone knocks at my door at night I only open the window. I keep the door closed and don't let them come in. To tell the truth, I was a little frightened to be here alone at night at first, but now I'm used to it. Still, I keep a few stout clubs on hand just in case!

Stretching Limited Labor

Taili's two daughters married before they turned 19. They were even younger than Taili had been. When sons marry, the labor of women is added, but when daughters marry their labor is lost. Since Taili's eldest son was living in town, his marriage added no labor. We wondered why, given that her husband was dying and she would soon need all possible labor, they had chosen not to delay the marriage of their daughter. Farmers prefer young, strong daughters-in-law, Taili advised us, so a girl that marries late loses some value. Hence parents prefer to see their daughters marry young. There was little choice, and Taili would have to carry the whole burden alone for some time, since her remaining sons were still too young to marry.

Seeing her plight, friends and relatives urged Taili to remarry. She was still young enough, and would have a hard time raising two young sons by herself. There would be no shame in it. Most young widows remarry here. But Taili could not know how a second husband would treat her children. Nor could she be certain that her lot would be any better were she to remarry.

I'm afraid of ending up with a man not fitting to my personality. That would be a heartache for me, and the children would feel uncomfortable on my account. If a new husband argued with them, I'd suffer more than by living alone. Besides, I wouldn't want a new husband to bear the burden of raising my children. So I decided it would be better to live alone. My brothers and sisters and friends accuse me of being too rigid. Neither my husband's father nor his brothers want to keep me from remarrying, but really I don't think there would be much change for the better if I did. In the end I'd have to do the same work. So why not just live alone?

But to live alone and get everything done, Taili needs help. She and her two sons now share the work at home, in the store, and in the fields. Her sons tend store to relieve her for other work, and she asks them to go to town when she needs stock from her wholesalers. Since she lacks capital to build reserves, visits to wholesalers are frequent. Taili still works her fields, although now that her sons are approaching adulthood they help more there as well. Gradually they will relieve her of that burden.

It's getting somewhat easier now that they do more of the work, but it was really hard before. I worked hard to care for them, especially for my youngest sons. They appreciate my sacrifice and can understand me, especially my youngest. He graduated middle school this year and now helps me a lot. Making compost is hard and dirty work, and he does a lot of that. Not like my second son, who has not been so helpful. That one likes to watch TV and dance. He likes to visit his friends. Sometimes I get angry at him. I'd rather do it all than ask him to do something!

But both do help now, they even do some housework to relieve me. When I have to be in the shop, they cook and do the laundry themselves. Sometimes I work late, like during the harvest. If the electricity stops at night many people buy candles so they can continue to work. Because that keeps me up much of the night, it's hard for me to get up early in the morning. Then my sons pitch in and cook breakfast.

Although it's not easy, my boys and I now manage to cultivate nearly 20 *mu* of land. We also farm several *mu* of hillside land, too poor to be divided among families. With our four oxen, and now that my sons are nearly adults, we're okay. Although they know how to farm now, my boys are still young. They don't yet have the full power of men, so I must work with them. But now that they can plow, at least I don't have to do that anymore.

Working together, we get everything done without hiring anyone. During Spring planting, one of us leads the animals, another tends the plow, and one plants. If we are particularly busy, we may ask relatives to help. If someone helps us for a day or two, then one of my sons will help them. When we plant yellow beans or potatoes, we often exchange labor. We neighbors help each other as we can. So if people come to borrow my oxen, I never ask for money. They just give us some fodder in return.

Before my second daughter married (in 1988), she helped a lot too. The year before, I planted six *mu* of sugar beets. That's really hard work. When we harvested the crop in Autumn, we had 7,000 kg of beets. Then, she and I did everything by ourselves. We took off the leaves and earth. I borrowed a cart, and we carried the crop to town for sale. It was exhausting for two women alone. I haven't planted sugar beets during the two years since she married. They are profitable but just take too much work. If I always had to ask for help, that would be intolerable for me. I would be too deeply obligated. That's a widow's burden.

I seldom hoe now in summer because my sons are old enough to do it. I just remain at home to cook and tend shop. If I went to the fields, there would be too many of us there, and the boys wouldn't have their lunch on time. So now I stay home to prepare lunch so they can return to the fields early in the afternoon. Even during busy periods, I try to stay home as much as possible because many people come to buy things then, especially during the morning hours. When families can't prepare breakfast on time, they buy cookies to eat instead.

Autumn is the busiest farming season, and is busiest in the shop as well. But even then I avoid hiring help. I usually rise at 5 AM, make breakfast, and then start work. After the kids have finished breakfast, they relieve me in the shop so that I can eat. During the busiest period, we all go to the fields after breakfast and return at noon. I make lunch, while they tend the shop. While they take their lunch, I work in the shop. Then I go home to do housework, and they mind the shop. In the afternoon, we all return to the fields. We handle dinner much the same way, taking turns minding the store. After dinner they can rest, but I stay in the store. I generally go to bed after 10.

Now that her sons are reaching their full strength, Taili's burden is lightening and there is no longer any powerful reason for her to burden others. She has landed on her feet. Having sacrificed so much for her sons, Taili believes that they will feel an obligation to repay her efforts, that they will support her in her later years. But if her period of desperation was transitory, so may be the growing relief she is now experiencing. The future is still uncertain.

I must prepare for my second son's marriage. I have only one pig. I won't be able to kill it this winter, because I will need it for his wedding. I don't really know what will become of me after he and my third son marry. It's becoming more common here for young couples to partition when they marry. I don't know if they will want to do that or not. Certainly I don't want to interfere with their lives. If I can get along with one of their wives I will probably live with her. But if I have trouble with both, I suppose I'll just have to live alone and depend on my shop for a living.

Taili's story shows how hard people may have to struggle in the new economy if their families are short of labor. Today, five years later, Taili still tills less land than average, and earns less from the land she does farm. Yet, with great effort on her part and by straining her children's capacities, Taili has managed to achieve an above average standard of living. In 1987, her income was 3,588 RMB, most of which (2,388 RMB) came from farming, the rest from her shop. She earns one-third less from farming than the Su family, with its more abundant labor and larger area of land. Her small store adds to her income without imposing an overwhelming demand for labor. But it brings in less than the more labor demanding sand sifting and carting sideline of the Sus. If it is hard to farm and run a profitable sideline with only young labor, it is nearly impossible to do so without any extra labor at all, as the next family shows.

An Elderly Couple: The Dilemma of Success

Farming is a demanding, uncompromising regime with little tolerance for weakness. A successful farmer must do things correctly, and to do things properly one cannot be very old or infirm. Much of youth's vitality is given to preparing for its own decline. In this society, without old age pensions, social security, or personal savings, people build family relationships that offer the support that the larger society does not give. When powers ebb, people look to their families. The family is at the center from beginning to end. Unfortunate indeed is an aging couple without support of their children.

Such are the Yangs, to whom we now turn. At the time of our first visit in 1988, Guofu and Gueiying lived comfortably with two of their four children, their married second son and his family, and their second daughter. There were several able workers in the household; Guofu and his wife were then 59 and 56, their son was 24, their daughter 18, and their daughter-in-law was 22. There were more than enough women to care for the granddaughter they added to their household that same year.

The family lives in a simple, two bedroom earthen home. In 1987, they enjoyed an above average income -- 3,482 RMB, or 697 RMB per capita. That year Guofu's son earned 1,104 RMB at an iron foundry in Genghis town. Guofu himself earned an extra 70 RMB doing a bit of carpentry for neighbors. Gueiying sold some of the pigs she had raised and with the 523 RMB she earned bought the family a new TV, their only luxury. But they earned the bulk of their income, 1,785 RMB, from farming.

Several of their children held city jobs, enviable by local standards. Nonetheless, the Yangs had arrived at a bitter turning point. Their very success in finding jobs for their children had created uncertainty about the future of their farm. How could they hope to wind down their own activity, to find a peaceful and secure old age for themselves, if there were no sons and daughters-in-law on the farm to depend on?

Family Background

Guofu was only 11, the third of 10 children, when his father migrated from Shandong. The whole family came, and five of Guofu's brothers still farm in Tranquillity. Another left to become a lumberjack. Kinsmen, especially those well placed, can be counted upon in need. Guofu's brother thus went out of his way to find forestry work for several nephews who are, as a result, also now gone. The family has frequently also called on Guofu's younger sister's husband, a cadre in Zhalantun City, for such help. And within the village Guofu's siblings commonly help each other. The brothers are especially attentive to the needs of their eldest brother who, at 70, is poor and lives alone with a deaf mute son.

Yang Gueiying's parents had been petty merchants. Her mother sold donuts and candied fruit from a stall. In 1939 they brought her and her second sister from Shandong, following a Great Aunt on her mother's side. Her third sister was born here. From the time her parents died just after the war, Gueiying raised her two younger sisters. Even after she married, they continued to live nearby and she attended to them like a mother. Her second sister would become a cadre in Tranquillity brigade. When that girl reached 18, it was Gueiying who arranged a marriage for her. It did not work out well, however. After a short and childless marriage, she divorced. Although she would later have four children by a second husband, her first mother-in-law was convinced that it was her fault that the marriage was childless.

Guofu and Gueiying are familiar with life in a large family. When she married (1949), Gueiying entered a joint family. Better than most, she and her husband appreciate the security such a family can provide.

> When I married, there were 16 people in his household. Apart from his mother and father, there was his eldest brother and wife with their child, my husband's second brother and wife with their child, the two of us, and all his unmarried brothers and sisters. We three daughters-in-law took turns doing the housework. We'd each cook and feed the pigs for five days, and then work in the fields. There were always half dozen of us in the fields. Our mother-in-law supervised us. She organized us all very well and, when conflicts arose between us, she would speak for the one that couldn't stand up for herself. Three years after I entered the family, my father-in-law passed away.
>
> At the time of my marriage I was still responsible for my sisters. So when I joined his family, I had to find some way to take care of them. I found a house nearby, where they could live and cook for themselves but still be under my eye. We had to arrange it that way because it wouldn't look good if these unmarried girls came to live and eat with my husband and his brothers. People might gossip were we to do that. They might suspect that something was going on between them and our men, and their virtues might be compromised.

The Yangs remained together for a long time, dividing only in 1966. Because farming was collectivized then, there was no important family property to divide.

> In fact, we can't even call what happened a family division in the old sense, since there really was nothing to divide. Further, my husband's fourth and sixth brothers had married by then, so we really had a lot of people in our

household. This created a lot of conflict, so we decided to divide the family. Since my father-in-law by then had already passed away, we had no reason not to.

My eldest brother-in-law remained with my mother-in-law. The others all left to set up their own families. We divided the family compound into two parts. My husband and I lived in one, his elder brother and mother in the other. A year later we sold our part of the house to my husband's second brother for 150 RMB, and bought the house we now live in from his fourth brother. The house was empty because he had gone off to become a logger. It was a big improvement for us because it was larger than the family house, and it had a nice garden, a courtyard, and some trees. We paid 500 RMB to get it and we've been here ever since, for over 20 years now!

Another Way Besides Farming

Guofu never saw a great future in farming, so he tried hard to find some other way to make a living. Although he never undertook a formal apprenticeship, after he married he did learn to make woodworking tools and to use them well enough to make simple furniture. Then he found work as a carpenter in Manzhouli City. It seemed a promising way to a better life so, leaving his wife behind in the care of his extended family, he left for the city. Everyone thought he was lucky to have this chance to live in the city and learn a useful skill.

I heard that a factory there was hiring labor so I went to ask. They took me on, and I stayed with them for 11 years. They made lathes and various kinds of wood working tools, not precision tools, of course, just tools of a rough sort. I learned to make them by watching others. It seemed that there was a future for me in Manzhouli so, after five years of separation (in 1960), my wife joined me.

Gueiying brought along her youngest sister and her own four year old daughter. Soon after they had a son. The prospects looked good indeed. But they continued to maintain close contacts with family at home and visited from time to time.

We returned to Tranquillity every year at Spring Festival because my mother-in-law really missed this son of hers. At the same time, we were sinking deep roots in Manzhouli. I found temporary work there pulling down brick walls, that brought me about 40 RMB a month. I did that for quite a few months. So you see, even though the country faced serious economic problems during the "three bad years," we were doing quite well.

And while we were there, my youngest sister, who was then still living with us, found herself a mate. I respected her choice and didn't interfere. So, she married him. But the course of our lives changed quite suddenly when the state started to send urban residents down to the countryside, and we had to return to our village.

That was in 1966. Manzhouli is a trading town on the border of what was then the Soviet Union. Sino-Soviet relations were not good at the time, and there was a rumor that war might soon break out. People were encouraged to return to the countryside. Besides, as the Cultural Revolution built, political factionalism disrupted work in the shop. It was a time of confusion and tension. Guofu painfully described the time:

> The story was that the Soviets were threatening to attack, and there we were, right on the border. I really worried about our safety. In fact, my work unit urged many of us to go back to the countryside. They didn't press me, however. In fact my unit cadres actually tried to persuade me not to. You see, I was by then a skilled worker, I had experience. They wanted to keep me. But I really believed that the Soviets might invade right there in Manzhouli, and my mother was repeatedly writing, urging me to come home.
> Once the Cultural Revolution was underway, moreover, there wasn't enough to eat. Everything was in disarray, with all sorts of groups struggling with each other. Then our grain coupons were stolen and, after a short time, the grain stores closed altogether. Eventually there was nothing to eat. By then I really wanted to go home, but still my unit refused to allow it. They simply wouldn't authorize my move. So I sought out my leader and threatened him physically. He was so frightened that I might beat him that he agreed to let me go. You know, with the Cultural Revolution underway, threats like mine had to be taken seriously. He had no choice but to let me leave.
> But I can tell you that, very soon after I returned to my village, I really regretted my decision. I had been a fourth level worker, earning 80 RMB, not many earned that much. Later, when the Cultural Revolution was over, many of those that had left Manzhouli returned, but I didn't. Do you know why not? To tell the truth, I was too embarrassed to return because I had argued with, even threatened, my unit leader. The same people were still there. Once, on a train, I ran into the head of my unit. He asked, "Why don't you come back to work? Everyone else has returned!" I answered, "Because I don't have the face to return."

Returning to Familiar Roots

Guofu became a carpenter and farmer in the collective. His wife earned work points cultivating commune fields. But their return to Tranquillity was a let down to them both, as Gueiying recalls:

Because he had been a carpenter so long, he had little farming experience. In fact he had never really farmed before. But I had spent most of my life farming, so I went down to the fields and earned 10 points a day. But my husband earned more than I possibly could. He earned 14 points a day making carts, plows, and door frames for the collective. Together, we earned enough to feed the four of us. But the work was hard, and we were no longer used to that way of life. We had a very difficult adjustment to make.

For the next 15 years they made their living that way. As their children were too young to bring in work points, the family depended on their efforts alone. But wood working paid less on the commune than it had in Manzhouli, a reality difficult to digest.

On paper, I earned a lot. I worked every day without stop, and got as much as 4,500 points a year! I only stopped working when it rained. I did carpentry for the brigade, and also some for private families. If someone wanted to build a house, I might make doors, or windows, or even the house frame itself. Sometimes I repaired carts and wooden plows. But I didn't make furniture anymore because that would have taken more time than I had. Still, with all that work, most of my earnings were swallowed up by the collective. In 1976 they assigned me elsewhere, to the commune water conservancy team. I worked there for six years, during which time I rarely had time even to go home. I earned 120 RMB then, more than anyone! My wife farmed for the brigade, worked our garden, and raised chickens.

But don't be impressed by my earnings, I couldn't keep a single penny! At the end of the year our wages were given directly to our brigades, not to us, and the brigade gave me work points instead. Because I earned a lot, they gave me an additional three points. But in the end I just earned labor points, 15 a day, much like everyone else. Later, when land was allocated to families, I gave that work up and returned to my village.

Farming and Family Reproduction

Because the labor of women was much needed in the fields, particularly during busy periods, Gueiying was often separated from her children. Sometimes, she could not find time to nurse. In her case, working during her pregnancies ended tragically.

I gave birth nine times, but only four survived. While I was pregnant with my first, I hurt myself uprooting hemp. I yanked on it too hard and fell over backwards. The child was still born. My second also died at birth because of my work. I was pulling up grass to feed the pigs when I began to feel ill. I ran right home where I immediately delivered a dead child. My third baby lived only 11 days. I really don't know why that one died. I lost my seventh and eighth as well. One came down with convulsions and died after four days, the other was born with no strong bones at all.

When I had infants at home, I used to leave the fields to nurse them only during our regular morning and afternoon rests, and at lunch time. I tried to get home four times a day. Your mother-in-law can tend your infant while you work. If you can't get home to nurse, she may even bring the child to you in the fields, or just give it something soft to eat until you get home. That's how we handled it at first. But later, after we partitioned, I had to let my older children watch the younger ones while I worked. Some women can't even do that, and just wrap their infant up tightly and leave it home alone on the sleeping platform.

Shrinking Security

Their first daughter helped with farming from her teenage years. But when she became ill and could no longer endure the rigors of farm life, Gueiying and her husband found a way to exchange her demanding rural routine for an easier life in the city. That was the beginning of a shrinkage in family labor. Gueiying described how it came about, in the context of a more general discussion of marriage.

She finished primary school and then, at 14, went to work in commune fields. In fact she became the women's leader in our brigade. But when she was about 21 she hurt her legs and could no longer work. My husband and I felt that a grown up woman incapable of field labor wouldn't have much of a future here. So, when his younger sister (in Zhalantun City) asked us to send our daughter to help care for her newborn child, we were eager to do it. Soon after, she found a job in a garment factory there. And about one year after that my sister-in-law found a husband for her. She married at 23.

Her husband is from an urban family in Zhalantun; his father is a cadre there. Before they married, she brought him home to meet us. We were quite satisfied. The marriage itself was very simple. We had a nice meal, but there was no dowry or bridewealth.

It worked out well for her. After a short time, her husband's family used connections to get urban registration for her, and now she works at home, making blankets and clothing to order. Her aunt helps find clients for her. Even though she lives in Zhalantun, we still see her quite often, during holidays. Now she has a son and daughter to keep her busy. The eldest is 10, the youngest only one. There was no penalty to pay when she had her second because there was a long interval between them. But, she thinks two's enough, she doesn't want any more.

My eldest son was born next. There's a four year gap between my first two children because, during that time, my husband was in Manzhouli and I was here. After my eldest son graduated high school, he farmed for two or three years. Then (in 1981) he became a teacher in the village school. My second sister, a women's cadre, helped get him that job. He was qualified for it, though, because he has good character, relates well to others, and is a high school graduate.

He married in 1984. They met entirely on their own, while working in the fields. They found occasions to chat during labor exchanges, and then she started coming around quite often. They spent a lot of time talking. Clearly they were pleased to be together. So, after about a year, they asked my opinion. Well, I considered her straight forward and content with her lot. I thought she would be a good worker. So I agreed to the marriage.

They had a "travelling wedding." They just went to visit her native place in Hopei province. Train tickets were still inexpensive then, only 100 RMB round trip for the two of them. They gave her folks there 100 RMB as a gift. I suppose the whole trip didn't cost more than 500 RMB. And because they had a travelling wedding, we didn't have a big, expensive ceremony here. We just prepared a small dinner for three tables of relatives when they returned. We didn't give any bridewealth, and spent only 90 RMB for the dinner, that's all. We didn't have much money then, so we couldn't buy much furniture for them either. My husband made a chest of drawers and a clothes wardrobe for them, and we gave them four suitcases and a sewing machine.

Their eldest son remained with them until their next was ready to marry. All that time the young couple saved for a home of their own. Although custom here does not require that parents build a home for children when they leave, if relations are good they often help out. Guofu and Gueiying paid a quarter of the cost of the house bought when the couple left. Guofu described that family division:

After marriage they lived with us for nearly two years. Their first child arrived after the first, and they partitioned when the infant was about seven months. Actually, we divided at my suggestion. You see, any daughter-in-law is an outsider to the family of her husband. Because of that it is easy for her to conflict with her husband's siblings. I wanted to avoid such conflicts, and that's why I suggested a family division. But she said, "I really don't want to move out, your other children are still small and I can help you care for them." So I said, "If you move out early you can build your own family sooner." Finally it was agreed, and we gave them 1,000 RMB to help them buy a home of their own. He also borrowed some money from his wife's brother. Altogether they borrowed 3,000 RMB, which they used to buy a well made, brick home.

He earns very little, about 900 RMB. Apart from his modest teacher's salary, they have 20 *mu* of land, on which my daughter-in-law does most of the work. Of course teachers all take a few days off during the busy season, so he gives her some help then. I suppose they must earn about 5,000 RMB a year from his wages and the farming they do. They concentrate on cash crops, like onions, which sell well, so in the end they make a pretty good living.

Further Shrinkage

Although their son continued to help them, he was not really able to do much. His teaching responsibilities made it difficult even to help his wife. So Guofu and Guoying could not count on his labor. They really felt his loss, and the problem did not end there. Subsequent marriages became increasingly costly and removed ever more labor.

Unfortunately, our eldest son can't give us much help during the busy seasons. They have their own land, and they, too, are very short on labor. His job fills his days, and since their children are in school, they can't help much either. When he left we had hoped to be able to depend heavily on our second son. But now he is away as well, a contract worker in the metal factory. Like his elder brother, he graduated high school and then farmed with us, for about four years. He married a girl from nearby Yonghe village, someone her older brother introduced. You see, her older brother had taken my first daughter-in-law as his god-daughter, and that's how he got to know our second son. Anyway, he married in 1986, three years after his engagement. They had to wait that long because we didn't have enough money pay for the wedding.

Altogether I guess his marriage cost us about 3,700 RMB. We bought them a wardrobe, a small chest, a sofa set, four chairs, several suitcases, and some clothing. We held a feast of eight tables. The banquet alone cost nearly 600 RMB. Her family didn't want any money from us, no bridewealth at all, but we gave her 300 RMB anyway. When she came to live with us she brought a television set, that was her dowry.

They lived with us for three years. After their daughter was born they signed a Single Child Certificate and she had an IUD inserted. But she got pregnant again anyway. When her son was delivered the device came out with him! So it really wasn't her fault. She wasn't fined, and even got a piece of land for the lad. But one thing you can be sure of, she doesn't want any more children!

Three years ago, our second son found work in a steel factory in Genghis town. Last year, when it moved to Zhalantun, the two of them moved as well. We still see them often, though, they come to visit on holidays. Because they live in the city, they have no one to baby-sit. My daughter-in-law can't go out to work for that reason. After the harvest I go to give them a hand with their children.

They still haven't formally changed their household registration from rural to urban yet so, for the present, we still farm land allotted to them here. After the factory moved to Zhalantun, they expanded and hired more workers. The new ones all had urban registration. But to date none of the original workers from here have been able to get urban registration. I tell you, it is not easy to transfer household registration! It depends on whether or not the state wants to make a special effort to support a particular shop. If it does, then they make it easier to change household registration.

Our last child, a daughter, also finished high school. Afterward, her aunt helped her find a restaurant job in Zhalantun. She worked there for several months until she met her future mate. Her fiancé wanted her to quit her job, he was afraid she would run into the wrong kind of people working in a big city restaurant. But he himself was still waiting for a work assignment at the time, he had no job of his own.

His father was a cadre in a drug company, so he found work there. He earns about 100 RMB a month. They married last year, and have a son. Perhaps next year they may succeed in changing her household registration. You have to have the right sort of connections. If they can't do it, we'll turn to my husband's brother-in-law for some help.

Guofu was most vocal about rural-urban differences in privilege. Recall that he himself had sacrificed urban registration when he left his job to return to the countryside. Now he believes that the decision to leave Manzhouli was a serious mistake. Had he not panicked at that time, he and his family would now all enjoy urban registration. As it is, he worries that his second son may not be able to keep his present urban job unless he manages a change in household registration. While aware of the implications for himself and his wife of having all their children living in the city, he is nonetheless intent on assuring them a better way of life. Through them he will, in a sense, undo his own mistake.

Except for my eldest son, all of them went to high school. It was not easy to support them that far, as I'm sure you understand. It meant sacrifice on our part. It was costly, and we had to do more work ourselves than would have been necessary otherwise. But we felt that, as long as they want to go to school, we should do what can to make it possible. Even if we had to work harder, we felt we should do it. But as time passed, we came to feel that education, by itself, was no use. What good would it be if they ended up farming like us? And we thought that because we were just plain people, not cadres, we would have no powerful relationships to call upon for help. So we were really worried that our children would not be able to translate better education into a better life. Well, so far so good, things have not worked out badly for them. As you see, our children are all arranged for.

Strange Fruit of Success: Living Alone

Guofu is at the point of achieving the success he worked so hard for, righting the balance by placing his children back in the city. But he and his wife will remain in the countryside, to spend the rest of their lives farming. While both were still vigorous enough to work hard, they could not manage on their own all the tasks that needed to be done on land allocated them and their son. As old age approaches, Guofu already feels his loss of power.

As their children's lives improve, their own situation becomes more precarious. What will become of them now that everyone has left? After his eldest son partitioned, Guofu could still count on the labor and support of his second son and daughter-in-law. Now that they too live far away, he and his wife can only depend on themselves. At a time when life should be getting easier, it has actually been getting harder. Theirs is a far cry from the old age Guofu's parents enjoyed, surrounded by married sons and their families.

It was a lot easier for us last year, when the foundry was still in Genghis. My son lived at home and could help us when he returned from work. Actually he didn't help a lot even then, because he worked all day. You know, they had three shifts there. Sometimes he worked terrible hours, but he had no choice. All the workers were from farming families, so if they had allowed some to choose their shifts there would have been terrible arguments. During the time he worked in Genghis, I depended mainly on my daughter-in-law's labor. She did his work. Now neither of them can help us, they're both too far away.

I have even more land this year than last because of my second daughter-in-law's second child. The village has already given us land for it. I'm not sure how our farming will work out this year. It turns out that the owner of some of the land I received in the last redivision had planted soybeans on it. Without knowing that, I went ahead and planted them again. So I don't know what sort of yield I will get this time, perhaps nothing! I planted more corn this year than last, and that's a crop you don't have to rotate. So on that land I may actually do better than last year.

But if my yield is substantial this time, so too will be my work. Last year my second son and his wife were here to help, but now they're gone and my second daughter-in-law has had a child, she can't come to help out either. So I think it will really be hard for us this year. I'll have to get up very early and go to bed very late to make it. If my second son can't take a holiday during this year's harvest, I will certainly have to hire someone. I'll admit to you, I already had to hire help during planting this year, six or seven labor days. At planting time there are always some people who come from other places looking for temporary work. Most have little land but lots of labor.

This year, I think I may actually have to hire 15 to 20 labor days during harvest. It costs 7 RMB for one day of labor; we don't have to feed or house them, but usually we do. If I was really determined not to hire any labor, I suppose I could do it all myself, but I would have to do everything very slowly, and it would take much more time. And you know, when you see everyone around you working quickly during harvest, you get anxious if you can't keep up. I'd also worry that, if I couldn't harvest fast enough, people might steal crops ripe and standing in the fields. Once we cut and bring them home that's not a problem. And if I can get my crop in fast, I can take my time threshing it, perhaps ask some neighbors to help when they have time.

I will really have a big problem when it comes to preparing compost because that takes a lot of work. To make it, I collect rich earth at the stream's edge and carry it home. Sometimes I pull up grass to add to it. But I can't do that work anymore, I simply don't have the labor for it. Last year, I just carried some poorer mud from nearby, and added horse manure and chicken droppings to it. I'm too old now to do such heavy work, but so long as I have land I have to do it. If you don't add compost, you waste your land, it will just grow weeds. And if you let that happen everyone will laugh at you and say you are lazy. Nevertheless, this year I didn't even haul mud for compost. I'm just too old, I have to give up on that. So, now my land hasn't really been well prepared.

Not having enough labor is a serious problem. Other families are making good money collecting, sifting, and transporting construction sand, but I can't do that either. What bothers me most is to see others, especially people from other places, making money on sand when I can't. During the busy sand collecting periods more than 20 tractors may come from outside. The brigade has stipulated that only local people can sift sand, but outsiders can come and haul it away. That really makes me angry! Our cadres say that we local people get upset about this for nothing. They argue that, since we don't have enough tractors of our own to haul all the sand, we should let outsiders do it. But many of us feel that these outsiders are stealing our wealth!

There are many times when I keenly feel our shortage of family labor. For example, when the sprouts appear and it's time to weed. We have to grab the right time, not too late, or else you lose the chance and the weeds grow too fast to be well controlled. We must get that work done quickly. But because of my age, I'm very slow. So that's a problem for me. Last year, my second daughter-in-law helped. My first daughter-in-law weeds her own fields so she hasn't got the time. She can only come over when we plant potatoes, and we go to help her too during that period. Except for that we don't exchange labor with her.

There is a slack of about two months between weeding and mounding, and harvest. Last year I just kind of frittered it away. Normally that's when we cut wood and grass for winter fuel. My second son helped me do that last year. We went to the hills after he got off work and cut wood and grass together. We cut it and hauled it back to dry in our courtyard. Then it has to be turned periodically. My wife sometimes does that job. Last year we cut two carts of wood, and two carts of grass.

It would be better to go to the mountain further away to cut grass, but my cart isn't good enough for that. In any case, there is no one to help me now. In fact, this year I didn't go at all. There is only one of me, and I can't do it alone. The wood we gathered last year lasted only one winter. I really don't know how we will solve the firewood problem this year. I can't cut any. I can barely even work the land on time.

I manage to get the basics done, either by myself, by hiring workers from time to time, or by exchanging labor with neighbors. I exchange labor during corn harvest, for example. Harvesting corn is troublesome. You have to pull the cobs from the stalks, and strip them. Then you've got to haul them home and put them in the courtyard to dry. Seven neighboring families exchange labor to do this work. My wife helps with pulling cobs and stripping. As a group we hire someone with a machine to come and separate the kernels for us.

Well you see, there's a lot to be done. Even if my sons were with me, I'd find it harder to farm each year simply because I'm not as strong as I used to be. Neither is my wife. With our sons and daughters-in-law gone it's only worse. I really don't know how we will manage in future. But my situation is still not as bad as that of my elder brother. He lives alone with his deaf mute son. The fellow is also retarded; he can't walk, talk, or do anything. My brother's wife died after having only given him that handicapped son. When it comes to working in the fields, the boy is of no use at all.

So my brother really has a bad time of it. The brigade helps him out. They have assigned them 6 *mu* of tax free land upon which to grow food. He can still build mounds himself, but he can't plant by himself. So when he has to do that, we brothers go over to help. He has so little land that it really doesn't take much of our time. We plant it for him and then he builds the mounds. At harvest we all pitch in to help bring his crop in.

Some time ago, we tried a different solution. My second elder brother gave him a son in adoption. We thought that would be a long term solution, but it didn't work out. The boy was only 10 or so when he went to live with them, but he was old enough to decide that he didn't like his adoptive father. In the end, he went back to his own parents. So now we still help him out.

Guofu's brother is proud, uncomfortable about accepting unbalanced, uncompensated help from his younger brothers. If Guofu's future looked bleak because of age and insufficient family labor, his brother's can be expected to be even bleaker.

Even though he is very sensitive about this, we will continue to help and support him, even when he becomes much older. What else can we do. We will probably always have to do that. Still, it's hard to know how long I will actually be able to do it, since I really don't know what our own situation is going to be in future. We'll just have to wait and see what happens.

The Woman's Side

From Guoying we have a woman's view of things. If Guofu has a hard time of it now that his sons have left, her lot has become even more so since hers is a double burden. In addition to contributing labor to help her husband in the fields, Guoying also manages the household and in that domain she works alone. As her description of housework shows, the added responsibility is substantial. It is little wonder that Guoying expresses some resentment at the division of labor.

My husband certainly has his hands full, but with no daughter-in-law in the house so do I. I do the housework and the cooking. I make the fires, feed the pigs, work in the garden, wash clothes. Now that there are only two of us it doesn't matter much if we get up early or late, but normally we get up at 5 or 6 AM. Then I put the chickens out and start cooking. I feed the pigs while my husband puts the horses out to graze. Sometimes when he isn't home, I haul water from the well, and do all the garden work. I do most of the gardening, although he helps a bit when he's free. We eat at noon, and take our evening meal at 8. Now I have a new habit. I watch TV every night. If I didn't, I would have nothing else to do. I don't do much in the fields anymore although I do still help weed.

The chickens and pigs are my responsibility. I prepare their food and feed them myself. It take an hour just to cook up food for our two pigs. One large pan of pig food will last for three days. Two years ago I raised three, and mainly cooked pumpkin for them. Pumpkin is so soft that as soon as you cook it, it reduces to nothing. So it's a lot of work to feed pigs, especially once they've grown.

The year before last we bought three piglets. They cost a lot then, about 200 RMB each, more than now. We sold them for 1,300 RMB and I used the money I earned to buy our TV. Pigs mature in a year to a year and a half. They gain a lot of weight during the two or three months before you slaughter them, and then you have to feed them a lot. You have to add millet husks and beans to their feed. If you give them all they can eat when they are really large, they can eat three pots of food a day. That's a lot of work for me.

During fall harvest, we're very busy. And that's also when I put vegetables up for the winter. It takes a lot of time to do that too. I work late into the night, under the electric light. Last time I salted two large earthenware jars of vegetables, and gave one to my second son when he moved out. I only have one left, but that's enough for my husband and me to eat until next New Year.

I also dry eggplant and other vegetables. I can just leave them outside to dry for about five days, or dry them inside on the warm *kang* in only two days. We begin to dry vegetables as we bring them in. We dry whatever we grow. Of course we produce more vegetables than we can eat ourselves, so we give some to our children and sell the rest to the brokers who come to Genghis at harvest time. We have to carry our vegetables into Genghis every three days and I help with that too.

Between Women

Despite the heavy workload of women, and perhaps in part because of it, cooperation is not always easy among them. Indeed, a daughter or daughter-in-law may actually increase the burden, as Guoying's account of her daughter-in-law's childbirth makes clear:

It is also my job to make clothes and wash the bedding. We usually do the washing of winter bedding just after the summer busy season. But my second daughter-in-law's being here threw me off, she only left a few days ago. She came to have her baby at the busiest time of year, and brought her eldest child with her. Although we were all very busy, I cared for her child and for her until one month after the baby was born. So now my winter bedding isn't done yet. I've taken them all apart, but I haven't washed or sewn them back up yet.

She didn't have anything at all to do all that time. I made four meals a day for her. In the morning, after getting up, I fed her and then the rest of us ate. After washing the dishes it was time to wash her baby's diapers. Her older child slept with us and cried often. Luckily her husband was visiting the day she gave birth, but he had to leave the very next day. He returned a few days later, but then left again. During her month of rest after delivery, he probably came to visit four or five times. When she was about to give birth we called the midwife from town. She went into labor just as the woman arrived. Everything went smoothly. But to tell the truth, childbirth is exhausting even when everything goes without a hitch.

Of course we were all very happy and congratulated her. I killed a couple of chickens and cooked them to make her strong. I steamed them and made noodles to go with them. I made it a point not to put much salt in her food. As is our custom, everyone sent eggs, and we bought some as well. A new mother should eat lots of eggs. She had 10 with each meal. She must have received over 1,000 eggs! Of course she couldn't possibly eat them all, visitors who came to wish her well ate some.

For a whole month she remained in the house. She was not to go out, but could walk around inside. I kept the *kang* warm for her all that time. At the end of the month we had the usual full month feast. You may know that we have to invite guests then. If you didn't, people would say you were stingy. So we invited two tables of guests and spent about 20 RMB for each table. I also made two suits of clothing and a couple of small blankets for my grandchild, and I turned a couple feet of cloth into diapers.

I did that for all my grandchildren. My oldest daughter-in-law can't make these things or do housework, and to be quite frank she isn't willing to learn how to either. She simply buys everything she needs, all her clothes and shoes, in the market. As a matter of fact, I didn't even teach my own daughters to sew or do housework. My eldest was over 20 when she married, but I still had to make clothes for her! After she married, she gradually learned to sew by doing it. It wasn't that I didn't want to teach them, they were just too busy with other things. From the time they were very small they had to farm. They really had very little time to learn these other things.

Coping with Success

By local standards, Guofu's children are all doing well, all of them have found a better life in the city. As he and his wife survey their accomplishments, they also wonder about the price they may still have to pay. What will become of them? How will they manage alone?

> We just can't go on doing what we did in the past. My wife and I simply can't do it all by ourselves. Next year, I won't plant my land at all, I'm too old to do it by myself. We don't have young labor in our household, so I suppose we will just have to give it up. My wife has been suggesting that she wants to go to live in the city with our second son, but I don't want to. She tells me I should keep an open mind about it, but frankly I'm not keen about the idea. I really don't know whether we will move there or not in the end. But I don't know what else we can do. I have no other way to make a living, I'm too old now for everything. Although I still have carpentry skills, my eyesight has been getting worse for some time, and now I can't see well enough to do that sort of work. You can't get away with making crooked things! I guess I will rent my land to someone with more labor, let them meet my quota and tax and just give me a little in return, perhaps 11 RMB per *mu*. I'll only farm enough land to feed us.
>
> I'm happy that my children are all grown up and have gone out to take up their own jobs. But being happy won't feed us. My son earns a good salary, but he spends what he earns. His child spends 2 to 3 RMB each day on cake, food, and ice cream! Of course, that's none of my business, but if they spend money that way, how could they possibly have anything left for us? It doesn't matter, I don't want his money. I'm already old, I don't have many days left to live anyway.

Gueiying also has reservations about living with her children. She knows that there would be drawbacks to such an arrangement.

> It's not easy to be an old person here. You not only have to bring up your own children, you have to raise their children as well! That's why I am not entirely happy to live with my children either. With everyone together like that, it's tiring. As long as we are able to continue working, perhaps we should try to do so. And when we're no longer able to work, our children can send us rice or grain and I can simply cook it up. That arrangement might save us a lot of heartaches.
>
> There is no clear custom here about when people should retire. It all depends on circumstances. If your sons and daughters-in-law are smart and work hard, then old folks can retire very early. If not, they may still be working when they reach 80. Just like Eldest Brother-in-Law! His only child can't do anything, but depends on him! He has no choice but to work hard in his old age.

So we really don't know what will become of us right now. It's possible that our second son will return to live with us. If he can't get urban registration, he may lose his job in the factory. It that happens and he does come home, we will repair the house for them. If he returned, that would make life easier for us. But as yet we can't be sure he will come back.

When we first met this elderly couple, they lived in a three-generation household and enjoyed income from wages as well as cultivation. There were younger men and women to help with farming and domestic work. Gradually those advantages slipped away. When his first son and daughter-in-law left, Guofu could still depend on his second son. When that son took a city job, his wife took on more work. But eventually she, too, left. By our second visit, the Yangs lived on their own resources, trying to do everything themselves. They were increasingly sensitive to the harsh realities created by their success in placing their children elsewhere. In their declining years, life was getting harder, when it should have been getting easier. Now they were cutting back on their farming, cutting corners and cultivating pessimism.

Their futures are uncertain. A lot now depends on whether or not their second son will return to the village, his failure, their relief. If he does get urban registration, the Yangs will have to negotiate some support from their children because they cannot hope to live indefinitely on their own declining powers. The demands of farming are uncompromising. When people grow old they must be replaced.

Tranquillity villager at home after a day's work.

Middle Village daughters gathering vegetables for a meal.

Middle Village lads at play.

Middle Village men helping a family replace a roof.

In Sandhill, the annual visit of the artificial inseminator from Hailar

Grasslands Mongol woman shearing.

Grasslands woman storing her personal effects.

Grasslands lad at play.

PART THREE

Pastoralists: Another Kind of Society

6

Chinese Herders:
Sandhill and Great Pasture

In their advance to the south . . . the Chinese had only to master problems of magnitude -- the scale of transport, the reach of administration, the adjustment of the imperial superstructure to the provincial and regional substructure. As they spread northward and began to approach the steppe, on the other hand, they encountered problems of a different order. Here successful adaptation to the environment required a reversal of tendencies that were already at work. Southward spread did not set up any confliet between the colonizing margin of advance and the solid core of China. Expansion to the north did set up a conflict because if carried out too far it began to create at the margin a different kind of society (Lattimore 1962:470).

What became of the Han Chinese who left the world of cultivated fields and crossed over to that grassland margin? Where they have not remained in farming, forcing their will on resistant lands, where the grassland won out and Han migrants turned to herding, did the new adaptation create "a different kind of society"? And did this society overwhelm the cultural differences that set Han apart from others? As we cross the Daxingan range into some of China's best grasslands, we visit Han Chinese who tend livestock for a living. Here they use grassland resources to expand family income far beyond what they could get from farming. To fulfill the promise of their pastures, however, they have had to adjust to the needs of animals. In this and the next chapter we explore that adjustment.

Sandhill and Great Pasture open two very different windows on pastoral life. Sandhill is an administrative town. Dairying is the main industry, but pasture is limited. Great Pasture is a rural township with more abundant, lusher pasture that supports sheep, goats, and horses, as well as cows. The potential for pastoral growth is much greater than in Sandhill.

When Han migrants sought refuge on this frontier, they did not intend to shed a way of life rooted in the peasant village, but the grassland presented new opportunities and challenges. Livestock and grazing techniques greatly influenced their behavior. Raising cows or sheep requires doing things in certain ways. Even under the commune, herdsmen could change the way they cared for livestock only at great risk. Indeed, the animals challenged collective management. And so, the Han had to alter their peasant ways. In many respects, Han and Mongol productive behavior and social structure drew closer together. Both have adjusted to the needs of animals and, somewhat less well, to each other. In this and the next chapter, we will see how reliance on livestock gives rise to like actions from these very different folk. We will find that the type of animals tended, and the nature and availability of pasture constrain behavior. Since each group has long established ways of doing and seeing things, their cultures have also colored their adaptations.

Sandhill Town

Sandhill has a short history; recent Mongol and Han migrants and their first generation descendants live here. Most residents arrived after 1949. Population growth, government attempts to collectivize a decentralized herding regime, and frequent political struggles led, in the course of time, to a series of administrative changes. In 1947, Sandhill was a village of Gasumu township. It became a township of two villages in its own right in 1952. In 1956, Sandhill became a Higher Level Agricultural Producers' Cooperative with two production teams. Han who earlier worked for Russian herdsmen had already begun raising cows. When Sandhill Commune was organized in 1958, and with the end of small family business, all Han turned to dairying.

Sandhill Under the Commune

The first commune was a large one, embracing Gasumu and Sandhill townships. Unmanageable, the two finally separated and have remained apart since. In 1962, Sandhill was raised in administrative status to a town (zhen). It then ran Sandhill Commune along with several work units -- cadres in banner government offices, and workers attached to three nearby railway stations. It became hard to migrate to this area, and unregistered rural residents had to leave. Sandhill Commune itself had three production teams -- a shepherding pastoral team, a team that raised dairy cows, and one that grew vegetables. There was no brigade between commune and team.

In 1965, a "four cleanup team" (siqing dui) of district level cadres arrived to conduct a campaign against corruption. During this campaign and the

Cultural Revolution that followed soon after, able local cadre were detained. This seriously disrupted administrative functions of the commune and town. The teams then took over many of their functions and became self sufficient. Now, all three teams herded, grew vegetables, and had sidelines. Although team one men mainly raised sheep, they also pastured cows and fished in the nearby Hailar river. Women wove baskets and fences from local rushes. Team two added haying and net and ice fishing to dairying. Team three gardened, raised dairy cows, and women wove river rushes.

The collective was poorly suited to raising animals. Members had little incentive to care for collective livestock, and cadres could not effectively control how members tended them. Poor pastoral practice lost livestock. Since the animals would have given birth to future stock, the reduced numbers depleted generations of animals, and collective resources did not expand. And because women and youth did not herd on the open range, a great deal of labor was untapped. Despite early promises, herdsmen did not benefit from commune economies of scale.

The team tried several times to give households a couple of dairy cows to raise, and those in home care fared better than those in collective care. But because commune leaders constantly worried about family level management under a socialist regime, such efforts did not last long. Shifts in policy, now in favor and then against family management of dairy animals, further reduced their benefits. Even when cadres condoned household production, members' bad past experiences made them cautious.

In 1963, individual families were allowed to raise one or two cows. But a short time later, the cadres took them all back. You know, these were animals we had raised at home, that we had taken good care of. Suddenly our living situation was changing very fast. After our cows were returned to the commune, herdsmen were careless. And in a short time most of the cows we had returned were thin, sick or dead. Then the policy changed again, and families were once again allowed to have one or two cows. Every family wanted a quality animal and grabbed for the best. Yet again the policy shifted. In fact it shifted back and forth many times. Each time the commune took back animals, many died. The worst was in 1963.

Towards the end of the commune era, every family was allowed to raise one cow. We sold our milk to the collection station each day then, and earned a few tens of RMB a month. Before, the rule had been that whenever our cows had calves they were to be returned to the commune. Now they urged us to raise the calves ourselves. But none of us fell for that. We knew that once the animals had grown, they would take them back and that all our care would go for nothing. The cost of raising them would be ours, but the commune would reap the profits. But since the responsibility system was put into effect, and animals became the property of individual families, people have been willing to work much harder and to take better care of their animals. As a result, nearly 90 percent of all new calves survive now. That was unheard of under the commune.

Dissolution of the Commune

In 1983 the family replaced the production team as the basic accounting unit, and Sandhill town took over administrative functions that the commune once handled. With limited grassland and livestock, it was easy to divest team property. Together, the three teams controlled only 347 sq km of land, of which only 247 were suitable pasture. The town continues to manage this grassland. Too small an area to be divided, it is shared by all households with livestock.

Not many town residents wanted to raise sheep on the open grassland. To persuade the few people with shepherding experience to buy sheep, cadres set a low price, but only a handful of families bought them. Everyone wanted to raise cows. They were graded and priced according to their milk producing ability. Team members drew lots for cows and sheep, and winners were expected to pay over time -- one year for cows, ten for sheep.

When township and village replaced commune and brigade, families took over many functions that the collective had performed. Now, with the family responsibility system, cadre control livestock management indirectly, and their power has greatly eroded. And so, they have not strictly collected payments on animals. Cadres assert that they have not brought pressure to bear on delinquent households because they "do not need the revenues at this time." Yet in other contexts, they complain about lack of funds. This suggests that, in these domains, cadres cannot exert the control they once did.

People of Sandhill

Han, Mongols, and the few Daur, Manchus, Hui, Ewenke, and people of Russian ancestry, all live together in this modest town of earthen roads and simple houses. Nearly half the Han are migrants, mostly with peasant backgrounds. Even more Mongols (61 percent) had been migrants, mainly from herding locales elsewhere in Inner Mongolia. As well, some urban registered migrants arrived to take up wage earning jobs. Although born elsewhere, most migrants have spent their adulthoods in Sandhill. Conditions here have shaped their home and work lives.

With its sizable minority population, Sandhill is characterized by a jostling and mixing of cultural elements, the uneasy compromise of the pastoral region. Distinctive Mongol cultural markers speak to their nomadic life spent on the range -- a separate language, boiled mutton eaten with knife rather than chopsticks, milk-tea, a preference for strong grain wine, ceremonial wrestling, and the mobile yurts used by shepherds. Many still wear traditional long robes, slit from the waist so the wearers can straddle horses. Horses and horsemanship play an important role in Mongol life, in town less an economic role than one of show. Cultural markers for the Han reflect their peasant origins -- fixed earthen houses, work pants and shirts, grain and vegetables, pork, fish from local streams, bottled beer, and bicycles.

Where people live together, traditions combine. Town-dwelling Mongols live in homes like those of the Han, and grow vegetables in their compound gardens. Most Mongol adults can speak Mandarin, and most dress like the Han. Mongol youngsters, too, carry their milk cans to collection stations on bicycles. But here the Han favor beef and mutton, not pork. Like the Mongols they drink milk-tea, and share the regional penchant for hard liquor. They too come forth with mournful grassland ballads when they drink alongside Mongols. And when they cut hay or herd on the open grassland, they, too, live in yurts. Our Han friends were amused by our encounters with *shoubarou*, the traditional Mongol mutton dish prepared for guests. Hosts slaughter a mature sheep for the occasion. They boil large haunches in water without spices, leaving the desired strong mutton taste. Our Han hosts, noting our discomfort at tearing the fat-larded mutton apart with hands and knife, recalled their own difficulty getting used to this dish, which many now favor.

There are also traces of the earlier Russian presence. A white haired, blue-eyed, Russian-born woman married to a Han Chinese, the matriarch of a three-generation household, still lives in Sandhill. Some Chinese occupy the wooden houses with gingerbread facades built by Russian railroaders near the train station and along the track. Many families also enjoy locally made Russian-style bread (*klebbao*).

Despite some erosion of authority, cadres conduct important business. They monitor grassland use and promote artificial insemination to increase milk production. Cadres carry out regular animal counts, the basis for taxation. Herdsmen pay a small tax for each head they own and graze on public pasture. Owners of tractors, trucks, and jeeps pay a road tax to drive their vehicles on public roads. Fishermen rent surface rights to river locations, and merchants pay business taxes. Local cadres manage to collect all these taxes efficiently.

Sandhill is run on these taxes, but there are few town amenities. All roads are of earth. There is poor drainage, so that during the rainy season,

148

roads turn into mud lakes that are impassible on foot. Town leaders argue that the cows that enter and leave each day would quickly destroy any road repair. The town infrastructure is simple, and apart from the various town, township, and banner offices located here, includes two clinics. Education, once available through high school, now stops with junior middle school. There is a small old age home, residence only for a few old Mongol men who have given up the open grassland. There is a post office and a small market square with a dozen modest stalls. Sandhill also has several small cafes, a few artisans, and entrepreneurs run small shops of their own.

Making a Living in Sandhill

Despite its simple looks and modest facilities, Sandhill's population was the most urban of all the sites we studied. Many earn their livings as salaried white or blue collar staff, local government administrators or railway workers. But there are also many dairy farmers and shepherds, and even people with urban registration usually raise some cows. Their shared herding concerns create common features in their lives.

The town oversees a mixed population of wage earners and dairying folk, Mongol as well as Han. In addition, some shepherding families live in town. A separate township (*sumu*) government, with offices in Sandhill town, oversees grassland dwelling shepherds, who once belonged to the same commune. Shepherds that reside in town hold jobs in those offices. But most other shepherds in the vicinity live on the open grassland outside; nearly all of them are Mongols.

Family herds are small, and few town dwellers raise sheep. Dairymen here try to increase milk yields through breeding and costly feed supplements, rather than by raising more cows. Sandhill thus features a relatively intensive form of dairying. In this form of the pastoral economy, herdsmen apply labor and some capital to extend natural resources.

Great Pasture Township

Han first came to Great Pasture, with its open spaces, large herds, and sparse population during the 1930s. They came from the same areas of China and for much the same reasons as Sandhill Han. More came after 1949, to fish, mine, or transport for a newly opened, but short lived, nitrate mine nearby. As yet, none were herders. Nomadic Mongols lived and raised sheep on the open grassland nearby, but few lived in town. As elsewhere, the proportion of migrants surged during the Great Leap Forward and its aftermath, and again in the 1970s. Two-fifths of the current Han population came as migrants, mainly from rural areas. Most were in their twenties and early thirties when they came, so Great Pasture herding conditions have shaped their lives.

Great Pasture Under the Commune

Han began to herd only with collectivization. Four Mongol families moved into town and joined two dozen Han in the first collective. Members paid an entrance fee or put in productive property of equal value.[1] The collective put together a herd of 106 cows, 27 horses, and 630 sheep. Later, in 1958, a commune was formed of one Han and four Mongol brigades. The Mongols joined from their pasture base; new Han migrants arrived through the 1970s. Even though the Han took up a pastoral way of life and some Mongols settled in town, Han and Mongol brigades continued their specialties. Mongols mainly raised sheep, Han raised dairy cows.

Division of Labor: Women and Men in the Commune

Livestock require constant attention. There are periods of greater labor demand, but these are little marked, and there are no slack times. Herdsmen must care for their animals daily. They pasture sheep year round and move them often, to feed them and preserve the grasslands. The great distance they travel and the importance of highly skilled, experienced labor, underlie sharp differences in the tasks that women and men, young and old, do.

In the Mongol brigades, families with recognized skills had responsibility for flocks of about 1,000 sheep, herds of 100-150 cows, or 800 horses. Men from other families helped under their management. The grassland shepherding encampment had teams of four men: a daytime shepherd, a night shepherd, a cook, and a foreman who did all tasks.[2] Men pastured the animals. In those days, they did not corral livestock at night, but grazed them continuously so they could fatten well. There was enough labor to watch them round the clock.

Herdsmen did most of their work far from the commune center. Although the tasks men and women did were quite different, if the wives of grassland dwelling Mongols were on the spot, they would help birth and shear the sheep. When men drove the flocks to distant grazing pastures, the women remained in home camps to care for lambs and cows left behind. Husbands and wives lived apart at such times.

150

As in Sandhill, Han families remained in town throughout the year. Teams of men pastured dairy cows, and brought them home for milking. A dozen women milked brigade cows for two hours in the early morning and again in evening. Women (and a few older men) gardened during the short growing season; they also wove baskets at home, the brigade sideline. In Great Pasture, as in Sandhill, the daily care that livestock demand made it hard for women and men to do anything other than their proper tasks. Because of the distance between herds and homes, the same person could not combine several kinds of work. Thus, among the Han, too, men and women did different work.

In Great Pasture, Han men also dominated brigade sidelines -- fishing and cutting hay. During spring, summer, and autumn, eight boats were hauled to the nearby Hailar river, each manned by two men. In winter, groups of a dozen men went ice fishing. Each summer, teams of 40 men cut grass for winter fodder. Some women took part as cooks. Construction and transportation were also men's work. Thus, men could earn work points at many tasks all year round, and cadres calculated points in their favor. From the outset, women and older men were considered "half labor." If their families wished, they could remain at home and not earn work points. Han women did only limited and seasonal work outside the home in any case. And whether Han or Mongol, women's chores outside were considered "lighter" than those of men, and were therefore less well paid.

Cadres chose experienced males for most tasks. Harsh weather, mismanagement, predation from wolves, or disease could decimate herds and flocks. Workers had to be able to lift heavy animals and other objects. They also spent long periods away from home, often in severe weather. Children and youngsters lacked judgement, and women had to remain close to home to run the household and care for children. Neither were strong enough to handle grown animals.

Dissolution of the Commune

Great Pasture Commune was dissolved in 1983. As in Sandhill, collective management had created problems. During most of the period, the brigade assigned more work points for harder and longer tasks. But workers earned a day's points no matter how well they did the work. The Cultural Revolution carried the system even further. Then cadres gave the same number of points for all tasks, whether heavy or light, according to the number of days worked. Whereas workers had not expected to choose their own task assignments before, they now began to argue about who would do what. Animal management suffered. One informant described the situation from 1968 to 1973 this way:

They only required that you do a day's work. It didn't matter how well you did your work. You could just go to the office or to the pasture and do nothing and you would still be paid. At that time you were paid monthly, according to the number of days worked. Your age, sex, the season, or what you did, didn't count, only how many days you had gone. But at the end of the year, the head of the brigade always found that members owed money because their expenses exceeded their incomes. It seemed as though the more you did, the more you owed them. Income and expenses were clearly not in balance, and it was the collective members that had to make up the difference. So people no longer saw any reason to work hard, you couldn't earn more and you ended up in debt anyway.

Then, in 1968, the brigade recalled all the cows that they had lent us. Once they were back under collective management, there were many deaths and losses. Many of us ate or sold the animals, and no one paid attention. By 1973 there were only several thousand sheep left to our brigade, whereas before there had been between 10 and 20 thousand! In 1976 some cows were again given out to individual families. So, by the time the responsibility system was formally begun, many cows had actually already been distributed among brigade families.

Mongols and Han viewed livestock differently. Mongols had long raised sheep and cows to eat and trade. Collective ownership encouraged their willingness to consume. Mongol shepherds were also aware that good weather might turn, and that flocks might not survive. Perhaps reflecting this awareness as well, they were ready to slaughter and eat healthy animals rather than increase flock and herd sizes. No one could be sure the animals would survive the next winter season. It was an attitude that may have helped maintain a delicate balance between pasture and numbers of sheep.

Han herdsmen are sharply critical of this attitude. While admitting that collective management contributed to laxity in their brigade as well, Han nonetheless associate it more with the Mongols, and they point to it as one sign of Mongol economic backwardness. One Han shepherd observed that,

Under the commune it was really true that more animals died than now. The main reason was that the shepherds gave healthy, strong animals to brigade members to eat. Because the sheep were not their own, they didn't worry. They killed too many animals. Besides, they should have only slaughtered the weaker, older, lame sheep and not the healthy, strong ones. But this was a problem that was particularly serious in the Mongol brigades.

When the commune was dissolved, administrative responsibilities passed from commune to township; brigades became villages. The animals were distributed among teams, and there were enough cows and sheep for each family. Livestock thrived on a broad expanse of pasture and grassland. But because Han families had migrated to Great Pasture at different times, some gave the commune more labor and money than others. Those who were members longer got more animals. Members of the Mongol brigades had lived in the area throughout. Every Mongol adult therefore got the same number of sheep, and each household the same number of cows. And Mongol families ended up with more animals than the Han because their brigades had more to begin with.[3] Han resent this difference even today.

Pasture and grassland have remained public property. The brigade handles hay cutting areas differently from public grazing pasture, however. Each year during the haying months, the Han brigade assigns grass cutting areas to member households based on the number of animals they have. Since the Mongol brigades have much larger grass cutting space, each family, independent of herd or flock size, gets the same area.[4]

In dividing the animals, cadres subtracted from the price of livestock all fees and property given when members joined the collective. Herdsmen could pay the rest over time. As in Sandhill, however, cadres soon stopped collecting payments. They concluded that there were enough funds for administrative functions and infrastructure.[5] In their view, it was better to leave these monies with brigade members to encourage investment in livestock. Of course, there is no way to ensure that people will so invest, and cadres admit that the debts would be troublesome to collect. Although they do collect the taxes and assessments required by the state, cadres clearly prefer to let these debts slide.

In addition to administering the township, local leaders make important decisions affecting production. They allocate land for home construction. They collect taxes and fees, count livestock, resolve arguments and disputes, and pay stipends to demobilized soldiers. They supply veterinary services, assign fishing rights, manage brigade pasture, and regulate seasonal flock movements and grass cutting. They underwrite the cost of artificial insemination, and offer incentives to encourage flock development. Cadres have retained enough authority to perform these tasks. But because they no longer have direct control over livestock, they have lost some power since commune days.

People of Great Pasture

Like Sandhill, Great Pasture reminds us of towns on the early North American frontier. Its dirt roads are unpaved. There is no running water and no courtyard wells. A single communal pump draws underground water to a holding tank. Families haul water home in tank carts led by cows. Here, too, there are Mongol and Han schools, and clinics representing both medical traditions. There is a post office, train station, several hay buying firms, a state store, and township government offices. Other services are not well developed. A few people sell vegetables along the street, but there is no central market. There are fewer artisans, shops, and restaurants than in Sandhill. Although it is the center of township government, Great Pasture is more a dwelling place than a service town.

Making a Living in Great Pasture

Now that families depend on their own resources, the daily round of animal needs sets household schedules. Each type of animal has its own rhythm of activity, and the mix of animals raised defines options.

Dairying. In Sandhill and Great Pasture, people earn most from cows. Pasture, water, winter fodder and milk collection stations are the crucial resources that set work patterns. These are as important to Mongol as to Han dairymen, which is why they raise their cows much the same way. Herd and flock sizes, too, shape pastoral strategy, and here Sandhill and Great Pasture differ. Because they have less pasture and grass cutting land, Sandhill's dairymen make modest use of scientific methods to increase yields from smaller herds, and they cut hay only for their own use. In Great Pasture, dairymen try to increase the numbers and types of animals they tend; they give little attention to breeding for higher milk yields. They can herd more livestock, and the more they have the more worthwhile it is to cut hay for sale as well as for use.

When the Han first turned to pastoralism, they found that dairying better fit the sedentary way of life they knew as farmers. Mongols, used to a more mobile way of life, favored sheep. In recent years, many Han have added sheep, while Mongols have bought milk cows. As the specializations that once set Han and Mongols apart erode, their ways of life also become more alike. In looking at who does what and when, we focus on Great Pasture where dairying is important and complex. But most of what we have to say applies to Sandhill as well.

Dairymen anchor their animals near home. Cows move much less than sheep, which graze on the open grassland year round. In summer, they graze close to population concentrations where there are milk collection stations. Men work hardest in winter, when the animals are penned much of the time. Women labor most during the summer peak milking time. But the sorts of tasks men and women do and when they do them change little throughout the year. Men bring the animals in from pasture each evening. Women milk and send the milk cans to the collection station at the same time of day. Men and women do different things, and since men all do their work at about the same time, just as women all milk at the same time, exchanges of labor between sexes and between families are not easy to arrange.

Cows yield most from early spring through late autumn, with June through August the most productive months. During this eight month period, townsfolk deliver their milk to one of several collection stations twice a day. Trucks collect milk from shepherds as well, at a few central points on the grassland not far from town. In the early winter months, trucks collect only once a day in town and not at all on the grassland, where transportation is poor and shepherds raise fewer cows. So Mongol shepherds and the few Han dairymen who raise cows on the open grassland earn nothing from milk during the winter.

After the morning milking, men drive livestock to pasture. Most Great Pasture families graze their own cows, but in Sandhill professional cowboys do this work. When they bring the animals back in the evening, women milk them a second time, and pen them in courtyard stalls for the night. Cows that have recently calved and have more milk return at noon for an extra milking. Women remain at home and milk their cows whenever needed. Milking machines are still too costly for small herds and are hard to maintain.

Once the family cows have been put to pasture, men clean the pens, replace the top layer of earth, straw, and manure, and lay in new hay. They fertilize family gardens with some of the manure mixture and throw the rest on the dirt road in front of the house. During winter, Sandhill cows remain in pens. Great Pasture cows spend more of the winter in pastures, and some remain on the open grassland year round. But when the snows are heavy, dairymen in both places must feed their cows at least twice a day because, in contrast to sheep and horses, cows do not paw through snow for grass. Dairymen must also lead their cows to the river to drink, or carry water to their pens. Winter feeding, watering, and pen maintenance are heavy tasks, and dairying is labor intensive.

Most Han and Mongols in Sandhill and Great Pasture own cows. As shown in Table 6.1, herds are largest in Great Pasture, where the average Han household owns over twice as many cows as in Sandhill and nearly four times those in Middle Village. In Great Pasture, where larger herds spend more time in open pastures, and where men put more labor into cutting hay, dairying takes so much time and energy that neither men nor women can easily do other jobs.

Grass Cutting. The more cows a family has, the more worthwhile it is to cut hay. The scale of hay cutting is therefore greater in Great Pasture, where it has become an important money making sideline. Great Pasture exports hay to other parts of China and abroad to Japan through private and government firms. Here, haying demands an ample supply of strong men. Only those 20 and over cut grass. Brothers often join to do this work. They work together even after family division, pooling their machines

TABLE 6.1 Cow Ownership in Sandhill, Great Pasture, and Middle Village by Nationality: 1988*

							Cow Owners	
	Households (No.)		With Cows (%)		Mean Cows (No.)		% Owning > 15 Cows	
Location	Han	Mon-gol	Han	Mon-gol	Han	Mon-gol	Han	Mon-gol
Sandhill	136	45	83	96	6	6	3	7
Great Pasture	85	31	98	90	15	15	51	50
Middle Village	132	--	89	--	4	--	--	--

*Significantly more Han own cows in Great Pasture than in Sandhill. Han and Mongols do not differ in mean number of animals owned, and for both groups the means and the percentages owning more than 15 are significantly higher in Great Pasture.

and labor. They may also hire workers from outside. Just before grass cutting season, temporary laborers travel to Great Pasture looking for work. Local Han are all away cutting grass, unless they have few cows.

Fodder grasses grow in pastures without fresh water far from town, where few animals graze. Grass cutters remain on these distant grasslands for several months at a time. They must cut the grass and bring it in for delivery as soon as possible. Men ready their machinery and buy supplies in July, and cut their assigned areas in August and September. They drive several tractors at once, one worker at the wheel of each. A single machine pulls one or two hay cutting machines, also run by workers. Collecting machines, each operated by a man, are then drawn through the fields. Piling and stacking cut hay is heavy work. From October to mid-December, the workers transport the cut hay home without stop, to store for use or to deliver for sale. While hay is still in the fields, someone must remain there day and night to prevent people from stealing it or animals from grazing it.

While gainful and needed for dairying, haying can put a heavy burden on family labor. During all this time, there must be enough men at home to pasture cows and do the regular dairying tasks. Families with large herds, but without enough men to both cut grass and tend cows, may have to hire cowboys to pasture their animals during the haying season. Where labor is short at home, women or young children clean cow pens and do "men's jobs." Given the competing needs for male labor, families that cut hay cannot easily handle other, nonpastoral sidelines.

Shepherding. When Great Pasture Han turned to the pastoral way of life, they were not eager to spend long, uncomfortable periods on the open grasslands engaged in a risky pursuit. When the responsibility system began, therefore, most placed their small quota of sheep in the care of grassland dwelling Mongols. Sandhill families still do that. Sheep are most efficiently herded in sizeable flocks (over 200), and only those that specialized in sheep found it worthwhile. A Great Pasture Han described this earlier arrangement:

> When the responsibility system began, I was given 72 sheep because we had six persons in our family. Because we lacked labor, I put them into the care of a shepherd. He kept the lambs and wool and each year gave us six sheep to eat. The arrangement was that whenever we might want our animals back he would return the same number we'd given him. When the responsibility system first began, most of us were afraid of losing sheep and of being unable to repay their cost. In those days, it was even hard to find a willing shepherd to take your animals, because the risk in raising them was simply too great. My own solution was, eventually, to sell all my sheep.

But when the selling price of sheep began to rise, this man and others like him took that risk. Very few families raised sheep in Sandhill in 1987, and most of them were Mongol. There is not enough pasture there. More families, Han as well as Mongol, raise sheep in Great Pasture (Table 6.2). Mongols are more likely to have them, however, and their flocks are larger as well. Twenty-seven percent of Great Pasture's Mongol families owned over 200 sheep, but only 6 percent of Han had flocks that large. And while nearly half the Han in Great Pasture owned no sheep at all in 1987, more had acquired them or had enlarged existing flocks by the time we revisited that site two years later.

Sheep demand even closer attention than cows, they must be moved often and watched constantly. Mongols manage sheep differently from the Han. Before the collective era, most Mongols lived in yurts on the open grassland year round. Most still do. They carry their few belongings with them as they move. Mongols greatly prefer the open spaces and the convenience of the yurt. But as they expand their dairy herds, Mongols compromise their mobility and build fixed dwellings like the Han.

Some Mongols maintain three seasonal base encampments not far from Great Pasture. During spring, fall, and winter, women, the elderly, and pre-schoolers live in these camps while the men work elsewhere. The camps

TABLE 6.2 Sheep Ownership in Sandhill and Great Pasture by Percent with Sheep, Mean Number per Owning Household, and Nationality: 1988

Location	Households (No.)		With Sheep (%)		Mean Sheep (No.)	
	Han	Mongol	Han	Mongol	Han	Mongol
Sandhill	136	45	9	22	99	119
Great Pasture	85	31	56	71	76	174

are close enough to town and milk collection stations for families to market their milk, but still too far for children to attend school. For that reason some Mongols, even those without dairy cows, build or rent housing in town, temporary *pied a terres* for women and children that they leave once schooling ends. Others send children to town, to live with kin or in a dormitory, while both parents remain on the grassland.

Pastoralism had not been a part of the cultural legacy of Great Pasture's Han; the turn to dairying led to changes in familiar living patterns. The addition of sheep called for even greater adjustments, and the Han had much to learn from the Mongols. Han men began a more nomadic existence out on the open grassland, a life similar to that of the Mongols. Since they earned the most from dairying, however, the Han could not give up their fixed quarters in town, as principle residences for their families and dairy cows. The shepherds themselves live in yurts out on the open grassland, where they move the family flock from pasture to pasture. Some live in a third, permanent lodging on the grassland when they graze large cow herds year round.[6] Thus, whether Han or Mongol, all who raise both sheep and dairy cows need a fixed place to live in where they herd cows, and at least one movable abode where they tend sheep. They also need workers in both places.

Raising Sheep: Mongol and Han Ways

If cows demand sedentism, sheep are pastured on open grassland year round and require movement. Shepherds shift their yurts and flocks six times a year. There are also shorter moves of sheep. All shepherds fit their behavior to the flocks' seasonal movements. These bring Han and Mongol shepherds' living patterns closer. Indeed, Han shepherds have become the new nomads of China's northeastern frontier. Shepherding, not assimilation to Mongol culture, has brought about shared ways. Nevertheless, Han shepherds are more sedentary and use their family labor somewhat differently. We now turn to the round of seasonal shepherding activities. We shall see how dissimilar cultural legacies find their way into the details of flock management.

Spring. When the snows begin to melt, mounted shepherds lead their flocks from winter camps to pastures where grasses are exposed. They move out early so the sheep can quickly recover weight lost during winter. Because the weather can change suddenly at this time of year, still weakened sheep must be closely corralled at night to maintain body temperatures. Even with the closest attention, the animals can get sick because of the weight they have lost.

Mongol men, having earlier left their families to tend flocks in winter pasture, now return to their grassland winter quarters. Together, humans, cows, and sheep journey to spring camps some 15 km from Great Pasture. In contrast, when Han shepherds grazed their flocks in winter pastures, they left their families and cows behind in Great Pasture town. And when they move to spring camp, their families continue to live in town, with the cows. Han shepherds move their yurts and flocks closer to their families in spring, but continue to live apart, although visiting is easier.

Spring is also the time for lambing and shearing, both of which take much work. Each Mongol family has its own corral to protect lambs from the elements, and they lamb and shear near the family yurt. Han shepherds share more sturdy, stone lambing corrals built by the commune. Because they are all in one place, Han shepherds make an extra move in spring. From winter camps they go to spring encampments, then to the common lambing place, and finally back to spring camps for shearing. In all these grassland encampments the Han live in yurts. Most significantly, their families do not join them on the grassland but remain in town with the family cows.

It takes about 40 days for a large flock to lamb. During that time, the sheep demand attention day and night because they can birth at any time and need help. Several men work together. One watches over the sheep that will not deliver young; another helps the animals birth. A third handles the lambs, and a fourth cooks. Should the weather suddenly turn, the workers will have to corral carefully to keep the weakened ewes and their fragile lambs from catching cold.

Workers gather the ewes in covered corrals and watch for signs that an animal is about to birth. When a sheep stops moving and lies down, that is the signal that she is about to deliver. The men then carry her to a smaller protected enclosure to birth. The space is only big enough for a single ewe and her lamb, so the two can readily bond.

Unlike cows, sheep produce only enough milk for one lamb. There is no surplus to feed a second lamb. If the ewe rejects her lamb, therefore, the shepherds must force her to feed. They place her in an even smaller corral for several days. If that does not work, they bottle feed the lamb with cow's milk. After about a month, well fed lambs should be strong enough to graze with their mothers.

Shepherds shear in June, near their grassland yurts. A good sized flock takes about 20 days to shear, depending on weather and worker's skill. One by one, the workers toss animals over the corral fence into a smaller holding pen. There they tress their feet and shear them. The shepherds must do this work carefully and quickly. If the animals are shorn too late they will begin to shed on their own. That would slow their growth and put them in danger of cold during the coming winter. Temperatures on the grassland are changeable at this time of year and the animals are still weak. Bad weather can slow shearing down: a sudden rain could easily chill a freshly shorn animal. Shepherds therefore stop shearing when the weather turns bad, and start again only when it improves.

Summer. Shepherds travel far to the south for water and suitable pastures in summer. Sheep crop close, so if they are allowed to graze an area too long, they can destroy vital root systems and degrade the pasture. To allow grassland to recover, the township requires that all households with sheep move their flocks to pastures some 30 km to the south, near the Hui river. The animals graze there from early July through mid-August. Township cadres decide when this mass movement of people and animals will begin and end. They will fine any family that refuses to make the trek. From a command post set up on the banks of the Hui, cadres regulate pasture use and settle disputes over summer grazing areas.

In July, over 100,000 sheep will be led to these summer pastures. Families all make the necessary preparations at the same time. They prepare wagons, yurts, and supplies well in advance. A flock can move about 20 km in a single day, so the journey takes two days. Small tractors and horses pull carts bearing yurts and supplies. Once settled in, the shepherds move their flocks within the general area about twice each month. Cows travel at a different pace, and milk cannot be collected on the distant summer grasslands. For that reason, Mongol families with dairy cows usually split up again in summer. Wives, the elderly, and small children stay behind in spring camps with the cows and some lambs. There they tend their herds and deliver milk to the collection trucks each day. The families and herds of Han shepherds, as always, remain behind in Great Pasture.

Without constant attention, sheep can easily be lost or injured. Animals may go astray as the flock passes on two sides of a grassy knoll. They can be lamed when taller grasses get caught between their toes. Shepherds must also adjust grazing patterns to the weather. When it is unseasonably hot, sheep refuse to graze. To make up for their lack of daytime appetite, they must graze in the evening, lengthening the herder's day.

Fall and Winter. In mid-August, all shepherds return to camps closer to Great Pasture, to the same general area where their spring camps are located. Families that cut hay must send some men back earlier, a reason why Mongols with large flocks cut little grass. For Mongols this is a time when family, flock, and dairy herd come together again. But for Han, living patterns return to what they were in spring. Han shepherds return to grassland dwellings near town, while their families continue to live in town with the cattle.

Rams and ewes, shepherded separately in summer, are joined for breeding in autumn so their lambs will be born in early spring. The lambs will have time to grow large enough during the warmer months of the year to survive the harsh grassland winter. Shepherds here do not improve their flocks with artificial insemination. They claim that it is not practical to inseminate so many animals over so wide a space. Furthermore they believe that the procedure produces weak and slow growing lambs, with short wool that is hard to sheer. Such animals would be at risk in winter.

In November, shepherds again leave women, children, and the elderly behind in sheltered winter camps with the family cows, and lead their flocks to winter pastures. For two to three months, they move the sheep within the area several times. Shepherd and flock are constantly exposed to the elements. At night they pen the animals in metal corrals while the shepherds rest in their yurts. Mongol shepherds do not use valuable labor to cut winter fodder solely for sheep, and the larger the flock, the less practical cutting hay for them would be. They graze their animals on the open grassland throughout the winter instead. They lead their flocks to pastures with high grass, to places where, even when the snow is heavy, sheep will be able to dig through and find grass.

At this time, infectious diseases spread rapidly; injuries and losses are common. A sudden, unseasonal snow squall ("white disaster") can rapidly wipe out a flock if the animals are unable to find grass beneath. If winter snows are light, animals may not have enough to drink ("black disaster"). There is little that shepherds can do, although Han flocks are less at risk in a white disaster because they can divert some stored grass to feed their sheep. Nevertheless, all shepherds and flocks are exposed to nature's caprices. And at night family dogs may not be able to chase off the wolves. The discomforts and very real hazards of life on the open grassland underlie the common view that men are by nature more suited than women for the rigors of shepherding.

Division of Labor

Men tend their livestock every day, often in far flung locales, and much of what they do requires strength and experience. Herding is thought of as men's work, by women as well as by men. But the pastoral way requires the labor of women as well: men, women, young and old, all have their tasks.

Labor and Gender

Women and men both point out that, as in commune days, each sex has different work to do. Each family must pay constant attention to animals. The work often requires having family members in different places at the same time. Men have principle responsibility for the work away from home, and for the tasks that demand great strength. In Great Pasture, men hitch up tank carts and haul water home from the community pumping station each day. Only they have the strength to free fully laden water carts stuck in the mud. They shovel out cow pens, feed livestock in winter, and haul and pile hay, all of which also call for concerted power. Pasturing sheep through the deep cold of winter, too, imposes heavy physical demands. Women and men both classified such jobs as "heavy work," which is why people think of tending livestock as largely the domain of men.

Women do most of their work within compound gates. They care for children, build and maintain fires, clean, cook, wash, repair and refill the padding in winter clothing, sew new clothing, make shoes, garden and put up vegetables. They milk family cows in their own compound courtyards; they do not need to leave home even for that. An able woman can milk a dozen cows a day, although that would be considered a heavy load. If the family herd is larger, she will need help.

Women also have the unpleasant task of converting cow dung into cooking fuel. They shape it into disks, which they then turn and dry in the winter sun. Then they pile and store them. They also make the mud bricks used in summer to fix the house. They do all this with bare hands in bitter cold. Women also milk with bare hands, which takes much endurance.

People believe that women are built differently from men. They have more stamina. They can maintain long term, low levels of energy. Doing "lighter" work, women spread their energy evenly over time. While women are capable of short bursts of intense power, men are believed to be more so. On occasion, when there are not enough men, wives, daughters and young sons may help shovel out the family cow pen or pile straw, but most consider such work too taxing on a regular basis. There are few herding tasks for which Han women and men readily replace each other. Certainly, no one counts on women alone to do such work.

Lambing and shearing take strength as well. And shepherds and herdsmen must be able to lift and carry animals, once again work better left to men. Women and youngsters do even less in winter than at other times of the year. A woman may stand watch over sheep in deep winter, but relying too heavily on her limited experience could be costly. There is little room for error, especially with sheep, and loss of animals has an impact on later animal generations. We often heard comments like, "What would happen if there was a sudden rain storm and the sheep began to scatter? How could an inexperienced girl handle that?" For these reasons, women and young people do not normally do this sort of work.

Where the place and nature of the work of women and men vary, traditional ideas about the innate differences between women and men have been reinforced. Herding men and women do dissimilar work. They are taught separate skills, which confirms the original beliefs that they are inherently unlike and should be trained differently. By bolstering traditional concepts, the pastoral economy feeds a self fulfilling prophesy. Once culturally defined capabilities become the basis of task assignment, people considered wrong for certain jobs are not trained to do them. For that reason, it is hard to know how well women might perform the full range of herding work if they relieved themselves of child care and domestic obligations. People generally think of women's work as "domestic" and thus downplay its economic significance. This does not mean that they consider such work unimportant or easy. Indeed, while men often referred to the "lighter" work of women, they often also expressed respect for their endless efforts. Some even suggested that women may actually work harder than men.

While they may undervalue it, family members do notice women's input to the domestic enterprise. But in the popular view, women and men must do different things because they "differ physically" and "women need to stay close to home." The lines are more clearly drawn here than among the farmers and, for that reason, men show even less willingness to do "women's work." Once they enter the house, men are free to "rest." They may milk cows, even do housework, but only when female labor is short. And while women would appreciate having men do more around the house, they comment that what men and women do is natural and reasonable.

Even though they cannot fully take part, women work beyond the compound gates. A young woman may move with the shepherds so long as there is someone at base camp to care for the cows. There are cases in which young, unmarried daughters travel to summer or to winter pastures with their fathers or brothers. They go not to shepherd, however, but to cook and maintain the yurt. If shepherds leave summer pastures early to cut grass, and there are not enough men, women may watch over the flocks. Similarly, when dairymen go away to cut grass, there must be someone to pasture the family cows and clean the pens. If there are no young men at home, cowherds may be hired to graze the family cows. But sometimes a woman will put the animals out and bring them back. She may even do the heavy work of cleaning pens under such circumstances.

Han women, unlike their Mongol counterparts, remain in town year round and do most of their work there. If they are to tend family and milk cows, they cannot go to the open grassland to help shear and lamb, or cut grass with the hay cutters. Only where a serious shortage of men cannot be resolved some other way, and where a family has several able daughters, might a young woman play such a part. But she would then mostly cook.

Women assist but do not replace men in shepherding or grass cutting. Men simply have to work harder if they lack grown sons. A young Han woman can only provide short term relief watching over grazing sheep. Certainly she will not remain on the open grassland through winter. When the weather turns cold, she returns home and a brother or hired shepherd will replace her.

The types and numbers of animals a family has, along with cultural understandings, shape what different family members do. Thus, women in Mongol families with many sheep help with lambing and shearing. They can do so because their families are usually together on the grassland. Since young Mongol women live closer to grazing flocks, moreover, they can also relieve the shepherds. In these ways, differences in Han and Mongol economy and living patterns affect work and management styles.

Cooperation

But if Han women remain closer to the family compound, how do their families manage their animals and cut hay? In most cases, a family of two men and one able woman can handle regular tasks without help. People who need more labor cooperate with others or hire men. Han believe they can work best with close kin (Parish 1985). Just as the collectives lost efficiency when many different families worked together at a wide range of pastoral tasks, so today, small scale cooperation based on close ties work best.

Mongols, too, cooperate with closely related families to get work done. In summer, they usually pitch their yurts 0.5-1.0 km apart. They may set up their yurts even closer to join flocks and pool labor. Different families may work together, or in turn watch over the flock for several days. So long as the number of animals is manageable and the families few enough that everyone can be counted upon to meet their obligations in full, cooperation can be effective. Apart from such limited exchange of labor, they may also hire temporary workers to shear, lamb, or cut grass.

Labor and Age

Age is also considered in the assignment of work. Youngsters are too inexperienced to work much until about age 14 (much later than among the farmers). Until then they do only a few tasks, usually close to home. Children lead calves to nearby pastures at daybreak, and carry milk cans to the collection station. Teenage girls help milk. But in general, people under 20 do not fully participate in herding sheep or cows, milking, or cutting grass. They may fill in for adults but they cannot replace them. The work is too demanding and important to be entrusted without supervision to inexperienced youngsters.

At the other end of life, retirement comes later than among the cultivators. The elderly do vital work longer than among farmers, and their burden may be greater now than in the collective since families tend more animals, and a greater variety of animals, on their own. Apart from looking after the family gardens and doing some domestic work, men tend cows and sheep and women milk cows until they are quite old. The daughters of herdsmen go to school longer than those of farmers, another reason why women toil at household tasks longer among the pastoralists. Indeed, in contrast to the village elderly, couples here can make a living entirely on their own until they are quite old. They can reduce the number of cows they manage, the amount of pen cleaning and winter feeding they do. They can hire a professional cowherd to pasture their few cows. Their children will cut the hay they need, or they can trade their grass cutting rights for hay. Once they scale back their dairying operations and find help for the most strenuous tasks, people well on in years can care for several cows.

Birthing and shearing take more strength than dairying, but old people can handle a small flock, again with help. Experience is what counts. Even men in their seventies mount horses and watch over flocks in winter. Watching the flocks is boring, lonely, and cold, but does not demand great strength. Thus, pastoralists can remain independent until late in life.

Combining Tasks

Because herdsmen make a better living tending livestock than farmers can from simple cultivation, they take on few unrelated ventures. And because they work continuously at raising their livestock, often in distant places, they have little time for such ventures. Sidelines are therefore less popular here than among the farmers. Nor can Great Pasture families that cut large amounts of grass for sale or herd large flocks of sheep easily shift labor to scheduled jobs in Great Pasture or elsewhere.[7]

Herdsmen lack the slack periods of farming, and their division of labor is also less flexible, allowing fewer opportunities for women to stand in for men. As a result, herding families have less time and fewer workers for sidelines. Even weaving fences and baskets, the few sidelines women did during the commune era, are now gone. With the shift to a family based economy, families simply cannot spare the labor.

Instead, people expand their herds and flocks and change the mix of animals to increase their income. Here, too, there are constraints. Each type of livestock has its own needs. It is hard to shepherd and do other things because sheep and goats must be moved about year round. A great deal of time is spent astride a horse, and it is not possible to do much else at the same time. It is hard enough to combine grass cutting with dairying, but it is more difficult still to combine haying with shepherding. No matter, sheep and goats graze year round so they do not need hay. That is why Mongols cut less grass than Han, and often transfer cutting rights allotted them to Han dairymen in exchange for hay.

Nor can households easily combine sheep with dairy cows. Shepherds can increase the number of cows they tend only if they have a lot of labor, and specifically male labor. They must also alter their living styles, anchoring part of their families during some of the year. And for dairymen to add sheep, they must keep some men on the open grassland and maintain their town-based dairying life at the same time. In both cases, some family members must remain near a milk collection station, while others move with the sheep.[8]

Moreover, families with sizeable dairy herds must cut large amounts of fodder grass, which itself takes many men weeks of hard work far from home. So it is hard to combine shepherding, dairying, and grass cutting, although a few large Han families, with many able men, manage it. In short, herdsmen cannot easily combine pastoral activities or combine them with unrelated sidelines. To do so, they must have many family workers, cooperate with other families, or hire workers.

While farmers raise pigs and poultry, these do not much enrich the domestic economy or diet here. Smaller barnyard animals cannot easily travel and do not fare well on open grassland. They require costly and hard to get nutrient supplements. Women would have to feed the pigs and clean their pens, adding to the work of milking cows and helping to clean cow pens. Like the farmers, they would have gather, chop and cook leaves. But their minuscule backyard gardens barely suffice to meet family needs. Pigs would thus constitute a heavy burden.[9]

More surprising, in neither pastoral site do families process animal by-products to increase their incomes. Apart from the milk-tea drink that Han and Mongols enjoy at home and the sun dried cheese that Mongol families make, milk has little place in the local diet. Families have neither the machinery, capital, transportation, refrigeration, nor market for processing milk into cheese or other by-products for sale. A small collective factory that made powdered milk in Great Pasture failed. Another is still running in Sandhill, but at half capacity. There are problems of transport and quality control, and this modest operation cannot compete with Hailar's large modern milk processing plant.

For all these reasons, pastoralists still prefer to expand their herds and flocks to improve their incomes. Or, where they have too little pasture, they raise the productivity of their animals through scientific breeding and feeding. And the more successful they are at tending animals, the less likely they are to take full time jobs or try sidelines that remove them from their livestock, their main source of livelihood. As Sandhill's Mayor put it in a discussion of his town's prospects for the future, "The only option available to us now is to do better what we are already doing." In his view and that of others, it is not likely that outside capital will find its way to Sandhill to open new ways for making a living apart from dairying.

> Any industry built here would have to make use of local resources. But our resources are limited. We have few skills to offer, apart from herding. And because of poor quality and quantity of our livestock, we don't have enough animal products to meet industrial demand. So in order for us to attract investment, we will first have to deal with the problem of supply. If we can't expand our pasture then perhaps we can improve it. Only then might we increase the number and quality of our animals. But even then, we won't increase them by much.

Great Pasture people believe they have sufficient pasture to expand their livestock almost without end. They expect that they will continue to profit from the energy and money they invest in animals, which are their capital. But even here, they can only increase their livestock to the limits of grazing and hay pasture. Although labor need does not increase lock step with animal numbers, if they greatly enlarge herds and flocks they will need more workers, since machines cannot yet replace humans on the grasslands.

Because herdsmen make a good living from livestock, and can hope to do even better by raising more, outsiders without animals find a niche here. A Sandhill carpenter, hard pressed to meet a growing demand for new housing, cannot find local workers willing to toil:

> I never hire local people. For one thing, they lack the skills. For another, they aren't eager to do such hard work. And they need to go home to take care of their cows. Local people usually begin working for me at 8 or 9 in the morning. At noon they go home for lunch and rest. In the afternoon they want to finish working early, usually about 6 PM. So in the end they are only willing to work six or seven hours a day. Finally, the living standard of local

people is high. They can make a good living raising cows and fishing, and they feel that earning a living that way is much easier than construction.

So all my workers come from the south, from Hubei or Anhui provinces. They come in groups, looking for work each year during the construction months from May through October. They come from regions where there is little land but a lot of labor. Their wives and children manage the farm tasks while they are away. And the outsiders are prepared to work 11 to 12 hours a day! That's certainly more efficient for me than hiring local people.

The profitability and ongoing work of pastoralism deprive the carpenter of a local labor force. For families with a serious investment in pastoralism, other activities have little attraction. Not only are most of them are not easy to combine with pastoral work, but they are also not as rewarding.

Fishing

The Hailar river passes near both communities; livestock drink its waters, and men fish there. In summer men cast nets from boats; in winter they ice fish. Some Sandhill men and even more in Great Pasture work this lucrative non-pastoral sideline. Some Great Pasture Han earn even more from fishing than from animals, but none have given up pastoralism.[10] And this point is crucial.

Herdsmen cannot easily mix fishing and pastoralism. A dairying family that wants to fish needs a lot of money to lease a site and pay for equipment.[11] It must also gather men who know how to fish. Families bid for rights to river sites each year. Several men pool capital and labor to get one. Because more people fish than in the past, cadres limit the fishing period to prevent over fishing. Competition is keen, and obtaining a good site often requires a "back door" connection.

During the commune era, only Great Pasture's Han brigade fished. After privatization, a few Han families turned to fishing. Some did so because they were desperately trying to make up for livestock losses. They soon found that they could make more fishing than herding. But because fishing is uncertain, pastoralism remains to be their main work.

While fishing can net windfall profits, a lot depends on site and weather. Rights to specific fishing sites on the nearby Hailar river are gotten from the brigade. Members bid on specific sites and, if accepted, they get approval from the township government. They pay a fee to register the contract at the banner level. Every site has a different value, depending on location and past performance. Bidding competition is fierce.

Fishermen leave home for long periods, during which time they stay fixed on the river banks and cannot move about. Few shepherding families can afford to place men in fixed sites for such a long time. For that reason, Great Pasture Mongols rarely fish. They do not eat much fish anyway. More crucial, fishing would compete with shepherding.

The men let their sheep graze alone along the river banks while they fished. Because they paid too little attention to them, however, dozens of sheep followed each other into the river and drowned. Han shepherds, too, are not likely to fish. Nor is it simple to combine fishing with dairying or cutting grass without extra family labor or help from others, since haying and net fishing take place at the same time. We were told of one unfortunate Han family that did try to combine the two. In Sandhill and Great Pasture a successful family pastoralism encourages only more of the same.

Summary

Han and Mongols have their own distinct political, cultural, and economic interests. Although both make their livings from dairying and shepherding, dairying continues to be the main work of the Han, while shepherding is the Mongol specialty. But herding dictates a distinct division of labor that pulls Great Pasture Han away from their farming heritage. Pastoralism calls for patterns of work unlike those of farming. Livestock determine what must be done, by whom, when, and how, and prompts other changes in family and community life. In the next chapter we highlight some of the differences between pastoral Han and Mongols, and detail how the lifeways of Han pastoralists and farmers differ.

Notes

1.   The fee, 60 RMB for men and 30 for women, reflected the lesser value placed on women's work.

2.   One worker was added to these shepherding teams during lambing. In Mongol teams the day and night shepherds each earned 12 points per day, the cook (sometimes a woman) only 8 points.

3.   In the Han brigade, households were divided into three groups according to how long they had been in Great Pasture. The earliest residents, present from 1956 when the first collective was organized to 1959, got two grown cows and two grown horses. Members from 1960 to 1973 could buy one large and one small horse or cow, and families that joined after 1973 could buy only a calf and a young horse. Group assignment had no effect on the distribution of sheep, which were allotted by household size. Each Han, regardless of age or sex, was entitled to 12 sheep. In the Mongol brigades, every adult was entitled to 43, and larger animals were

divided equally among families. Each could buy a couple of steers or bulls, two milk cows, a pair of mares, and two geldings or stallions.

4.   In the Han brigade, strips 10 km long are allocated each household, the width determined by type of animal. To accommodate changes in the number and types of animals each family raises and in numbers of households, cadres redistribute grass cutting pasture every year (Han brigade), or every three years (the Mongol brigades).

5.   For example, cadres of the Han brigade used these funds to pay for electrification. Outside wiring cost nearly 10,000 RMB. It cost about 257 RMB per household to bring electricity to all homes in the brigade. Although debts to the brigade have not been removed from the books, brigade leaders decided to make further collections only "from time to time" as additional funds are needed.

6.   Shepherds often build semi-subterranean winter dwellings, structures more like the Chinese earthen home than the Mongol yurt. They dig a hole around five feet deep, and build a shallow wooden structure over it. During the bitter cold months, Han shepherds live either in such semi-subterranean houses, or in Mongol style yurts. The Mongols still usually prefer their traditional felt covered yurts even in deep winter, but an increasing number have now also adopted the more fixed, semi-subterranean abode for winter use. Because it is warmer than a yurt, some Mongols consider this healthier for women and infants. Tibetan nomads have similar structures. Ekvall (1968:33) records that one high pastoral tribe in southern Tibet moves once every three years and builds half cave, half sod houses at each move.

7.   In only 3 out of 85 Great Pasture Han households were family members living away, 9 persons in all, and only 1 was a worker. The rest were students or children. More people were reported away in Sandhill, not surprising given its urban classification and the greater ease of movement that allows. Out of 136 Han households there, 24 reported a total of 39 members living away. Only a few are workers or their spouses (9 people), the rest are students who left for better schools.

8.   Steers, cows without milk, and one to two year old calves can graze with the sheep. They move at a different pace, however, so it still takes more labor to manage both.

9.   Only 28 percent of Sandhill town residents and 7 percent of Great Pasture residents own a pig or two.

10.   Twelve of the Great Pasture Han households reported fishing income, but no Mongol families there did. In Sandhill, seven Han and seven Mongol households earned money from fishing.

11.   The annual costs vary greatly but, on average, a fishing site cost 7,000-8,000 RMB in 1990.

7

Chinese Herders: Economy and Society

Herdsmen care for livestock every day, and shepherds and hay cutters make long treks to grasslands far from population centers. These key features of pastoral production, daily care of livestock and management of distant grasslands, structure the rhythm, timing, and places of work. Although Han and Mongols have kept their discrete cultures, they work, marry and build their families in similar ways. We begin with the ethnic markers that Han and Mongol herdsmen carry forward from the past. Then we highlight the rewards of pure pastoralism, whose high profits attract Han and Mongol alike. We then explore how herdsmen form and reproduce their families. By comparing herding and peasant families, we see how pastoralism has forged a unique set of goals and means to achieve them, for Han as well as Mongols.

Ethnic Boundaries

Although Han and Mongols have both adopted the pastoral way of life, in crucial ways they are still culturally and socially far apart. At one level, they are members of the same community. They share many public and private facilities and have many community goals in common. They use the same post office, veterinarian, and animal inseminator. They shop in the same stores, sell animals to the same buyers, eat in the few local restaurants. They listen to identical cassettes; parents waltz at common social functions, while Han and Mongol teenagers play pool together and compete in sports.

But at another level, Mongols and Han still form their own subcommunities. We see this in dress, speech, political competition, the rarity of intermarriage, and occasional fights. Their separate nurseries, primary, and junior high schools instruct in different languages. Medical staff in two clinics treat from distinct traditions. More important for our study of how economic roles shape family organization, the mix of animals they prefer

170

and the way they manage them are not the same. The Han mainly raise dairy cows and in Great Pasture add to dairying by selling hay, raising sheep, and fishing. The Mongols are mainly shepherds. Although many raise dairy cows, they rarely cut hay for sale, and do not fish. Their economic pursuits reinforce ethnic traditions. Whereas the Han live in town with their cows, Mongols prefer life with their flocks on open grassland. The yurt is still the principal dwelling for 29 percent of all Great Pasture Mongols. Some Han own and use yurts as well, but none call them home.

The formal and informal understandings that govern political life in the Inner Mongolian Autonomous Region also reinforce ethnic boundaries (Gladney 1990). Mongols now take top civic seats, as well as many jobs in judicial, police, party, and state bodies. Although only a third of Sandhill's population, they hold most key positions. Two-fifths of Great Pasture's population, Mongols enjoy even firmer control over township administration there. Han and Mongols each promote their own political interests.

Whereas few of our farming Mongols speak anything but Mandarin and in habit and custom have all been thoroughly sinicized, this is not the case here. An ability to speak Mandarin is important in Sandhill, an administrative center, and nearly everyone there can speak it. But on the grassland, and notably in Great Pasture, there are more Mongols than in the farming area, and their way of life prevails. Mongol language is very much alive, and those living on the open grassland differ most from the Han. In fact, Mongols living in yurts go about their lives with little contact with Han. Nearly all Great Pasture Mongols speak their native language, even a few Han can manage some Mongol.[1]

Given the enduring cultural and political differences and the larger pool of marriageable minority men to choose from compared to the farming area, intermarriage is less common. Only 12 percent of Mongol women married Han in the pastoral area, and only 5 percent of Han women intermarried. But fully 69 percent of the minority farm women married Han. While only 7 percent of Han farm women intermarried, there are fewer eligible minority men there.

Ethnic apartness in the pastoral area reflects sensitivities and antagonisms just beneath the surface. Memories, experiences, and scars reinforce a silent division. Both sides voice distrust and look down on the other's culture. There was ample evidence of this during our stay. For example, six Great Pasture girls, ranging in age from 12 to 14, once came to look at us foreigners in their midst. When we asked if they had any Mongol friends, they laughed but didn't respond. When we pressed the question we learned that not one had a girlfriend among the many Mongol families living in town. They first mentioned language: "We can't speak Mongol." When we pointed out that most of the Mongols living in town can speak

Mandarin, the girls seemed embarrassed. "But they have different customs and eat different kinds of food," they protested. In fact there is little to distinguish the diets of Mongol and Han townsfolk. Pressing the question still further, we learned that Han and Mongol school boys sometimes fight. Disputes among boys from the two schools may easily expand; support aligns along ethnic lines (Jankowiak 1992).

Among adults as well, many Sandhill Han complain that Mongol cadres have little respect for education, resist change, and stand in the way of ambitious Han entrepreneurs. As one put it, "If a talented person does emerge, even if he becomes a cadre, he will soon find himself opposed and will in the end have to give up." Great Pasture Han complain that Mongols control the best jobs and grass cutting areas. They claim that Mongols benefit most from local development programs. They suspect that more state subsidies flow to Mongol grassland constituencies, and to the Mongol school and clinic. As one person bitterly put it, "We are all the children of one mother, but she favors one child over the other. All the best things she gives her Mongol child." During our stay with the farmers, we heard few such expressions of resentment from either side. In fact, the farmers were hard pressed to come up with any substantial differences between Han and non-Han. Their descriptions of wedding and funeral procedures, food preferences, and other cultural events turned up no variations of note.

Other Important Distinctions

Ethnic contrasts are not the only ones that divide people. Everywhere in China, type of household registration, a designation passed from parent to children, has until now defined privilege and opportunity. People with rural classification do not usually enjoy the variety of benefits available to non-rural folk (Davis 1988; Lin and Bian 1991; Walder 1986). Urban registered townspeople of Sandhill have better schools, cheaper grain, and a chance to work in government offices or factories. They have retirement pensions. Some get housing and a number of special services from their units.

In Sandhill, Mongols and Han make their livings mainly from dairying, but many also earn wages in the various state, banner, town, and township offices located there. The sort of work people do can also create social and political differences, and here Sandhill is the most diversified of our four sites. For example, some Gasumu township residents have left the grassland to live in town because they work in government offices, yet their economic and political interests are still in line with those of their grassland kin.

Likewise, households with railway workers form a distinct social sub-community in Sandhill and Great Pasture. Most live apart in special housing along the railroad track. Their work more closely links them socially to railway workers in other communities than to the other residents of Sandhill or Great Pasture. When their women deliver children, they do so in the better equipped hospital in Hailar City, rather than in a town clinic or with the help of a midwife. Their children attend the railway workers' school in Manzhouli City, and when they graduate have an inside track to railway jobs. Townspeople with government jobs also enjoy special privileges, and they, too, mingle mainly with each other. In Sandhill, Han hold most of the railroad and other specialized jobs, which further enlarges ethnic divisions there. In contrast, registration and occupation form little basis for identity in our farm villages, where all work the land.

Despite the greater diversity in Sandhill, most families there and all of those in Great Pasture raise livestock. Cadres, craftsmen, and artisans, whether Han or Mongol, urban or rural in registration, earn some income from animals. And when people raise the same mix of animals, and their ways of handling the animals are alike, other differences, including earnings and even those arising from ethnicity, narrow. Herding calls forth like ways of doing things, and earnings and spending patterns of the two pastoral communities are also alike.

The Pastoral Bottom Line

With the great profitability of pastoralism, Sandhill and Great Pasture families have enjoyed a rapid rise in income. People in Sandhill claim that real income has risen a lot since the shift to a privatized economy. The data in Table 7.1, given us by Great Pasture cadres, trace this rise in earnings.[2] The basis of this improvement is pastoralism. That income differences between communities exceed those between the ethnic groups within each site reflects the power of the economy to set family earnings.

Income is higher in Great Pasture, which specializes in herding, than in Sandhill, with its more restricted herding. For Han, the mean per capita income in 1987 was 1,156 RMB in Great Pasture and 811 RMB in Sandhill. Mongols earned nearly the same. As Table 7.2 shows, the larger part of all production value in both sites comes from animals and related products sold to state purchasing agencies.[3] But the overwhelming importance of pastoralism in Great Pasture (where herding and haying produce nine-tenths of all value) pulls up income there.

The two areas have their pastoral specialties: Han earn more from milk in Great Pasture (3,286 RMB) than in Sandhill (1,645 RMB). And, reflecting their vast grassland and ample herds, Great Pasture Han also

TABLE 7.1 Income Improvement in Great Pasture: 1985-1989*

Year	Township		Han Brigade	
	Net Income per Person (RMB)	Adjusted Net Income per Person (RMB)	Net Income per Person (RMB)	Adjusted Net Income per Person (RMB)
1985	410	410	363	363
1986	558	587	286	301
1987	480	473	417	411
1988	584	538	605	558
1989	783	---	851	---

*Using the rural cost of living index for Inner Mongolia, with 1985 as the base year to adjust for inflation, the mean real income per person for the whole township increased 31% between 1985 and 1988, 53% in the Han brigade.

TABLE 7.2 Income by Source, Location, and Nationality: 1987

Item	Sandhill %		Great Pasture %	
	Han (N=136)	Mongol (N=45)	Han (N=85)	Mongol (N=31)
Cultivation	6	7	1	1
Fishing	3	4	3	--
Hay	1	1	24	6
Pastoral animals	52	55	65	83
Pigs, poultry & eggs	3	4	1	--
Remittances	2	1	1	--
Sidelines	6	2	3	1
Wages	27	26	2	9
Totals (RMB)	580,008	229,174	608,668	214,875

bring in much more from cutting hay. Only 6 percent of Sandhill Han report income from hay (944 RMB). In Great Pasture, 61 percent have some, and the mean there is 2,808 RMB. Mongols earn far less from hay.[4]

More Sandhill families report earning some wages: 61 percent of the Han there compared to 12 percent in Great Pasture. The proportions of Han and Mongol families with wages, and the amounts they earn, are the same in Sandhill. Fewer families enjoy wages in Great Pasture, and more of them are Mongol. One-third of the Mongol families there had wages, only 12 percent of the Han. Mongols with few animals earn wages pasturing Han sheep, or helping with shearing or lambing. They also hire on at grass cutting time. And because Mongols control the administrative structure of Great Pasture, they also seize most of the regular jobs that come along.

Where people herd different livestock, expenses also vary. Since Sandhill has less pasture, feed constitutes a higher proportion of expenses (Table 7.3). And because many have jobs and herd fewer animals than in Great Pasture, over half the Han pay small amounts to have cowboys pasture their animals. In Great Pasture, ample herds and flocks make full time pastoralism worthwhile, so fewer families hire cowboys. Only 31 percent of Han there report paying wages, mainly during hay cutting. Since most hired workers are outsiders, wages add little income.

While recurrent production expenses listed in Table 7.3 comprise about the same proportion of income in both sites, Great Pasture Han spend more on costly, but less frequently bought, items.[5] In both places, for example, many families have bought large tractors to cut hay and transport goods. Because many more Great Pasture families cut hay, and in larger quantities, half now own a tractor (a third in Sandhill). And machines are far more common in our two pastoral sites than in the villages.[6]

In Sandhill and Great Pasture alike, animals are the basis of livelihood. The requirements of these animals are responsible for a distinctive pastoral way of life. But when it comes to income, pastoralism can also create diversity, particularly under the family responsibility system. The mix of animals, herd and flock sizes, and the other sources of income people can tap, give rise to new types of community hierarchies.

The Responsibility System and Socioeconomic Differentiation

Whether Han or Mongol, herders earn more than farmers. Table 7.4 shows that income decreases as we go from extensive pastoralism to pure cultivation. Tranquillity farmers earn the least despite the supplement of sidelines. Shed dairying adds a fillip to Middle Village earnings, just as wages greatly increase income in Sandhill.[7] But Great Pasture households, with their more exclusive and extensive form of pastoralism, earn the most.

TABLE 7.3 Expenses by Type, Location, and Nationality: 1987

	Sandhill %		Great Pasture %	
Type Expense	Han (N=136)	Mongol (N=45)	Han (N=85)	Mongol (N=31)
Equipment Repair	3	14	8	6
Feed	61	50	45	67
Fertilizer	2	--	--	--
Fuel	6	12	21	16
Insecticide	--	--	--	--
Labor	5	8	14	1
Remittances	14	10	4	1
Seed	--	1	--	--
Sidelines	--	--	--	--
Taxes	4	2	6	3
Veterinarian	5	3	2	6
Totals (RMB)	130,992	51,995	184,234	47,187

TABLE 7.4 Net Income by Location and Ethnicity: 1987

	Han			Mongol		
Location	No.	Mean per House- hold (RMB)	Mean per Person (RMB)	No.	Mean per House- hold (RMB)	Mean per Person (RMB)
Great Pasture	85	4,993	1,156	31	5,409	1,125
Sandhill	136	3,302	811	45	3,937	814
Middle Village	132	3,240	712	--	---	---
Tranquillity	106	2,837	594	--	---	---

Associated with disparities among communities are differences in the way wealth is distributed within them.

Measuring "Wealth" -- A Problem

Extensive herders are wealthier than others but income differences are also greatest among them. Still, we found no evidence of widespread poverty in any of the sites we visited. This becomes clear if, in comparing communities, we keep in mind that the income a family earns in any one year is not, by itself, a sufficient indicator of wealth. It is most imprecise for pastoralists, because while we use the value of all production (sold and consumed) to calculate net income, we could not evaluate their capital assets, livestock, and machines. Animals embody expendable as well as expandable capital; they represent wealth on the hoof.[8] The dairyman or shepherd invests care, feed, and capital in them and, if all goes well, they multiply. Farmers also invest labor and capital in their land, but the area they cultivate does not grow.

Even herdsmen with ample livestock and equipment may experience years of low or negative income. They may have to replace animals they lose to natural catastrophe. They may buy or repair the large tractors and other machines they use during grass cutting. Unavoidable social expenses, too, can produce negative incomes, even for those with large herds or flocks. For example, parents spend heavily when a son marries, and herdsmen spend far more than farmers. But these are all episodic and usually short term challenges to the budget.

Overall costs, like incomes, are similar in Sandhill and Middle villages, and levels are far below those in Great Pasture. Tranquillity, most outside the money economy, has the lowest production costs. Pastoralists (including the part-pastoralists in Middle Village), spend more on equipment repair, labor, and animal feeds than the pure cultivators. Because they raise many animals, they need substantial feed. But taxes comprise a larger proportion of farm expenses. They are higher in absolute terms as well. Perhaps cadres can more easily assess fixed land area than determine numbers of animals, the basis of much taxation in the pastoral areas. They also have more trouble collecting taxes on the grassland.

The regular production costs of farmers are lower, but so is their income. As a result, even a small rise in expenses can throw a family into enduring debt. They, too, contend with unusual, temporary shortfalls, but they cannot easily make them up. Although farmers pay less on marriage, they also sell animals or equipment to meet these expenses. Yet they have less to sell. For these reasons, a comparison of net per capita incomes alone does not take into account the levels of risk families take on or their ability to rebound from setbacks. We must keep this contrast between the economies of herdsmen and farmers in mind when we assess income levels in the four communities.

Income Distribution

Privatization and diversification have increased income inequalities within, as well as between, communities. The more extensive pastoral regime enlarges income inequalities the most. As Table 7.5 shows, Great Pasture has the largest proportion of wealthy households and the widest income spread (Gini scores) of all four communities. Sandhill, with its substantial wage supplement, has the second largest proportion of wealthy households, Tranquillity the lowest.

Although some herdsmen have benefitted from the new economy more than others, people do not complain about grinding poverty. To the contrary, they perceive a rise in living standards for most people. They believe that while some have become much wealthier, there are fewer poor households than before. Indeed, our Sandhill survey does not find many

TABLE 7.5 Per Capita Income by Location: Han 1987

Income (RMB)	Great Pasture (%)	Sandhill (%)	Middle Village (%)	Tranquillity (%)
200 or less	12.9	4.4	6.8	6.7
201-400	5.9	14.1	18.2	25.7
401-600	10.6	20.7	23.5	26.7
601-800	14.1	18.5	15.2	21.9
801-1000	4.7	12.6	16.7	7.6
1001-1200	10.6	11.1	6.8	3.8
1201-1400	10.6	5.9	5.3	4.8
1401+	30.6	12.6	7.6	2.9
Gini	.42	.31	.32	.34
No. households	85	135	132	105

"poor" households. Only 4 percent of Han there have per capita net incomes of 200 RMB or less, fewer than in our cultivating sites.[9] But in Great Pasture, 13 percent earn this little. Yet, if we exclude those that reported unusual expenditures for animals, tractors, or homes, and those with sizeable herds (capital), we are left with only four "poor" households. That amounts to only 5 percent of all Great Pasture Han households. There is no evidence, then, that privatization results in significant impoverishment in any of these sites.

Herd Size and Income

Keenly aware of their grassland limitations, Sandhillers have been improving the quality of their herds, while cadres plan to limit herd sizes. The number of cows continues to grow there nonetheless, and even more dramatically in Great Pasture, along with the demand for hay. And reflecting their rising value, the number of Great Pasture sheep has also increased (Watson et al. 1989).[10] Han think of livestock as forms of capital -- savings on the hoof. Dairymen stated that the more animals they have and the heavier when sold, the wealthier the family will be. Chasing numbers, the Han hold their animals longer than might be sensible (Hinton 1990). They may do that not simply because they value size and numbers, but also because they anticipate a need for large amounts of capital for a marriage, a start up herd for the new couple, or a new house. Families that have more animals can also weather sharp changes in earnings or expenditures. When the Han apply this "more is better" strategy to sheep, it can be even more problematic since they are particularly hard on pasture. By damaging pasture, they can threaten the livelihood of all.

Somewhat different values and objectives guide Mongol practice. Before the rising price of milk induced them to take up dairying for the market, Mongols only sold sheep and wool. They are accustomed to eating and selling animals, and mutton continues to be their staple food. And raising sheep in itself limits the number of dairy cows they care for. Given nature's caprices, it is risky to hold sheep long. Mongols are keenly aware that they must keep flock sizes in check to balance the needs of animals and pastures over the long haul. Thus, a more conservative view of the grassland's animal carrying capacity may underlie their lesser concern for numbers.[11]

In contrast, Han noted with contempt that Mongols worry less about the number of sheep they have and are all too willing to eat and sell animals. As one Great Pasture dairyman explained it,

They make their livings mainly by selling wool and mutton. Since they earn relatively less from milk, they have to rely heavily on sales of sheep for a living. And because of that their flocks don't grow as quickly as ours. Since our dairy herds are larger, it's less urgent for us to sell off our sheep.

Less generous Han impute this supposed Mongol trait to laziness, even irrationality. They credit the Mongol failure to expand their flocks to "poor managerial skills," or to the absence of a strong "entrepreneurial tradition" like that of the Han. One assured us that grassland dwelling Mongols,

> have a cultural block against development. They see no virtue in expanding their herds or flocks. While ours increase in size, theirs do not. They're not good businessmen. When they get money by selling wool or animals, they don't invest it wisely. If they decide to buy something, they simply go into a store, plop down a fist full of money and say "take whatever it costs."

Clearly, powerful cultural as well as economic factors underlie the different attitudes and pastoral strategies of Han and Mongols. Nonetheless, both make a good living from livestock, certainly a better one than the farmers. And despite their differences, both believe that they will do better still so long as they can raise more animals.

Education and Income

Young pastoralists begin working later than farmers and, as Table 7.6 shows, they also go to school longer. Because important herding tasks call for experience and not simply for hands, the pastoralists make less use of children's labor. Even shepherds expect to see their children complete elementary school. Mongol girls and boys attend school as long as Han.

Education has improved over time for all pastoralists, especially for women. Indeed, many Han and Mongol children now attend school through junior high. Because girls do less herding work than boys, and much of that takes place in or near home, in the morning or evening, the girls are more easily spared to attend school. As a result, younger females are now somewhat better educated than males; a higher proportion go to middle school. In contrast, because they begin working earlier, farmers get less schooling than pastoralists. Farm girls receive the least.

Education levels are of course high in Sandhill; indeed, for several years the town had its own high school. We might also expect boys to be better educated there, since herding is smaller in scale and hay cutting less important than in Great Pasture. This is not the case. Girls are better educated than boys before age 20; only older men have more education

TABLE 7.6 Level of Education by Age, Sex, and Ecoarea: Han 1988

Age	Sex	Area	No.	Percent			
				Illit.	*Prim.*	*Middle*	*High+*
10-14	Male	Herder	72	6	83	11	--
		Farmer	58	3	83	14	--
	Female	Herder	75	5	72	21	1
		Farmer	75	4	88	8	--
15-19	Male	Herder	70	4	26	61	9
		Farmer	84	4	48	49	--
	Female	Herder	75	4	7	80	10
		Farmer	74	4	54	37	5
20-39	Male	Herder	165	6	27	48	20
		Farmer	196	1	54	31	14
	Female	Herder	151	10	27	41	22
		Farmer	184	14	59	24	4
40-59	Male	Herder	75	12	59	23	6
		Farmer	89	18	56	25	1
	Female	Herder	86	47	41	12	1
		Farmer	78	51	46	3	--
60+	Male	Herder	37	43	57	--	--
		Farmer	51	65	33	2	--
	Female	Herder	29	97	--	3	--
		Farmer	38	87	11	3	--

than women their age. Further, educational levels in the two herding communities are the same. So Sandhill's more urban character cannot explain why herdsmen study longer than farmers.

That pastoral youngsters go to school longer than farmers is not so much because education has something more to offer them.[12] Indeed, parents grumble that the young work less than ever, yet enjoy themselves and spend money more freely. They criticize their daughters for being less helpful than in the past, and for having "more interest in clothing fashions than in milking cows or doing domestic work." They "spend a lot of time doing nothing." Such complaints surely reflect a generation gap, and might therefore be heard anywhere. But we did observe more youngsters in the pastoral towns lounging about, chatting or playing pool, at all times of day. It was common to see groups of well dressed young girls "hanging out." But farm children were busy hoeing tobacco, weeding, and helping out.

Herdsmen are likely to send their children to school longer mainly because they need them less at home. Still, some parents do want their children to finish high school which, by opening a route to urban jobs, might present an alternative to pastoral life. The path to sought after technical jobs is through high school, which few rural youth can get into. They must pass competitive tests and at graduation are still unlikely to find an urban job. Even when they do, the jobs are usually temporary and bring no pensions. But for most, once children begin to herd, parents usually lose interest in having them in school. There is little evidence that education beyond middle school will boost the earnings of these children destined to be herdsmen like their parents.

Responsibility, Private Enterprise, and Labor

Pastoral families can do well enough with relatively few workers. They can adjust the number and kinds of livestock to the hands in their family. The labor demand of pastoralism differs greatly from cultivation, with its four marked peaks. The harvest alone takes so much labor that farm households without several workers simply cannot bring in their crops without outside help. It is harder, then, for the farmer to adapt to changes in family workers. Farmland, unlike livestock, cannot be sold and bought back later. And when farmers are short handed, they cannot further reduce already tiny farms without threatening their basic livelihoods. But pastoralists can expand their herds and flocks without adding much manpower. In the other direction, a family that has partitioned or a household of old folk may not have enough labor for a sizable flock or herd. But it can always reduce its work if it sells some animals and raises one kind of livestock. Herding households can also temporarily merge herds and flocks when labor is short, and take them back later when they have more workers.

Although pastoral families can make do with less labor than farmers, they now need more than before. The new economic policy allows them to expand and diversify to enlarge their incomes. Only families with many workers, and in particular with several males, can take full advantage of the new opportunities. So, herdsmen may begin to delay or avoid family partition. In the future, however, we may begin to find more pastoral "joint families" of married brothers, until now rare.[13]

Since they can expand and mix livestock, herdsmen cooperate to increase their manpower after they divide the family. Separated brothers, even in-laws, combine workers and machines to cut grass, shear or lamb, or to graze their animals. The farmers we visited rarely hire workers, but the Great Pasture dairymen that cut large amounts of hay commonly do. They hire outsiders, farmers who travel to the grasslands during their slack periods. A few hands can also be found among the so-called "black households," unregistered immigrants who fled the strict family planning regulations of their home villages. Han shepherds are also likely to hire help with their sheep to free their household members for dairying. Their women cannot help much with the sheep, since the family cows keep them in town year round.

Herdsmen can make a basic living with fewer hands than a farmer, but with ample family labor they can do even better. We find a significant relationship between household size and income; larger households earn more.[14] Families with many workers can expand their herds, raise different sorts of animals, and even cut grass for sale or fish.[15] Multiple regression indicates that in the pastoral sites only the number of men in a family is significantly related to income. Household size and income are related for farmers as well. Here, however, the number of women a farming household has is also related to income, evidence of the more important and more varied role of farm women.

Household size, income from animals and their products, from sidelines, and grass cutting, all contribute to overall income.[16] Multiple regression lets us sort out the relative contribution of these, and several other income sources, to differences in households' income.[17] In Sandhill, earnings from animals and from wages add most to income disparities. In Great Pasture the pastoral track is really the only one. There, dairying, and especially grass cutting, account for most of the income variance. Wages and sidelines make a smaller contribution to differences of income than in Sandhill; fishing is somewhat more important. With privatization, the pastoralists increased animal husbandry and hay cutting, but did not develop sidelines. But among the farmers, sidelines enlarge income disparities between households more than does the amount of land people farm.

Rising Living Standards

While families in all four of our research sites are much better off since privatization, the herdsmen have profited most. It is true that both peoples produce much of what they need to subsist. Herdsmen, like farmers, raise or grow much of their food.[18] They butcher their own meat and grow vegetables in small family gardens. In both pastoral sites, people use manure for cooking and heating. But both lay out cash for other daily needs. As Table 7.7 shows, herdsmen spend far more on food, nondurables, durables, housing, ritual, medical expenses, education, transportation, telephone, movies, and gifts at weddings. In addition, twice as many herdsmen support kin.[19] Because herdsmen earn more than farmers, their living expenses claim a lower proportion of household income.

Han herdsmen not only spend more on tractors, but also on TVs, radios, and other previously rare household goods (Table 7.8). They buy more clothes washers and sewing machines than the farmers. Of course the Mongols, as they move about on the open grassland, cannot carry large machines. TVs only make sense for the few that own mobile power generators. Mongols do buy battery driven tape recorders and peddle-operated sewing machines. Standard of living can also be measured in years of education achieved, and herders enjoy the edge here as well. They also spend much more than the farmers on their weddings.

The Cost of Marriage

New found prosperity has driven up the cost of marriage. For Han herdsmen, expenses for both groom's and bride's family rose from the period 1960-1978 to 1979-1988. In both periods, every man that married spent something, but the mean nearly quadrupled.[20] Hardly anyone paid over 3,000 RMB to marry during the first period, but 25 percent did during the second. In one case, total cost reached 13,000 RMB.[21] The farmers, who sorely need the labor of brides, spent more marrying sons during the first period. By the second period, as herders displayed new affluence, their sons' marriage costs outstripped those of the average farmer.

The cost of marrying a daughter has also risen, although her parents still pay only a fraction of a groom's expenses. The proportion of Han brides' families paying for dowries and banquets increased significantly from 63 to 83 percent. The mean amount they spent also rose from 216 RMB to 666 RMB over the two periods. If we define "costly" on the bride's side as 500 RMB or over, we find that the proportion of costly marriages of Han brides rose from 8 percent in 1960-1978 to 55 percent during the 1979-88 period.

The labor of women is important in both areas, so men often repay their

TABLE 7.7 Living Costs by Ecoarea: Han 1987[a]

Cost Item	Herders Mean per Household	(%)	Farmers Mean per Household	(%)
Durables	171	5	86	3
Education	156	5	60	2
Food	1,631	47	1,432	52
Housing	566	16	259	9
Medical	222	6	242	9
Nondurables	379	11	289	10
Other Social	181	5	150	5
Ritual	179	5	250	9
Totals (RMB)	3,487	100	2,768	99[b]

[a]"Living costs" include amounts paid for purchased items and the value of food produced calculated in local market prices. "Food" includes meat, grain, supplements, dairy products, tobacco, tea, and liquor consumed. "Other social" costs refer to transportation and miscellaneous expenses. The proportional contribution of all items to overall living costs did not differ significantly between pastoral sites.

[b]Short of 100 percent due to rounding error.

wives' families for their loss. Thus, bridewealth without dowry was more common than dowry without bridewealth. But here lies a crucial difference between ecoareas. Where women furnish less labor, their parents may need to give dowries so that their daughters can find a mate. In the pastoral area, where the non-domestic work of women is seen as less central, less diversified, and less easily substituted for the labor of men, families pay more to bolster a daughter's worth. Thus, the families of Han pastoral women give dowries far more often than those of farm girls. However, while it is true that herders spend more than farmers on the marriage of daughters, they do so for sons as well. They simply have more money.

Parents prepare for marriage long in advance, and they have to assume that the cost will keep going up. For herdsmen, marriage of a son is a heavy burden because, in addition to the wedding itself, parents build a home for the couple. While farmers more often live patrilocally when they

TABLE 7.8 Consumer Durables by Location and Percent Households Owning at Least One: Han 1988

Item	Sandhill	Great Pasture	All Herders	All Farmers
Bicycle	93	88	91	82
Clock	79	73	77	72
Clothes washer	58	58	58	8
Motorcycle	10	1	7	1
Radio	34	55	42	47
Sewing machine	82	79	81	61
Sofa	56	49	53	13
Tape recorder	46	39	43	15
TV	85	66	77	46
Watch	89	91	90	83
No. households	136	85	221	239

marry, it is the herdsmen's custom that all sons but one set up an independent family. A bridegroom's parents will sell livestock to meet these charges. And in addition, they endow the couple with a herd or flock. Such obligations give more reason to chase after animal numbers. Whether herdsman or farmer, with improved living standards, the cost of getting married and starting a new family has spiralled.

Patterns of Marriage

Pastoralists spend more on the education and marriage of children, although those children contribute later than among the farmers. The cost of raising sons is especially heavy. Herdsmen take on the burden even knowing that all but one of their children will likely leave when they marry. The break is not absolute, of course, since help continues after separation. Indeed, if parents can tap that potential, they can do better under the new privatized system. Parents can also survive without many grown children if they have to. This feature of the pastoral economy underlies distinctive patterns of marriage and family, and affects attitudes about childbearing.

Finding Brides

Herdsmen, like farmers, try to match prospective mates closely. Recency of migration and ethnic divisions all influence choice. Because they are migrants from distant places, or their offspring, few Han are so closely related that they cannot marry. They are also surrounded by people culturally different. The minority population is larger here than in the farming area. The pool of eligible Han spouses is particularly small and localized in Great Pasture. This fosters community endogamy.[22] Sandhill has more Han, many with urban registration. More come and go, and people have frequent contacts outside. Many are migrants who brought wives, or for whom spouses were found in their home towns.[23] Still, in both areas, most men raised in the community have married local girls.[24]

People prefer partners with similar education.[25] Because girls go to school longer than among the farmers, a higher proportion of brides here are better educated than their husbands.[26] Household registration also creates endogamous groups with different opportunities. The minority with urban registration marry like people, or do their best to upgrade registration after marriage. In Sandhill, where close to two-fifths of our sample have urban registration, nearly all such household heads married women with urban papers. Those with rural registration all have rural wives.

Even though there are more potential ethnic minority partners for Han here than in the farming area, there is little intermarriage. Where intermarriage does occur, it usually between a better educated Han with a good job and a Mongol woman. Similarly, in those rare cases where a Han women crosses over, she marries a Mongol of solid standing. In Sandhill, for example, a few Han women have taken as husbands Mongol state workers, staff, cadres, or soldiers -- all with urban registration.[27]

Marriage Age & Marital Residence

Because herdsmen cannot use youthful workers and need fewer women to work than farmers, they can delay marriage.[28] As Table 7.9 shows, they have long done so. Because farm women work younger, and what they do is seen as crucial, parents try to bring daughters-in-law into their families as soon as possible. Thus, they are more likely than herdsmen to marry before legal ages. From 1950-1980 (when legal age at marriage was 18 for women and 20 for men), 17 percent of the farm men and 13 percent of the

188

TABLE 7.9 Mean Han Marriage Ages by Sex, Present Age, and Ecoarea: 1988*

Present Age	Ecoarea	Women		Men	
		No.	Mean	No.	Mean
15-29	Herders	59	21.6	46	22.8
	Farmers	82	19.9	71	21.0
30-39	Herders	74	21.9	77	22.8
	Farmers	85	20.0	75	22.6
40+	Herders	105	19.5	109	24.1
	Farmers	94	19.7	126	22.7

*Ever married women.

herdsmen married younger. The difference for women was even greater --
22 percent of the farm brides but only 8 percent of the herding women
married early. From 1981, when the minimum ages at marriage were raised
to 20 for women and 22 for men, 45 percent of the farm men and 39
percent of the farm wives married younger. Only 14 percent of the herding
sons and only 9 percent of the daughters married before the legal age.

Herdsmen marry later, and divide their families later too. The Han
custom is for all but one son to leave home at, or just after, marriage.
Because they can adjust animal numbers and pastoral activities to fit family
labor, sons can more easily leave their parents at marriage. It is also easier
for herding than farming newlyweds to leave, because family division will
not set them back for very long. Animals are easier to divide than land,
and they reproduce afterward.[29] Both families may quickly recover.
Nonetheless, herdsmen delay marriage, and therefore partition, because
they must give sons a herd and a home when they wed. And parents who
lose their son's labor do suffer, because men do so many more things than
women, and also because women less easily fill in than among the farmers.

Cultivators usually partition some time after marriage. The division often
reduces earnings for both of the reorganized family units. When a farming
son leaves his parents, the small amount of land he takes has no growth
potential. Often it is not even the best land a family has. Therefore,
farmers try to avoid family division and more commonly achieve the
traditional goal of patrilocal marriage.

More pastoralists live neolocally after marriage than farmers, and this has
long been the case.[30] As Table 7.10 shows, nearly twice as many pastoral

Han women lived neolocally from the time of their marriages. And there is little difference between Han and Mongol pastoralists in postmarital residence. That post-marital residence is just as likely for both suggests that the way herdsmen use labor shapes marital residence more than does ethnic background.

Family and Kinship

After marriage, the different labor needs of herding and farming continue to affect family form and composition. In all sites, Han opt for the bride to join her husband and his family at marriage, which creates stem families. Whether herdsman or farmer, young adults care for the elderly. With family limitation, rising life expectancy, and an increase in the cost of living, this is a heavy task. Rural folk still lack the pensions that urban workers enjoy, and public services for the elderly have shrunk since collectives were disbanded. In all four locales, older folk most often live in stem families. Aging herders can gradually reduce the amount of work they do if they live with a son. The son and his wife also benefit because even the elderly can do some useful work. Stem families create a larger pool of labor.[31]

Where families have large herds, and especially where they combine different kinds of livestock and cut hay or fish, labor needs increase. In such cases, one son will remain with his parents after marriage. His brothers normally leave when they marry, however, and in some cases all sons may move away at marriage. Thereafter, they may give their parents money each month, send over fodder hay and contribute labor when

TABLE 7.10 Postmarital Residence by Ecoarea: Women Married 1949 or After

Postmarital Residence	Herders*		Farmers Han (%)
	Han (%)	Mongols (%)	
Patrilocal	47	52	74
Matrilocal	3	3	1
Neolocal	45	43	25
Duolocal	5	1	--
No. women	204	99	230

*The distributions for herders and farmers differ significantly.

needed. Married daughters often milk or do some housework for their parents. Some pay small sums to their mothers in return for baby sitting. Nearly half the herding households support kin. Among the cultivators, since parents remain with their son, only one-fifth support kin.[32]

Herding sons more often give their parents money than the farmers do, because older folk are more likely to live apart and be more independent. They can often earn a living on their own. By reducing the size of their herds and flocks, passing animals to children as they marry, or selling them off, by depending on children or buying hay or labor, an older couple can make a modest living. They raise and milk a few cows as long as they can. When they can no longer do that, they move in with one of their children. This does not usually happen until they reach their late sixties or seventies, however, a later age than for cultivators. Some make a go of it to a fairly old age by supplementing dairy income with pensions (in Sandhill), with part time wages, and with small remittances and other help from children.

Family imagery reflects this fact. Elderly herdsmen are proud that if they scale back, they can live independently, and they see that as acceptable until they are quite old or infirm. In this sense too, family division is a less traumatic event among the pastoralists. They do not accuse sons who leave of lacking filial piety. Indeed, parents often urge them to move out at marriage and view the separation as natural. They assert that a prompt departure can avoid tensions that might otherwise sour family relations.

In contrast, cultivators do not wish to live alone. It is especially important that farm households contain a second woman because it is hard for one to farm and manage domestic work. By caring for children, and taking on some of the burden of housekeeping, an older woman can relieve her daughter-in-law for work in the fields or in sidelines. By remaining together, then, a farm family can reduce dependence on others and increase its ability to diversify. Stem families are also more suited to the needs of cultivators because farm work is too hard for old people on their own.

We thus find that 9.5 percent of all Han herding households, but only 2.5 percent of farm households consist of single couples or individuals. Most were older folks.[33] Further, whereas 61 percent of all herding households contain people 65 or older, 84 percent of the farming households do.[34] As Table 7.11 shows, stem families are less common and nuclear families more common among the herdsmen.[35] Herding Han households are simpler and smaller with only 4.5 persons; farming households have 4.9 persons.[36]

Pastoralism and Family Reproduction

Herdsmen need to raise two or three children to do their full range of pastoral activities, and they need more males than females. Grown children

TABLE 7.11 Family Forms by Ecoarea: 1988

Family Form	Herders*		Han Farmers (%)
	Han (%)	Mongol (%)	
Nuclear	73	73	67
Stem	17	23	30
Joint	1	--	---
Solitary	2	--	1
Couple	7	4	2
No. households	221	75	238

*The distributions for Han and Mongol herdsmen are not significantly different.

care for the elderly, and aging parents prefer to live with a married son. And a family with many adults that diversifies its undertakings can increase its income. Still, since their children contribute to the domestic economy later but cost more to raise, herdsmen aim for smaller families than farmers. There are, as well, other indirect factors that limit reproduction.

Pre-Family Planning Fertility

Pastoral Han have long had fewer children than farmers. We believe that the way herders use labor and the nature of their family organization lowers their fertility.[37] We find no significant difference in mean parity between pastoral Mongols and Han, but pastoral and farming Han are unlike. This suggests that differences in economy and ecology are more important than ethnicity. Farm women marry earlier. They put in more time outside the home and are needed sooner. Since all women bear their first children as soon as possible, the earlier marriage of farmers could increase their fertility. Indeed, as Table 7.12 shows, mean parities have long been higher for the cultivators.[38] Parity progressions, too, show higher farmer fertility. Earlier marriage contributed, but is not the whole story. Farmers 40 and over bore more children even though they did not marry earlier. Each cohort of farm women had more children during the first 10 years of marriage (Table 7.13).

We wondered whether they might have had more because their children died earlier and more often. Mothers that lose infants stop nursing and

TABLE 7.12 Mean Parity and Parity Progression by Ecoarea: Han*

Area and Age	Married		Mean Parity	Parity Progression (%)			
	No. Married	% All Women		0	1	2	3+
Herders							
15-29	59	41	1.4	15	41	37	7
30-39	74	100	2.8	5	3	35	57
40+	105	99	5.4	6	5	4	86
Farmers							
15-29	82	50	1.7	17	22	41	20
30-39	85	99	3.3	1	--	26	73
40+	94	98	6.4	1	--	3	96

*Ever married women. The differences in mean parity for herders and farmers is statistically significant for cohorts 40+ and 30-39 and, while not significant, is in the appropriate direction for the 15-29 cohort. For Mongols the means were: women ages 15-29, 1.3 children; women aged 30-39, 3.1 children; and women 40+, 6.4 children. A comparison of progression distributions (Spearman's) finds that each cohort of pastoralists and cultivators differ significantly.

ovulate again. Unfortunately, we could find no credible local statistics on infant or child mortality. Our own fertility surveys help little because there were too few women, and they may have under reported infant deaths. It is not something people feel comfortable talking about. So we cannot reliably determine whether higher infant mortality among the farmers and shorter birth intervals contributed to higher fertility.

Disease can also reduce fecundity. In Tranquillity, goiter was common, but it would not raise fertility. On the grassland, however, venereal diseases were reportedly rampant and could have endangered childbirth. Endemic during the late 1930s and 1940s, sexually transmitted diseases were brought under control in the early 1950s, but only after many Mongol women and their infants were afflicted. Of course even after, women once infected might still have longer birth intervals and lower fertility.[39]

Venereal diseases were most severe for the grassland Mongols. We have no way of knowing how affected Han were, but literature suggests they were less so. But we find little evidence that disease dramatically reduced fertility in our sites, since we find no difference in the mean parities of

TABLE 7.13 Mean Parity During the First Ten Years of Marriage: Han*

	Herders		Farmers	
Age Group	No.	Mean	No.	Mean
15-29	47	1.5	78	1.8
30-39*	73	2.5	85	3.0
40+*	99	3.0	89	3.5

*Herder-farmer difference significant.

Mongols and Han. Further, the lower fertility of herders persisted after such diseases were eliminated.

Herdsmen often leave their wives for several months at a time to cut grass or lead sheep to winter pastures. But we do not believe that the separations lower their fertility because they are not absolute, and the men return to visit their wives. Moreover, cutting hay on large scale is recent, while the lower fertility of Han herders is not.

Frequent, longer nursing lengthens birth intervals and lowers fertility, and nursing patterns could contribute to the difference in fertility. Since their work rarely requires they leave home, and because neolocality and nuclear families are more common, many herding women have no built-in baby sitters. Nor do they give their infants cow's milk. Pastoral mothers are always on hand to nurse, and do so on demand. Cultivating mothers often work in fields far from home. Since most live in stem families, they can leave their infants with mothers-in-law while they are away. More often away during the day, they nurse less often than herding mothers. This seems to shorten their birth intervals.

Family Planning Policy

Pastoralists have never faced strict family planning policies, and the state introduced them later than in China's heartland. Recognizing the hard frontier living conditions and political sensitivities of the ethnic minorities, efforts were initially casual, for Han as well as Mongols. From 1985, they became more concerted, as cadres tried to persuade Han to limit themselves to one child, Mongols to two.[40] In 1987, Great Pasture entered into contract with the league to limit births. Family planning cadres who kept their charges within targets got a bonus. They were fined if they failed.

Still, herdsmen do not face heavy penalties, and a number of "special circumstances" qualify them for a second child.[41] Most important, couples who have been pastoralists for five years can have a second. This exception is liberally applied, to Han as well as Mongols, to dairying families as well as to shepherds. (Han with urban registration and with family members employed by state agencies are not exempt.) Although farmers cannot take advantage of this loophole, and regulations are stricter, fertility is higher.

During our first visit, Mongols could still have two or three children, without much interference. Han were under pressure to delay second births, but defiant couples could get authorization after the fact. With the birth of a third, parents have to pay a fine or lose property. Even then, they bargain with family planning workers. We were told that, in practice, cadres only impose fines on couples with "many" children, the amounts depending on the number already born and economic capacity. Penalties have not been heavy enough to halt all second or even third births.

More casual family planning in Inner Mongolia's pastoral area has even drawn a few households from interior China. Hoping to escape stricter regulations, couples move to what are colloquially called "special childbirth areas" (*shengyu techu*). In Great Pasture, they rent simple dwellings, make bean cakes to sell, raise a few cows, or hire themselves out to make ends meet. These "black households," so called because they are unregistered, are beyond the reach of family planning workers. Local cadres observe that, while they could assess fines, they could not collect them from people with little income. Local people prefer to look the other way.

Restraining Fertility

There is much now that now discourages parents from bearing many children. Farmers and herdsmen alike complain that, because they lavish so much attention on them, children do not appreciate the problems families face. They are harder to discipline now. Such concerns deter people from having more than two, even without family planning. But herdsmen most strongly feel the costs of raising children. Although more survive, they cost more to raise. Children stay in school longer, marriages cost more, yet they work later than among the farmers. Sons often leave at marriage, and daughters earn little. And while sons and daughters apart help when needed, herders need help less than farmers.

If the pastoralists limit the sons they have because of rising costs, they have more reason to limit the number of daughters. Girls are less costly for the farmers. Even young girls have a role on the farm, and after marriage they often continue to help. In fact, as their labor outside the home increases with recent reforms, the value of girls should also increase.[42]

TABLE 7.14 Pastoral Children Born by Parity and Period: Han

Period	No. Births	Parity (%)		
		2	3	4+
1969-1979	127	17	15	56
1980-1988	88	44	24	15

While herdsmen have reason to avoid having many children, they do not embrace the one child family pushed by the state. Most children born during 1980-1988, when the state tightened family planning, were not first borns (Table 7.14). However, compared with the preceding decade, people had fewer higher parity children. While mothers are clearly bearing fewer now, many still have second, even higher parity children.[43]

As Table 7.15 shows, pastoralists and cultivators alike also have second children sooner than the state would like. Despite the requirement that couples wait four years, only 6 percent of Han aged 15-29, and 11 percent of those 30-34, waited that long. While women are no longer eager to have as many children as they can, then, neither are they willing to limit themselves to one, or to meet their reproductive targets slowly. Given their greater interest in controlling reproduction, how do women manage it?

TABLE 7.15 First and Second Birth Intervals by Age and Ecoarea: Han

Age	Ecoarea	Months to Second Birth		Months to Third Birth	
		No.	Mean	No.	Mean
15-29	Herders	16	30.2	--	---
	Farmers	38	24.4	--	---
30-39	Herders	54	30.9	31	30.8
	Farmers	77	27.7	53	29.9
40+	Herders	68	36.8	64	37.0
	Farmers	61	29.3	58	31.0

Contraception and abortion are available. But abortion is available only at the banner hospital, far away. The inconvenience and cost of getting there discourage Great Pasture people from seeking the operation. They are also wary about using intrauterine devices (IUDs), fearing that they may harm a women's health. The most common form of contraception used is the pill, although some women complain of side effects. Nor is sterilization an acceptable option. Here, as in the cultivating area, people believe the procedure can weaken both a man or a woman who receives it.

But contraceptives are available to pastoralists and cultivators alike. We believe that there are other reasons why pastoralists have lower fertility than farmers, and despite a more casual family planning program. We think the difference is due to the way they use labor, especially that of women, and the effect this has on family formation. The age people marry, where they live on marriage, family form, nursing patterns, and the number of children they desire, together with the greater cost of raising children, reduces fertility most among herders.

Summary

Although Han and Mongols have not merged into a single culture, in many ways Han pastoralists resemble Mongol shepherds more than their peasant forebears. Pastoralism and farming call for a different way of life. Herders work more intensively and continuously throughout the year. Their division of labor is sharper, and men and women do very different tasks. The work of women keeps them closer to home. Children, especially girls, begin working later than among the farmers.

Herders can make a much better living mainly because livestock is expandable while land is not. If they have ample grassland and can vary their undertakings, they do even better. Income has increased along with inequality, but poverty has not accompanied the new order. Most have seen living standards rise. The profitability and requirements of herding discourage sidelines like those of pure cultivators. It is even hard to combine pastoral activities. Herdsmen therefore do more with animals.

Family life also differs from that of farmers. Since women are less urgently needed, and marriage costs more, herdsmen marry later. Marriage commonly coincides with family division. Neolocality and nuclear families are therefore more common than among the farmers. Family division is easier. Animals are easier to divide than land, and they multiply thereafter. Households recover more easily, and can better manage on their own after partition. Activities and animal numbers can be enlarged or scaled down to fit family labor. Even a few cows can provide a passable living, which is why we find more pastoralist elderly living on their own. Where families have more men, however, they can dramatically increase their incomes by cutting hay for sale, tending cows and sheep, or fishing.

These features of pastoralism also shape reproduction. The way herders deploy labor, especially women's, and the nature of family life lowers fertility below that of farmers, despite a looser family planning program. Although they have improved their incomes since the onset of the new economic system, herders pay more to raise their children, while the contribution of children comes later. This, too, restrains childbearing. The pastoral way of working and living thus bears deeply on the Han, and shapes families that while clearly Chinese also diverge greatly from their farming origins.

Notes

1. Nearly all adult Mongols in Sandhill (99 percent of the men and 94 percent of the women) speak some Mandarin. Even in Great Pasture, where there has been less contact with Han, over half can speak Mandarin (77 percent of the men and 60 percent of the women). But few Han in either place speak Mongol. In Sandhill only 13 percent of men and 6 percent of the women said they could speak some Mongol; in Great Pasture, 15 percent of the men and 2 percent of the women could.

2. We cannot verify the Sandhill government's claim of income improvement because authorities there could not provide credible year-by-year income figures. It is not clear how cadres in Great Pasture calculated annual income, but their figures take an upward trend.

3. See chapter 3 (endnote 3) for our definition of production value.

4. One percent of Mongols in Sandhill earned money from hay and only 10 percent in Great Pasture.

5. Sandhill Han spent 23 percent of all income on production expenses in 1987; Great Pasture Han, 30 percent.

6. Thirty-two percent of Sandhill's Han owned a tractor, 49 percent in Great Pasture, where many were of the larger, more expensive variety needed for cutting grass. In Middle Village and Tranquillity, only 24 percent of the Han owned a tractor in 1987, and most were small machines.

7. Sandhill's pure pastoralists earned about the same as Middle Village's mixed cultivation-pastoral households: in Sandhill the net per capita income was 711 RMB, compared to 712 RMB in Middle Village. But Sandhill's wage earners did better still. By combining animals with wages, they achieved a per capita net income of 966 RMB.

8. We cannot estimate the value of herds, flocks, or of productive equipment without information on the sexes, ages, and long term yield potentials of animals, or on the type and age of tractors and other machines owned.

9. See the data on the Hulunbuir League village survey above, chapter 3.

10. According to local statistics, livestock in the Han brigade rose from 9,421 to 19,366 between 1983 and 1990. The number of cows increased from 1,809 to 2,881. Reflecting rises in their price the number of sheep rose from 7,625 in 1986 to 14,897 in 1990.

11. See Ekvall (1968:18) on the careful ways nomadic Tibetan herdsmen assess the carrying capacity of their pasture.

12. There is only a hint that education may confer some advantage in earnings. Members of "poor" households had 5.7 mean years of education compared to 6.0 in "wealthy" households. If we compare only household heads, the difference is small and not statistically significant.

13. Still uncommon here as well, we find recent examples of joint families in the case studies which follow. They may herald the future.

14. Families with more income also appear to support fewer dependents. A "poor" worker supported 1.7 persons compared to 1.5 among the "wealthy." However, we are dealing with a small number of poor households, and the difference, while in the expected direction, is not statistically significant.

15. In Sandhill, income is positively and significantly related to size of herd and to income from wages. Great Pasture income is related to earnings from cutting hay as well as to herd size.

16. Income from wages is negatively (and significantly) related to number of cows owned in Sandhill. This reflects the difficulty of combining employment with large scale dairying; they are essentially alternative ways to make a living.

17. The Beta scores below are all significant, $p=.0000$. Family size is not included as an independent variable because, when other independent variables are controlled, its effect alone is not significant.

Income Source	Great Pasture (Beta)	Sandhill (Beta)
Barnyard animals	.02753	.09733
Fishing	.16589	.11990
Gardening	.02722	.08116
Grass cutting	.62181	.10740
Pastoral animals	.55621	.72854
Sidelines	.18666	.38855
Wages	.08473	.62643
Multiple R	.99932	.98890
R Square	.99864	.97792
Adjusted R Square	.99851	.97671

18.   Herdsmen consume 19 percent of what they produce in Sandhill; 11 percent in Great Pasture.

19.   Herdsmen also paid higher remittances -- 122 RMB per household compared to 23 RMB for the farmers. Sandhill Han reported the most remittances, probably because many are recent migrants whose kin live elsewhere.

20.   Han families with sons marrying during 1960-1978 spent an average of 584 RMB on marriage; during the second period, 1979-1988, they averaged 2,161 RMB.

21.   Similarly, the proportion of grooms spending less than 1,000 RMB on marriage dropped from 77 percent to only 22 percent.

22.   In 34 percent of all Han marriages studied, both spouses were originally Great Pasture residents. In Sandhill, only 12 percent were both local.

23.   Sixty-one percent of all Sandhill marriages were between people who both came from outside the town, compared to only 44 percent in Great Pasture. Moreover, only 30 percent of married Han males were raised in Sandhill, compared to 51 percent in Great Pasture.

24.   Of 96 Sandhill husbands with origins outside the town, 88 percent married girls from outside. Of 40 Great Pasture husbands from outside that township, 90 percent married women from outside. Fifty-nine percent of the men raised in Sandhill, and 67 percent in Great Pasture, married local girls.

25.   For Han, the mean difference between spouses is only 2.7 years of formal education, with the husband slightly better educated. The difference in education was only slightly larger than for farmers (2.3 years).

26.   Twenty-two percent of herding Han wives have more education than their husbands but only 14 percent do among the farmers, a significant difference. Where women are better educated than their husbands, the mean difference is 2.9 years for herding wives, and 2.4 for cultivators.

27.   While there were only three instances of Mongols marrying Han women in Great Pasture, in all cases the husband was a herdsman. On the other hand there were few people with urban registration or prestigious occupations in Great Pasture to begin with.

28.   Because Han marriage ages have been similar in Sandhill and Great Pasture we combine them for this analysis. Ages at marriage were, in Sandhill: 23.6 (men) and 21.5 (women) during the period 1950-1988. Great Pasture men married at 23.5 and women at 21.3. Mongol ages (in the two sites combined) were not significantly different from those of Han; Mongol men married at 23.8 and women at 21.6.

29.   Ekvall (1968:25) pointed out that yak herders divide their flocks easily. They easily distribute family wealth based on long standing consensus on how much belongs to whom, and so the relationship of family units continues to be amicable. The break up of parental extended families into nuclear families, so commonplace, is usually done in a matter-of-fact way with slight emotional turmoil or sense of violation of the proprieties. The resultant divided families remain in the same encampment, and there give much mutual help throughout the nomadic pastoral routine.

30.   We divided Han and Mongol pastoral women into age cohorts (15-29, 30-39, and 40+) and compared the proportions that married patrilocally and neolocally. We found the youngest are just as likely to marry neolocally as the eldest cohort.

31. Pastoral stem families, like those of farmers, are significantly larger than nuclear families, and also contain more adults (workers). Pastoral stem households have a mean of 5.6 persons, but nuclear households only 4.5 persons. If we define adults as persons 15 and over, then the stem households contain 4.4 adults compared to only 2.9 in nuclear households.

32. Eighteen percent of Sandhill women with living parents reported seeing their parents daily; 32 percent saw them at least once a month. In Great Pasture, 11 percent saw them daily, and 32 percent once a month. There were no Great Pasture women who never saw their parents, and only 6 percent of Sandhill women so reported.

33. There were 21 couples or solitary individual households, 37 persons in all. Of them, 28 were 60 or over.

34. Although an elderly couple can survive on a few cows, shepherds need more male labor. And if elderly shepherds raise a few dairy cows in addition to their sheep, it is harder still to make a go of it on their own. Since Mongols more often face this situation than Han, the problem is essentially theirs. Thus, only four percent of Mongol herding households were of this simple sort. Stem forms were somewhat more common among the Mongols, however.

35. There is no significant difference between Sandhill and Great Pasture Han in the percentage of stem households.

36. Sandhill Han households, with smaller herds, few sheep, less hay cutting and wage earning have 4.3 persons; Han in Great Pasture have significantly more with 4.7 persons. Sandhill Mongols average 4.9 and Great Pasture Mongols, 5.3. Within Sandhill, households that make their livings from dairying average 4.7 members, larger than the 4.1 of those that entirely depend on wages.

37. While we explore possible reasons for this difference between Han herders and farmers, our data do not allow us to sort out the relative importance of several factors. Partly our numbers of women included in our fertility surveys are small, even after combining sites. Too, there are potentially important variables for which we have no hard or reliable data. And so we present the following discussion as suggestive.

38. Figures from the 1982 census suggest a pastoral-cultivator difference for larger areas. The birth rates were Sandhill town, 17.4 and Great Pasture township, 15.2 per thousand; but they were 22.1 for Genghis town and 28.3 in Daur township (data provided by government sources).

39. A 1950 survey in Chenqi Banner (where Great Pasture is located), found that of 445 new babies born to Mongol women 40 and under, 218 had died after birth. Another investigation that year indicated that 56 percent of 333 new babies age 0-4 had a venereal disease (*Hulunbuir* 1986).

40. Our Chinese colleagues considered family planning particularly sensitive, and requested that we avoid systematic inquiry into this topic. From our formal interviews, casual conversations, and survey data we nonetheless get some insight into the situation. We know more about family limitation in Great Pasture than in Sandhill, so most of our observations refer to that place. Yet, we believe that the situation was much the same in Sandhill.

41.   For example, only children, or those whose father and paternal grandfather were both only sons, can have a second child even if their first is male. If a first born is retarded, parents can try again.

42.   Arnold and Liu (1986) explore the relationship between preference for sons and family planning in China by looking at married couples using contraception by number and sex of children, and one child certificate holders by sex of child. They find that every one of these measures provide evidence of the persistence of son preference throughout China.

However, we find while their daughters contribute less than those of the farmers, herdsmen also want daughters. Note that, of 16 Sandhill and Great Pasture women with second borns in our fertility surveys, 7 had their second after a son. Of course this does not prove that there is no preference for males here; indeed, it could mean that people prefer two sons. But their continued childbearing after one son is consistent with the herdsmen's comments that they want daughters as well as sons.

43.   The proportions second, third, and fourth or higher all differ significantly between periods.

8

Pastoral Families: The Haves

Herders, like farmers, plan their work around the number of hands they have. But those with plentiful labor can now enlarge the scale and complexity of their economic activities far more. Since number of men in a family is key, with grown sons or brothers, herdsmen can do more than simply survive. They can raise more livestock and mix animals or rural tasks in different places at the same time. Mostly, they find the labor the need at home. Herders can buy grass cutting equipment, livestock, or fishing nets, but they need family members to use them. Hired men work alongside family members. We look first at three families that have successfully expanded their undertakings to see how they align production decisions with family labor. When the collective was abandoned, they enjoyed a head start because both had many grown children living with them. They therefore received more livestock than others, and also had the manpower to tend them. The more workers a family had, the more ambitious it could be. One held sons in the family longer than usual, another worked closely with them after family division. Finally, a Mongol family does well through drafting its women.

The Wangs: A Family That Stays Together Can Do Well Together

Wang Laixiong and his wife showed their children that they had much to gain by staying together. They found a way to reduce the problems that normally lead to family division, and by delaying family division, adapted their family arrangement to the new economic climate. This family of 16 includes Laixiong and his wife, still vigorous at 58 and 52, three married sons ranging in age from 29 to 32, their wives and small children, and three unmarried adult children -- 22 year old fraternal twins, a boy and girl, and a son 18. This is one of Great Pasture's few joint families. Although it is a single family with a common, undivided family estate, Laixiong's married sons have their own separate households with kitchens. By allowing his married sons economic and personal space, Laixiong has lessened conflict. At the same time, joining labor and assets he has reduced overall costs and can diversify. This family is one of the largest and best off in Great Pasture. Still rare here, families like theirs could become more common in the new economic climate.

Laixiong's home is much like those of the farmers we met. The walls are of earth and brick, the roof of thatch. Bedrooms with their sleeping platforms flank a common kitchen and draw winter warmth from the kitchen stoves. A covered pit in the kitchen serves as refrigerator and storage. On the walls are a grandfather clock and calendar. Cash and small household items are kept in a locked wooden chest. Large mirrored wardrobes in the bedrooms of his sons reflect the family's new affluence as do the pedal operated sewing machines that each married woman uses to repair clothing.

Absent here are the kitchen wells with their squeaky hand pumps, so familiar in the farming area. Sandhill homes have wells in their courtyards, but in Great Pasture water is scarce, drawn from a common community well. Nor are there the large cooking pots farmers use to prepare mash for their pigs. Rickety fences of woven rushes, surrounding compound vegetable gardens, keep out wandering cows, and conceal the small family pit-latrine. A pile of dried cow chips for cooking, and piles of straw for use in the cowsheds, take up part of the backyard.

Family Background

Laixiong knows well the pitfalls of holding together a large extended family, having grown up in one himself. He had five brothers and sisters, all of whom left Hebei Province for Great Pasture together.

There were too many of us for the little land we had. So (in 1953) my elder brother set off for Inner Mongolia. The rest of us followed later (in 1958). We lived for a while near Teni River, a community north of the Hailar River, but later moved here to Great Pasture. In fact my wife is from Teni, that's how we met. She joined me here when we married, and brought her two unmarried younger sisters and a younger brother along. Most of our closest relatives on both sides still live here. We see them all quite often and help each other cut grass from time to time.

We're surely better off here than in Hebei. Farmers simply can't do as well. And I would even have to say that we Great Pasture people are better off than most who live along this rail line. We earn more, build better homes, and live more comfortably. We've been lucky.

When we first came, most people here were migrants from other places. There weren't all that many Han here then, so many settlers either brought wives or sent to their home places for wives later. Of course, we don't have to do this anymore. There are many local Han our youngsters can marry. But our eldest son's wife came from Shandong. Her elder brother came to Great Pasture first, and she followed (in 1977), met my son, and they married (in 1981).

First Daughter-in-Law migrated from a farming region, and knew little about cows. But, the change was worthwhile, she told us,

In Shandong I had to work in the fields every day. But after coming here, I remained at home to milk the cows and care for the homestead. Of course, I had to learn to milk from scratch, but once I knew how to do it, my life became easier. I worked less hard than in Shandong, and my living standard improved.

Building and Maintaining Domestic Dikes

Families, like rivers, build up to the point that they press outward, and eventually break through the dikes built to contain them. Because the Wangs have kept their familial dikes in good order, they have been able to put division off longer than any other family here. They have been creative. While they share a common family estate and income, and although the men work together, the daughters-in-law do not live together. The married brothers eat apart, and do some work independently. Physical separation and tolerance of limited economic independence helps the family avoid some of the tensions that might fracture it.

Laixiong and his wife live in the main dwelling with their three unmarried children. The three married couples each have their own residence. There is a fifth house out on the open grassland, where Laixiong's unmarried sons tend family cows without milk. Laixiong's second son credits this unusual arrangement to the family responsibility system:

When the responsibility system began, only my eldest brother was married, and he had not yet partitioned. Then we two younger brothers married (in 1984 and in 1985, both at 23). Even after, we continued as one family, unusual for this place. For one thing, our father simply couldn't afford to build a house for each of us at the time. Besides, we had already started out in a new direction that called for holding ourselves together.

My parents spent nearly 4,000 RMB on our marriages, the wedding feast, furniture, and the like, but it took longer to save enough to build homes for us. Because we all worked together, they finally managed it (in 1986). They spent about 30,000 RMB on that alone. But our animals remain family property, so even after we moved into our new homes, we continue as a single family in fact.

Family Economy, Past and Present

Laixiong and his two eldest sons worked as shepherds in the collective, and learned to live on the open grassland. According to Laixiong, they were lean years. The animals were so poorly managed that to save them the brigade handed some over to individual households.

During better times, each family was given a milk cow to raise and care for. We were supposed to return any calves born to the brigade. But no one really pressed us to do it so, by the time the responsibility system began, every family actually already had 10 or so cows and we just had to divide the rest. In effect we had already moved in the direction of family responsibility. We ended up with 20 cows. We decided not to divide them up among ourselves, but to build our family herd up instead by pooling all our resources. So in 1985 we borrowed 10,000 RMB from the bank, and the next year another 5,000 RMB, and bought 20 more cows.

Step by step we bought more of them. The more cows we had, the more grass we needed to cut, and we cut more than we needed for our own animals. We cut hay to sell and used the profits to pay off our debts and buy even more cows. To build our herd that way, we had to stay together. We needed a lot of labor just to manage it all. Right now we own about 160 cows, and we have sheep as well.

At first, when the responsibility system began, we decided not to raise sheep because of the risk and work involved. We got a small flock during the animal distribution, but sold them all the following year. The way we saw it, if we were to increase the size of our dairy herd, we wouldn't have the labor to tend sheep on the open grassland. We had to give something up. But we weren't without sheep for long. When the price of mutton started to rise, we bought a small flock of about 60 sheep for our meat. Little by little, their number increased, and we now have over 100.

When the government announced that families could sell grass (in 1984), we saw a chance to increase our herd and make extra money cutting and selling grass. Again, the best way to do both was to stay together. Since we have so many livestock, we get a large area of cutting land. We also rent cutting rights from 10 families that don't want to cut grass themselves, because they're short of labor or doing other things.

Now we spend many months cutting grass. It takes us nearly 50 days just to cut it, and 100 more to bring it home. My married sons do this work. They're men now, so I can count on them to drive and run our tractors properly. But if they're cutting grass, they can't also take care of our cows and sheep. The scale of our operation is now so large that we have to hire help from the start of cutting to the end of the year, at peak about a dozen men. There are more cows, more machines, and more people cutting grass, but the local labor supply is very limited. Everyone is busy cutting grass at the same time. Each year, just before haying, men come from other places, even as far as South China. They walk the streets, knocking on doors, looking for work.

They hire on for a number of days and get paid, rain or shine. We can't cut grass when it's wet, but they get paid one way or the other. Throughout, we all live out on the grassland. They live in our yurts, but cook their own food. We let some of them go once the grass has been cut, but the rest stay on until the end of the year.

We cut as much as 167 cartloads of grass each year. We keep 30 for our own livestock and sell most of the rest. In winter we allow our animals to graze near our grassland house. That's possible so long as the snow isn't too thick. Our dairying operation costs less that way, we can sell the hay they don't eat. But of course they can't remain out there by themselves, someone has to be there with them, which is why we built a house out there.

So you see, haying on the scale we do takes many men. In most families, brothers partition but still get together to cut grass. They divide the profits -- which person does what, and who owns what equipment gets so much. But our way is more efficient and lets us invest in future income. Since we are still one family, I can invest everything we earn in the large tractors we need to cut so much grass.

In 1984, we bought our first 55 HP tractor. Now we own two, and a 12 HP tractor as well. We could use our tractors for hauling as well, but we don't. There are already so many tractors here, that we wouldn't really be able to earn much. So we only use them for haying, carrying supplies to our grassland home, and collecting wood for fuel.

Cutting hay has become a big industry here. There are three grass collection stations now, two belong to the state, the third is a banner cooperative. They all pay about the same price, so we sell to all three. A ton of hay bought from us for 62 RMB goes for 230 RMB when it reaches Beijing. When it gets to Japan, I've heard the price can be as high as 700 RMB per ton. It's in our interest to unload it as fast as possible. We have no place to keep it here in Great Pasture, and the longer our cut hay stays out on the grassland, the more we lose. As it is, we lose over 10 carts to animals and theft each year.

We've done very well cutting grass, but it's getting harder. The costs of production have shot up. Diesel fuel gets more expensive all the time, and taxes have risen. Now we have to pay a bunch of special taxes to cut grass. For example there's a "transportation fee," which is supposed to offset the costs of road repair. For us that means 600 RMB! Then there's the "pasture management fee," which depends on how many square meters you cut. In addition there's the "business management fee," and the local "production management fee," both of which are a percentage of earnings. Everywhere you turn there are fees of one sort or another.

More and more people want to cut grass and have the equipment to do so. Each year there are more cows, and more demand for fodder. As people make money, they buy tractors. So grass cutting is very competitive. Last year we got 5 meter strips of grassland per cow, 0.5 meters per sheep. (The strip length was 10 km.) This year they are only assigning 3 meter strips per cow, and 0.3 meters per sheep. So you can see how the area is shrinking because more are cutting.

The wages we pay our workers have also been rising. Even when we first started to cut grass, on a smaller scale, we had to hire some workers, but then we only paid 8 RMB per person day. Last year we had to pay 13 RMB per person day! That's quite a change, isn't it? To top it all off, the selling price dropped 20 RMB per ton between last year and the year before, because more people are cutting. When we balanced our accounts last year, we found that we actually made very little. Because it now seems hardly worth it to work so hard for so little return, I'm changing my strategy. In future we'll do less grass cutting, expand our herd, and buy more sheep and some horses too. Sheep multiply quickly, and the price has been quite good recently, so we may be able to do well. I think that, in time, we'll be able to replace what we earned from hay by raising more sheep. Of course we'll still cut grass for our own animals, just less. We'll shift our attention and labor to sheep. Horses, too, have been bringing a good return, they're needed in farming areas.

Managing Labor

When the responsibility system first got started, Laixiong enlarged the size of his herd, and also the scale of his grass cutting. He could do both, because his household contained many adult males. At first he used more labor to work his herd than to cut grass. Then as the balance shifted, he had to bring in outside labor.

My two eldest sons cut grass while my third son and I herded sheep and cared for our cows. But by 1985 we were cutting so much hay that they couldn't handle it alone. Then the four of us had to work together, while the rest of the family took care of the animals. Soon even that was not enough, and my wife's younger brother began to help. Finally, we sent word back to our home place in Hebei to send labor. We put some Hebei men out on the grassland with my sons. They knew how to handle work cows, and we trusted them.

Meanwhile, their herd had been growing. To make that part of the family enterprise cost effective, Laixiong moved the less productive cows to the open pasture. He dug a well 20 km from town and built a house, four cow pens, and a corral there. His fourth and fifth sons, along with two hired people, lived out there and looked after the herds year round.

Recently, my fourth son got a job at a brick factory in Chenqi. He prefers that to herding, so I let him take it. So now, we're short handed out at our grassland home, when the rest of us are doing other things. Only my fifth son and two hired workers are out there full time now. I'm worried about that because my fifth son is only 18, a bit young for that much responsibility.

208

But we do want to keep animals out there. The quality of grass is especially fine around our grassland home, so the animals grow well. The idea is to increase the size of our herd and flock cheaply, so we let our calves drink their mother's milk out there. They grow faster that way. In any event, we couldn't possibly milk all the animals we have there with only four workers, and it's far from any collection station.

This family built its fortune by keeping together. They invested more, pooled labor, reduced expenses, and rapidly added livestock. They diversified their pastoral projects, adding sheep and cutting large amounts of hay for sale. Their success worked against family division, because not only would they have had trouble doing all this if they had not stayed together, but they would have earned much less. Working toward their success was Laixiong's willingness to let his married sons have some independence. It is often the women that first challenge family unity. Men overtly promote the unity of the patrilocal family, and it falls to women to pursue the interests of their own conjugal units. By giving his married sons their own houses, where the women live apart and milk their animals separately, Laixiong reduced the occasions for confrontation. He also minimized competition between brothers over family resources by granting them a degree of economic independence. He distributed the best of his cows among them, which they handle like their own property.

Now, apart from the 140 cows that we manage as a family, I've given each of them seven milk cows. They belong to the family as a whole, but my married sons care for them and keep the profits earned from sale of their milk. The animals are not theirs to do with as they like, but they give an income. And we only keep our best cows here in Great Pasture. So they care for our best cows here in town, and they work hard at it because they keep what they earn. Our daughters-in-law each milks her own cow and delivers her own milk. They each keep a few family calves, the rest we send to the grasslands. In winter, each couple tends its own animal pen.

This way, my wife and I no longer have to work so hard. Now we just stay home with our young daughter. But during the summer we all work, me included. We are so busy then that none of us men can afford to rest. We don't even have time to graze the cows we keep here in town, we hire a cowherd to do it. He takes them out in the day and brings them back in the evening for the women to milk.

The advantages of family unity were so obvious that no son spoke of family division. Laixiong's first son describes their arrangements:

We three married brothers have our own homes. We cook and eat separately, and we manage our own household budgets. Still, I can't say we are separate families because we jointly own and manage most of our animals.

We give what we earn from them, and from the grass we cut, to our father. Last year, we sold 20 large bulls for about 20,000 RMB. All of that went to him. He makes most of the decisions about how our family resources will be used and how we will invest.

At the same time, we each have income from a few cows of our own. We don't actually own them, though, they belong to the family. We only enjoy the right to sell their milk, but that gives us a fair income of our own. We also have income from the larger family. During Spring Festival each year, our parents give us each between 1,000 and 2,000 RMB. My unmarried brothers don't get that, because they're still members of my father's household. He takes care of all their regular needs. When they want to buy some clothes, they just ask him for the money.

My parents are getting on in years. They no longer milk cows of their own. When they need cash, they draw from our common family fund. We married brothers have no problem with that because, to our way of thinking, we earn more by keeping the family together than we would otherwise. The longer we remain together, the stronger we will become.

We do many different sorts of things, and by dividing up the work it's easier to pay more attention to each type of work. If each one of us tried to do everything alone, nothing would be done well. Although I'm certainly not wealthy, we all live comfortably and the family as a whole is doing alright. As things stand, there's really very little conflict. You know, many families in this brigade would very much like to do as we have done, but most fail because of dissension.

It's common here for brothers to work together after they divide. But we don't think that's the best way to combine efforts because, after partition, each brother knows which animals are his. If they put their animals together temporarily, each favors his own. We've none of these problems. The herd belongs to all so we pay attention to them all.

While Laixiong's son stresses the advantages of family integrity, his wife sees more promise in family division. Her focus shifts from the needs of the larger family to those of her own conjugal group. She talks of buying household items, and education for their children. New consumer needs, not seen before, now tempt couples to seek more control of their own budgets, and thus tend to pull families apart. First Son's wife revealed stresses not evident during our discussion with her husband:

The milk from our cows pays for our food. But we don't have a washing machine. Nor do we buy much clothing since that comes out of our own household budget. If we wanted to buy a washing machine, a TV, or a tape recorder ourselves, we couldn't get it from the common fund, and we can't afford to buy such things on our own. I wouldn't claim that we have a hard life; we get by on our milk earnings. And since the year before last, my parents-in-law have been adding to that at Spring Festival. So life isn't hard for us, but neither is it abundant.

We sisters-in-law don't quarrel much with our mother-in-law simply because we live separately. On the other hand, we do argue among ourselves even though we don't live together. I wouldn't want you to think that all we do is fight, we also help each other from time to time. If work at home becomes overwhelming, a sister-in-law will pitch in to help. If one of us is ill, or burdened with infants, then another may come over to help milk. But none of us is happy about the way the animals have been allocated. Each feels the other has been given better animals. We argue a lot about things like that. We'd like to see more of the herd distributed. But our husbands don't want to hear such talk. They think it's more important that we all get along and work well together. So whenever we start to argue, they calm us down.

Our parents-in-law don't even know we're fighting. Nonetheless, last year Father-in-Law told us that we'll partition once my husband's brothers have all married. He feels that once they've married, there'll be no way to get all the work done without arguing. I think he's right. With so many different couples and interests, there would surely be conflicts over how to divide family earnings. So by the time my kids have grown, I think we will have partitioned and then we'll use our own money to pay for their studies. My husband and I will raise our own animals then. I know we won't be able to earn as much that way, but at least everything we earn will be ours.

Although it may not endure much longer, the joint family lets the Wangs capture the moment. When they do divide, there will be more to divide as a result. But most families never reach this degree of complexity. Only those that try to combine different sorts of activities have any reason to hold back tendencies to partition.

The Lins: A Family Divided

Diversification can produce wealth even after families divide. The Lins are among the wealthiest in Great Pasture, with an income in 1987 of 27,356 RMB, over five times the community average for Han. Their per capita income was 2,022 RMB. They owned 30 cows; haying alone brought in 12,000 RMB. By 1990, they had added sheep. Their large, substantial home had two TVs, a sewing machine, and a clothes washer.

In 1990, Lin Dechang (58) lived with his father (79), wife (57), and three unmarried sons (20, 19, and 17). The Lins had six sons and three daughters. Their eldest son married and partitioned in 1975; two more married in 1987. One partitioned immediately, the other six months later. Three daughters married townsmen and live close by. Although independent now, Dechang's three married sons work with him because together they can achieve what would be impossible alone. Dechang's son-in-law also works closely with him.

Family Origins

The Lins married in Shandong, and Dechang came alone to Great Pasture in 1955. At first he cut hay as a hired worker, then on his own. Four years later, his wife, child, and father joined him. Like most migrants, they knew little about raising animals when they came. But when they turned from farming to a pastoral way of life, they found it afforded a better life. Little by little Dechang learned to handle animals. When he joined Great Pasture's Han brigade, he started to earn work points driving a cart, fishing, pasturing and doing other herding work. Danning, his wife, described their settlement:

> We followed him to Great Pasture during the "three bad years," when people were starving. The rest of the family didn't follow because, as time passed, things gradually improved in Shandong. My mother, an elder sister, two younger sisters, and a younger brother are still there, we haven't lost touch. In fact, two years ago I went back to visit them, and we often write.
>
> At first we just rented a room. It was very hard for us then. Families were allowed to have milk cows of their own, but we had no such rights because we joined the collective late and put in little. So we saved and bought a cow. It was still alright to do that then, until the Cultural Revolution. Then having your own cow was no longer correct.

When the responsibility system began, the Lins had their own milk cow, bought another, and the commune distributed several more. From this small beginning Dechang built his wealth.

> When the new system began, I was a "second level commune member" so, in addition to the sheep all of us got, I was able to draw a large male, a small male, and two milk cows. We also drew for horses, and I got three. For all of them I owed 2,000 RMB. After a short time, someone collected a payment from me. He came a few times more, but then stopped. I never did pay it off.

Raising and Marrying Children

The Lins had built a sizable family by the time the responsibility system came into force, which entitled them to more animals than most. Having a large family at that time was an advantage. Since then, however, Danning's views about having many children have changed.

> Now the state wants us to have fewer. But you know, women are not all that anxious to have as many children as they once were. Having a lot of kids

only increases a woman's work. And they're costly to raise, especially when it comes to marrying them off. It's true, as you suggest, that we need more labor now. In that respect, having a lot of sons is a good thing. But I think the more kids you have the heavier is your burden.

Nonetheless, women here still prefer two or three, even though they know they'll be fined. The cadres know we need labor badly, so they don't strictly enforce the regulation here. And most people will pay a fine to have more. The amount of these fines is not so great, and depend on how many children you already have, and other things as well. Last year, a couple I know insisted on having more than they were allowed. When the cadre went to persuade them not to have the child, they cursed her. As a result they were fined 8,000 RMB! But that's unusual.

Actually family planning is less strict here than in other places, which is why one or two "black households" come to Great Pasture every year. They can always find work here. They hire on to bind straw bundles at the grass collection station. That's hard work. Or they may hire themselves to fishing families. By doing odd jobs like that they make a living, so they stay on after their children are born. But recently, our cadres have begun to pay more attention to them. Last year, they took the TV of one such household when the wife delivered her third child.

Danning herself had been little affected by family planning and had never made any effort to limit the number of children she had. She nursed all nine children:

It was important to breastfeed them, because the food wasn't nutritious, and often I couldn't eat my full. Still, I always had enough milk for my babies. I nursed each whenever it cried to be fed, and I did that until each was about one and a half years old.

All her children survived. After elementary school, her sons became herdsmen and worked with the family until they married. Between the marriages of their first and third sons, living standards improved. The Lins did particularly well, but success only increased expectations. They would have to give their children proper marriages. Dechang expressed concern about doing it right, and especially about the rising cost of marriage.

Their marriages were all arranged through go-betweens. We normally have some sort of engagement ceremony now, although it's not as formal as when my parents were young. These days the two families exchange some simple gifts. In most cases the actual wedding takes place about a year after that. A girl's family doesn't expect much bride-wealth, although the groom's parents may buy new clothing for her. Before, we didn't have large dowries either. But these days, many girls bring a lot of things when they marry, especially if they're from well off families. Still, the overall cost of getting married is much higher on the groom's side. I figure that a groom needs 11,000 to 12,000

RMB to marry, a bride between 3,000 and 4,000 RMB. By our custom, sons usually move out when they marry. So in addition to the feast and furnishings, parents are expected to build a new house for a son when he marries. And most do manage it.

Danning's sons married at older ages as time passed, and each marriage cost more than the one before it.

Our eldest son married in 1975 at 20, young by local standards. I was already in my forties, and I really needed a daughter-in-law to help me, and I wanted to see grandchildren. Marriage wasn't as costly then. We just gave a pair of small clothing cases, two sets of quilts, and a set of pots and pans. The whole thing only cost us about 100 RMB. Then we probably spent close to 1,000 RMB on the wedding feast. About six months later, they partitioned to set up their own family.

When our second and third sons married (both in 1987), everything cost so much more! We gave each 5,000 RMB and three cows, which was much more than we gave our eldest. Our third son was 23 when he took a bride. He divided out immediately and moved into his paternal grandfather's house. That was very convenient at the time, because my father-in-law was living with us and the house was empty. Our second son was 25 when he married. We had to wait a bit, having just financed his brother's marriage. We had no money to buy him a house either. Fortunately we did find one soon after, the home of a Mongol family returning to live on the grassland because their children finished school. It was a fine house with two bedrooms and a kitchen. It cost us about 5,000 RMB.

None of their daughters had a formal engagement ceremony, but there were gifts and feasts. An old friend of Dechang, from his days of transporting goods to Hailar, introduced a mate for his eldest daughter, a young man working in a transportation unit. Dechang spent very little on her marriage in 1982. She simply joined her husband's parents in Hailar. Soon after the family responsibility system began, the enterprise for which her husband had worked was contracted out and became a private business. There was no longer any work for him, so the two of them came to live in Great Pasture, where Dechang brought them into the family economy. The marriage of his second and third daughters a few years later were progressively more costly.

My second married a man from Herhongde, about 10 km from here (in 1985). I spent about 500 RMB on that wedding. Her husband is the youngest son, and his parents live with him. He has good work on the railway line. They have a few cows as well. So she just stays home, milks their cows, and takes care of her baby. After her marriage came that of my third daughter. She married a Great Pasture lad (in 1988). We usually give sons some cows to begin their own herds when they marry, but not daughters. Still, when she married it cost me 2,000 RMB for her wedding!

A Great Leap Forward

Dechang gradually increased his herd and flock. In 1985, to stimulate pastoral development, the banner government lent a large number of sheep to the *sumu*, which passed them down to the various *gacca*. They were distributed to a few individuals who would likely do well with them. Dechang was willing to reorient from dairying to shepherding, and this promised an income leap.

I owe a great debt to the cadres for their confidence in me. Many were eager to get those sheep at that time because the value of mutton was rising, but they chose me. Although I already knew how to raise sheep, I was a bit awed by the responsibility. The gacca lent me 503 sheep, a larger number than I had ever handled. In an instant, my small flock had become a large one, and I had become a shepherd.

I had to return them in kind -- a large sheep for a large, a small sheep for a small one. It was certainly not an outright gift! If I were to fail and lose these animals, I would still have to return what was due. The *gacca*, *sumu*, and *qi* would not lose their investment in the end. But it worked out very well. Last year I returned all the animals I had borrowed, and they are now used to encourage others.

You know, if they hadn't supported me then, I wouldn't have been able to envision so ambitious a plan as I now have. Right now I have 1,500 sheep, 20 horses, 30 cows. Shepherding can make us a lot, but it's uncertain. Every year we lose perhaps 50 sheep out of 1,000. We eat 10 to 20, the rest die from sickness or get lost. Still, I think that by year's end, after selling some, eating some, and losing some, I'll have about 1,100 sheep, and that number will quickly grow. By next Spring, if all goes well, my flock should produce 700 lambs, so by the end of next year I should have 1,800 sheep.

We Han are new at this. The Mongols have more experience with sheep, but we Han have more tractors because we cut grass for our cows. So if the winter turns out really bad, and the snow so thick that the sheep can't find grass, we can feed them some hay. Because we have hay, we lose fewer animals. For example, of every 10 sheep raised by a Han, only one may die of starvation in winter, compared to 5 for a Mongol shepherd.

Managing Labor

Dechang may exaggerate the Han advantage. Nonetheless, he has done well with the animals he has, due as much to good management as to luck.

He would not have the herd he has, cut the grass he does, or raise the flock he now has, had he not been willing to diversify and take risks. He is also good at managing his family labor. Seven of his nine children still work together in various parts of his total enterprise. He described their cooperative arrangement:

I have a house about 10 km to the south where I dug a well and built large cow pens. My eldest daughter and her husband live there and take care of our cows. My sons and I send some cows out there. My son-in-law has urban registration, but luckily he learned something about raising cows. His Hailar transportation work unit diversified into livestock. Although we all have separate herds now, many of my animals remain with them. So we handle our animals as a single herd. They fatten well out there and are cheaper to raise since we don't have to give them much hay in winter under normal conditions. That way we can raise our cattle well, and increase the size of our herd rapidly. He herds them and she milks them. She's quite good, she can milk 50 kg of milk each day. A truck goes out there every day during the main milking season, so she doesn't have to come to town. But her children live here with us, because they go to school in Great Pasture. I pay my daughter and son-in-law to tend my animals, but I still earn about 200 RMB a month from their milk. My married sons tend their own milk cows here in Great Pasture and only send those without milk out to my daughter. So, though some of my sons have partitioned, we continue to manage many of our cows as a single family. The animals we put in the care of my daughter are separately owned, but cooperatively managed. In fact, we work together on everything. We couldn't raise sheep otherwise. Right now they're pastured south of the railway, quite near my home. My three unmarried sons, live in a yurt there and look after them.

But during shearing and lambing, when the work requires more labor than that, we all pitch in. We need a lot of men for about a month to get everything done. It takes all my sons, two hired workers, and myself to do it. Because we're so involved in shepherding now, we own a proper yurt we can live in year round. That's no small expense. They now costs about 3,000 RMB. You need the wooden structure, lengths of canvas for summer covering, felt for winter, a stove, and furniture.

All shepherds are busy shearing at the same time, so finding skilled labor is not easy. And everything must be done quickly. Catch the animal, truss it, throw it over the corral fence, shear it, let it loose. We do it morning and afternoon, about seven hours a day, day after day. But we can shear only when the weather is good. If it rains you have to stop. So we have to work fast in the time we have.

During shearing, we're always moving the animals about, corralling them and letting them out to graze. While they are grazing, they must be watched constantly. So we need labor for many related tasks. We can only relax at night, when we round them up and corral them. Once they're safely corralled near the yurt, the dogs can keep an eye out for wolves.

We have to shift labor around from one activity to another all the time. In a couple of days my three youngest sons and I will leave for the Hui river. We certainly need help from all my sons then. The usual way is to send the flock out first, tended by two men on horseback. Then others pull the yurt and supplies after them. We use our most powerful tractor to transport our yurt and supplies. We soon catch up with the shepherds. The flock can cover 20 km in a single day, so we usually start out in the afternoon and spend the night at mid-point. We could get there faster but we move slowly in order not to exhaust the sheep. The next morning we start out again so that we arrive by noon.

We also have to cooperate to cut grass, and you need a lot of equipment. My eldest son owns a 28 HP tractor, and I have a 55 HP machine that I bought in 1987. I also own a 12 HP tractor. I store all three in my barn, but any of my sons can use them. Besides tractors we need other sorts of equipment. I have four grass cutters and a grass collector. I have a 10 ton diesel fuel tank, and last year I bought five tons of fuel. I also own a four wheel cart, and a five ton cart. You need all these things to cut grass.

Apart from hauling our yurt and equipment down to the Hui river and back, we use our tractors to cut hay for our herds and for sale. We each take the grass we need to feed our own animals in winter, the rest we sell. I divide our profits equally with my married sons. Last year they each earned 2,000 RMB that way.

So you see, even though they partitioned when they married, we work as one family. My own view is that sons should leave when they marry. If they don't, then parents will find it hard to assign tasks. The sons, for their part, will shift responsibility to each other and shirk their duties. If they find living hard after family division, they can hardly blame their parents for that. But if we were all still together as a single family, then they would very likely blame us, and there would be nothing but conflict. So I think it's better for sons to leave when they marry. In our case, even when we are old we'll still be able to make a living and take care of ourselves. Even now we are saving for our future. But if we can't get by on our own later, then we will still turn to our sons even though we live as separate families. We know they won't abandon us. In the meanwhile, separated or not, we continue to work together for the common good.

Dadusulongmu: A Mongol Family

During winter, Mongol shepherds place their camp in protected gullies, where the snow melts quickly, exposing grass and watering the grazing animals. In summer they move their yurts to higher ground, where the ventilation is good and animals can find relief from the heat. Visiting them, going from one yurt to the other by tractor, jeep, or horse drawn cart, was easier when they were still in their base camps near town than when they were scattered near the Hui river. Although they did not expect us, our arrival was never a complete surprise, since we could be seen enroute for miles. Their dogs announced our coming well in advance. From afar we could see the domed yurt, white against an endless blue sky, itself a giant dome touching down on horizon in all four directions. In winter, the yurt is of felt on a collapsible wooden framework, to protect against the bitter cold and wind. In summer, the felt is replaced by canvas and woven rush mats.

The yurt is low against the wind, four meters high in the center, dropping to about one and a half meters at the lower walls. The pipe that rises from the simple central cooking and heating stove passes through the center of what looks like a wagon wheel circle. This serves as skylight and vent. Nearby are several large wooden covered wagons in a line, to carry belongings. They will be drawn by horses or tractors. Nearby, too, is the corral, home for the family sheep.

Our host greets us as we approach, chases away the dogs, and indicates his readiness to receive guests by opening the low, blue, wooden door of his yurt. By tradition it faces south or southeast, to avoid the cold winter winds. Inside, the floor is bare earth. A corridor separates two sleeping platforms. At its center is the family stove, in which our host's wife quickly prepares a fire. She throws dry dung into the stove, and an odorless smoke sends an army of mosquitos, ever present on the grassland, in sudden flight. Around the walls are clothing boxes and simple cabinets. A battery driven tape recorder and radio open the world beyond.

We bend low to pass through the entry, move around to the left, the proper direction for guests, and take our seats on the sleeping platform. Little is said at first. Milk-tea is poured from a thermos. After it produces the expected warm glow and sweat, the conversation begins.

The Mongol cadre, sent with us by the township government, now introduces us and explains the purpose of our visit. Conversation is quiet, with long pauses. It livens when a sheep, singled out to honor our visit, is slaughtered outside. And the conversation will become more animated still when, boiled in large chunks, it is finally served. As the knife is passed around, the host presses choice parts upon his guests, and it is all washed down with a grain wine of white fire. Finally broth from the pot and noodles, and our host breaks into song. Our Han assistants join with their village ballads, and some newly learned on the grasslands. And then a rest. Two or three hours later, we take up our conversation.

Dadusulongmu's family earned 7,000 RMB in 1987, more than the Mongol mean; but since his family was larger than average, their 1,140 RMB per capita income was at the mean. The family cuts little grass; they mainly use their small 12 HP tractor to move camp and bring in supplies. Dadusulongmu makes his living from sale of sheep, wool, milk, and steers. In 1987, he had 450 sheep, 35 goats, 5 horses, and 18 cows. When a milk collection station was set up on the grassland, he built a home seven km away and added more cows to his herd. That increased his need for labor, and he drew on the women in his family. Mongol women are at hand.

Family Background

When we first visited him, Dadusulongmu's household was already quite large. In addition to himself (aged 43), there were his wife (42), two unmarried sons (21 and 19), and two unmarried daughters (20 and 18).

> I come from a large family, I'm the eldest of 12. Most of them now live in a different brigade nearby, and we often visit and help each other. My mother lives with my fourth younger brother. I often visit her as well. But I have a lot of other relatives. There are more than 50 households in this brigade, and most of us are related.
>
> Unlike the Han, we prefer living in grassland yurts. But my brothers and sisters began to live in town when they built the school there. We kids had to go to school, and of course we had to have someone in town with us. So my folks rented a house in Great Pasture, and my mother lived there while we were in school.
>
> When I married (in 1966), my wife and I partitioned at once. There was plenty of labor in the family then, so they could easily do without us. And my parents were healthy. In fact they continued to work until they were nearly 70. Watching over sheep is not all that hard, even for an older person.
>
> My wife and I had four children in a short time. Three finished lower middle school, the fourth elementary school. Since my time, they built a dormitory for the Mongol school. All four of my kids lived there when they went to school, so we didn't have to live in Great Pasture with them. They came home once every week or so. Now that there's a dormitory in town it's no longer necessary to have a dwelling there when your kids are in school. And even those that do, usually return to live on the grassland once their kids have finished up.
>
> Now that my children have all finished school they live out here with us, and help us make our living. They'll most likely marry someone in this brigade and stay here then as well. Young people decide for themselves who they will marry, and usually they choose someone they know here. Parents don't pick their partner. As a result, most families in the brigade are somehow related.

The Commune Era

Dadusulongmu finished his own schooling in 1962 and immediately became a shepherd like his father. His grassland brigade, about 50 families at that time, had nearly 20,000 head of livestock, mainly sheep. He described life as it was in those years.

Each year the brigade chose about 20 experienced families to herd sheep. Because my father was an excellent shepherd, our family was always one of those chosen. They usually assigned a managing family a flock of over 1,000 sheep. These responsible families then organized labor and made their own pasturing decisions. They were responsible for any animal losses and were rewarded for gains. The brigade sent workers from other households to help. We especially needed help during lambing, shearing, and when the animals had to be injected. Workers were needed at other times as well.

Every couple of months, the cadres checked the number and condition of the animals in our care. If we lost too many we might be fined, or they might even decide to let someone else manage our flock or herd if we had repeated losses. But if we did our job properly, we made a pretty good living. Our family could earn an average of 24 work points for each day of work. We men tended sheep, the women milked brigade cows.

Other families were assigned around 100 cows instead of sheep, but they earned a bit less, perhaps 22 points each day. That's because cows require less attention. They can graze on their own without getting in trouble. But sheep have to be watched.

During normal times, we don't usually lose many animals, but shepherding has always been very risky. You can experience large losses quite suddenly. The worst years I recall were 1968 and 1969. There was an unusually big snow fall in 1968, and I still remember that nearly all the lambs born that year died. The problem was different in 1969. That was during the Cultural Revolution, when brigade members did little work and paid no attention to the animals. We lost a lot then!

In general, our losses were greater before the family responsibility system than after. Now we sell more than before, and fewer die except for one terrible year. Just after the new system started there was a "white disaster." I remember distinctly that on the 12th of April that year it was very hot. The next day it suddenly snowed, and went on snowing for two days. That was just after lambing. Although nearly all our lambs died, our losses were still less than during the white disaster of 1968. The reason for the difference is that, under the family responsibility system, we have fewer animals to look after than when we were managing brigade flocks, so we can pay closer attention to them. Even in a disaster, now, we lose fewer animals.

The commune promised that members would be better able to weather both black and white disasters because they could mobilize and concentrate more labor at such times. Now Dadusulongmu is persuaded that shepherds are more careful when the losses that would result from carelessness are directly their own. But, ironically, the greater attention people give to private flocks under the new system also discourages scientific innovation.

During a black disaster, when the snows have been insufficient and there is no water for the animals to drink, we have to carry water to them. That's heavy work for so many animals. If the animals are your own you're likely to be more enthusiastic about doing it.

From 1964 to 1979, I worked about 45 days a year at the Great Pasture artificial insemination station. We used artificial insemination to improve animal quality more than now. We had eight workers there from our brigade. We inseminated up to 2,000 sheep. Now every household has its own animals. None of us wants to leave them to spend 45 days working at the station. Besides, each household on its own decides to inseminate. And since most people here believe that the procedure produces very poor lambs, no one wants to have their animals inseminated anymore.

Making a Living the New Way

When Dadusulongmu's *gacca* divided the animals, he obtained 12 horses, 70 sheep, 3 milk cows, and 5 bulls. That was the basis upon which he began to build, by careful management and using his abundant family labor well.

Once we shifted over to the family responsibility system, I started to buy and sell sheep. I buy high quality animals and sell off the poorer ones. I sell when the price is high, and buy when the price falls. Last year I sold 50 sheep for over 100 RMB each, and a steer for 1,400 RMB. Now I have 12 horses, 200 sheep, and 30 cows, only 9 of which are milkers. I have nearly twice as many horses and cows as I did when you first visited me, but my flock is smaller because I've been selling off some.

In 1987, his *gacca* loaned Dadusulongmu 200 sheep, to help him expand his flock. Whereas the Lins used the opportunity to expand their flock, reinvesting all returns, Dadusulongmu sold many animals. He spent profits from his enlarged flock on a TV, tape recorder, some furniture, and a new yurt for his eldest son. He sold the 12 HP tractor he had bought three years earlier for 3,000 RMB and invested in a new one, for 6,000 RMB. The tractor itself can be considered an investment in production only in a marginal sense since the family cuts little grass.

We mainly use it to move our gear, it's transportation. It's less useful for cutting grass since we only cut a little for use, not for sale. A couple of weeks in August is all we need. There are a lot of reasons why we don't cut more. We're far from the collection stations and the road isn't good. Also we don't have enough people to do everything. We can't take care of sheep and cows and also cut a lot of grass. We can't be everywhere at once.

I have only two sons, so my daughters share some of the work. There is more to do in winter because the days are shorter and the cows spend more time in pens. We need to clean the pens more regularly, water the animals, and feed them fodder in the morning and again in the evening. But the busiest times for us are during lambing and when we cut grass. Everyone has to pitch in then. When it's time to cut grass, my wife and I stay home to care for the animals while all of the children cut grass. Our daughters go too. They drive the tractor, but they don't do hard work like piling cut grass.

Since we have more cows now, some of us must be near the milk collection station (in the fixed home) year round. So now we are together only during lambing and shearing. In winter, my eldest son and I tend the sheep in pastures about 20 km from here. We move the flock, and yurt as well, every month or so. If the snow is thick, we move more often. My daughters ride out to bring us food and clothing. While we live out there in our yurt, the rest of the family lives in the house we have near here. There is a well near it, so we can keep cows and lambs there all winter. In summer, my eldest son and daughter remain there to manage our cows while the rest of us go south to the Hui River with our flock. After we return, we have to move the sheep often because that's the time they grow quickly and graze a lot of grass. We generally move every 10 days then.

As you can see, life has changed a lot for us. Many Mongol families have built fixed homes. Personally I think the yurt is more convenient. Still I spent 9,000 RMB to build a permanent house to store my fodder, and keep my cows in winter. It's a better way to raise cows. Before we had our house, we used to bring our cows to Great Pasture. We lived there with relatives then. Now we don't have to do that anymore.

Looking Forward

Dadusulongmu had planned to enlarge both his herd and his flock. He may have to rethink his strategy now, however, because one of his sons has recently been offered a steady job he would like to take. With that son gone, there will only be two men to handle the cows and sheep.

In a few months he will go to Chenqi to work for a food company. Now that his uncle is retiring, my son will get work there in his place. And I expect that soon my daughters will marry, and I will lose their labor as well. Still, daughters-in-law will replace them. And if my second son finds a wife in Chenqi, and she remains there with him, we will adjust to that as well. I think we could make do here with just one son. My wife and I are still not too old to carry a full load and we could hire someone to help us from time to time.

When my first son marries we will still work together. We are not like the Han in that regard. In our case, when sons marry, parents usually set them up with some animals to build their own flock and herd. But still, partition is not total. After dividing, sons normally pitch their yurts nearby. We separated out some animals, but we continue to manage them together. That is what we do, and what Mongols in the other grassland brigades do as well. Fathers, sons, and brothers can cooperate better than strangers.

Dadusulongmu thus expects that when his remaining son marries, they will continue to work together. Each will know his own livestock, but they will be able to share responsibility well. As father and son they will trust each other, and by working together, they will be able to increase the number of sheep and cows they raise. Even so, two men alone cannot hope to handle both sheep and cows. They will continue to need the help of women, especially the help of daughters. But girls cannot do many things as well as men, and they will eventually marry out. For this family, labor limitations can be expected to restrain future growth.

9

Families at the Turning Point

In the course of family evolution, the number of workers changes often. Sometimes people foresee these changes. A newly married couple expects to lack hands after family division, treading water until their children reach adulthood. But other sudden changes can destabilize a family. A son may be lucky enough to find a job in the city, for example, or an essential worker may fall ill. Looking at families at such turning points underscores their inventiveness in getting work done, and also the fragility of any family's success.

The Fu Family: Holding Ground Won

Consider first a Sandhill family that worked harder than most to build a large herd. All along, the Fus expected their sons to handle and even expand the family herd. But realizing such expectations depends on family negotiations in a new setting of shifting, uncertain opportunities.

Fu Guoxi built his solid, three room mud and brick home in 1980. It stood alone at the edge of town. But then herdsmen began to pour their rising incomes into home construction, and by 1990 a whole neighborhood of new brick houses had risen around them. Their family income in 1987 was 6,000 RMB, nearly twice the Sandhill mean, their per capita income 998 RMB. They owned a TV, tape recorder, sewing and washing machines, and sofa. In 1988, Guoxi had 16 cows, more than most in Sandhill, and a small flock of 20 sheep. The Fus depend on their pastoral income. They earn no wages, have no sideline income, and sell no hay.

In 1988, the family lacked working males, and Guoxi brooded over the situation. He and his wife supported four nonworking youngsters. Apart from himself (age 51), the household contained his wife (49), two daughters (18 and 16), and unmarried twin sons (14). Two older daughters had already married, and his eldest son, still unmarried, lived and worked elsewhere. By the time of our second visit, his outlook had brightened

224

because, by then, his twins had reached an age when they could do the work of men. The potential for growth was there, and his plans were changing.

Family Background

Fu Guoxi came to Sandhill from Hebei in 1957. He was 20, and a farmer. His father had passed away when he was only five, and early on he had became the main support of his mother and younger sister. He left them behind in the care of relatives when he traveled to Inner Mongolia looking for a better life for them all.

His wife, Meilin, arrived in Sandhill from Hebei when she was four, and has known no other home. Two younger brothers and a sister also live here. Her brothers both hold low level positions in town, although, like most salaried people here, they also rear dairy cows. The Fus work often with Meilin's youngest brother, 15 years her junior.

Guoxi and Meilin met the year after his arrival, and married shortly thereafter. And soon after that, during the Great Leap Forward, his mother and younger sister joined them in Sandhill.

We had no idea my mother was coming. She just showed up! I wasn't home when she arrived, just my wife was there. My mother knew I'd married, but the two of them had never met. There they were, face to face, and they didn't even know each other! Well, it took some adjusting on all sides, but eventually everyone learned to get along. And it also took some time for my mother to adapt to a new way of life. At first the pastoral way of life was hard for her, she'd been a farmer all her life. There were so many new things to learn.

Under the Commune

In Hebei, Guoxi's father taught him the family sideline, making felt quilts for sleeping platforms. Guoxi also learned to handle work cows and sheep, skills that would serve him well later. But when hardship forced him to leave home, his first job was on the railway in Sandhill. Fellow countrymen found a temporary position for him, but he was soon laid off. That was when he paid the 60 RMB entry fee to join the cooperative.

I joined team three. (In 1959) I was assigned to manage the commune dining hall. My wife grew vegetables as a team member. She also wove fish baskets in winter, a sideline we no longer have. But communal dining was an idea that didn't work. So then they asked me to become head of team three, which I turned down. You see, I tend to be hot tempered. I felt I wouldn't be able to maintain cordial relationships if I took that job. In fact that's why I've never become a cadre. No, it wasn't because I was an outsider to Sandhill, in fact people didn't really consider me one. It was just a matter of my nature. Eventually (in 1962), I became an ordinary member of team one and turned to animals. I cleaned barnyards and built cow sheds, while I learned how to care for livestock. Then I herded on the grasslands. My wife joined my team and learned how to milk. She soon caught on and earned 10 points a day.

But living was not easy. In 1971 urban youngsters sent down to live and work in the countryside arrived. With them in town there wasn't enough work to keep everyone busy. Married women had nothing much to do, so my wife just stayed at home, took care of the house, and worked in our garden. The team did manage to find some milking for my eldest daughter to do when she finished school (at 15), and the 8 work points she earned helped a lot.

Guoxi's household grew, but still there were few able bodied workers. To make matters worse, his wife's health turned poor, the result of seven childbirths, with that of the twins the most difficult. Heavy household tasks were beyond her, and Guoxi, who returned every two weeks from the grassland, could not help. Fortunately, the commune was large and diversified, so when cadres learned of his family hardships, they gave him a new assignment that would suit his family needs.

We had many children at home, but neither my wife nor my mother were well enough to handle the housework and take care of them. I simply had to find a way to help. So I went to see the heads of my team and of the local commune factory. I asked if they would transfer me to the factory. That way, I would be nearby all the time and could help at home. They agreed, but I had to return our garden plot that belonged to the team, and the factory gave us no garden in its place. From that time, I depended on what I earned at the factory.

They had me making felt quilts, which I used to do in Hebei. I doubled my income at once, from about 440 RMB to 840 RMB a year. I really needed the added income since by then, I had a family of 10 to feed. I worked there until 1981.

Work and Infant Care

Meilin's collective work was periodic, and often there was no work at all for her outside. This flexible pastoral routine fit in with infant and child care:

You could take a break from work when you were pregnant and uncomfortable. About three months into pregnancy, you generally stopped entirely, or only did light work of some sort. When I conceived my first, I was weaving fish baskets for the team. I stopped before she was born and didn't start again until three months after.

I nursed her for more than a year. Even when I was weaving baskets, I could nurse her often. I started work at 8 in the morning, but went home to nurse after an hour, during our break. It took only 10 minutes to go home, and I could nurse for about 20 minutes before going back. During lunch break I nursed again, and once more after lunch. If for some reason I couldn't return, my mother-in-law would bring her, and I'd nurse her at work. Of course, once the work day was over she could nurse whenever she wanted.

I nursed all my kids much the same way, whether I was working or not. I only had a problem with my twins, because I didn't have enough milk for both. I had to supplement it with heated cow milk. That's not good because you couldn't be sure how hot it was, and mother's milk also keeps them from getting sick. But luckily my boys were okay.

Although I nursed all of them for about a year, it seems to me many women breastfeed even longer now. If they only have one, or are waiting a long time to have a second, they are likely to nurse a long time. These days it's even easier to nurse because we arrange our own work now. At busy times we work more, at other times we do less. And since we are home most of the time, nursing is really not a problem.

Raising Children and Planning the Future

Although their sons are just now reaching the age of full labor, one or more of them will probably leave at marriage. They hope to find town jobs and the Fus, like most Sandhill parents, would like to see them find trades with pensions. They would be quite willing to live on fewer animals they could handle themselves. But the Fus, with rural registration, do not qualify for sought after technical jobs.

For Fu Guoxi, the different prospects enjoyed by urban and rural townsfolk are a constant source of irritation. He resents the more limited school and work opportunities available to his children even more than the higher grain prices he must pay. Their children started out along a familiar rural path.

Our eldest daughter (born 1960) finished primary school and went to work for the commune. When she reached 22, she married a mine worker and moved away. We spent more than 600 RMB on her dowry. We gave her two sets of cotton bedding, a set of suitcases, some furniture, and a few sets of clothing. Now she has two children, and is a temporary worker. She sifts mud and carries bricks at the mine.

Our second daughter (born 1963) finished high school here. That's where she met her future husband. He's an accountant with the local government.

She also was 22 when she married. We gave her much the same sort of dowry, but their wedding was actually a simpler affair. You see, her husband's father was a cadre, which means that it wouldn't have been right for them to have a lavish wedding feast. When ordinary people invite a lot of guests, that's their business, but cadres are supposed to set an example.

Her husband didn't get his job by replacing his father (at retirement). He tested his way into that job. He was eligible to do it because he has urban registration. So now he goes to work each day, and she stays home and milks their cows. They live right here in Sandhill, so my grandchild often comes over to play, eat, and sleep. My wife babysits. In fact he's been here with us now for about a week.

Then a chance to break away did present itself, and the decision Guoxi and Meilin made affects their futures as well as those of their children.

Our eldest son, our third born, left home (in 1987) just after junior middle school. My wife's younger brother knew the director of an agricultural machinery factory, and he became an apprentice there. Then, after a couple of years, he responded to a notice that contract workers were needed to fix electrical lines in a mine over in Zhalanuer. Naturally, his ability to make agricultural machinery would be of no use there, but the move was worth it because he could make a lot more money. As an apprentice he was only earning 1.16 RMB a day. Now he has a basic wage of 70 RMB a month, and with bonus and other fringes his salary comes to 120 RMB. He's doing better than before, but we still can't depend on him financially right now. He makes barely enough to live on. In fact we have to send him money!

He likes what he's doing but the job doesn't really have much security. Nor does it bring a pension. The difference between the sort of contract work he has and working for the state is that they can fire him any time. It certainly is no "iron rice bowl." Never mind, I believe that an iron rice bowl is for lazy people! Our country now uses contract work to control the young, to keep them active and alert, and I think that's good. I just hope he can keep working there. If he works hard, maybe he will have a pension in future. Even with just a junior high school education, if he works hard, he may find a way to improve his position.

He already has a girlfriend. She works at the mine too. Once he decided to marry her, he asked our opinion. In reality, our consent was not the most important thing in his mind. And for our part, if he wanted to marry her it was alright with us. They will likely get married in October. Given his present job situation, there's no way he will be able to save enough on his own to get married. We still have to pay for the wedding.

People here expect the groom's father to buy them a home when people marry. Even a simple, broken down place is better than nothing. I've already bought one for them there in Zhalanuer, for 6,500 RMB. The groom's parents should also give some furniture, a set of bedding, and a couple of cows. They also hold the wedding feast. If we don't spend at least 10,000

RMB, we can't find a daughter-in-law. When my daughters married, I just invited three to five tables of guests, and that was enough. But I have to invite a lot of guests when my son marries.

Our third daughter (born 1970) graduated high school elsewhere, in Dongqi (in 1988). She lived in a dorm there. It wasn't expensive to keep her there, but it was becoming so. And even though she graduated high school it wasn't easy for her to find a state job. We don't have any well placed relatives or friends to help. Even if friends tell you about an opening, it's still hard to get it. There's always some sort of qualifying test, even to be a simple worker, and there are too many young people waiting for work. They all want a salaried job, but there are precious few of them, so testing is the only way to choose. If you pass, you get the job, if not you're out.

So after getting out of school, she returned to live with us. She did half the housework, all the milking, and carried our milk to the collection station if the younger kids were in school. Luckily, this year she found a job in the new local milk processing factory. Those jobs are supposed to be saved for the children of families like us with economic problems, but often they are given to people with good connections.

The twins, are a bigger problem, for they are at the center of the Fus' plans for herding development. Since their eldest son works elsewhere, only these young boys remain to help with the animals. But Guoxi and Meilin would prefer to see them find salaried work as well. If they are successful, however, there will be no way to expand the family herd.

I don't expect my remaining sons to be around very long. I certainly can't plan on it. In fact it's not really possible to make any clear plans for the future, because whatever I might think up won't much matter. They must follow their own desires. If they can pass the high school entry examination, then let them go. If not, then they can help me here.

Our (Han Chinese) tradition has always been sons take responsibility for the well being of aging parents and grandparents. But now the country has changed, and if you have pensions, sons don't have to do that. We older folks have also changed. We're more inclined to favor the children that are good to us, whether they are male or female. Whichever can't find work outside can stay to help us. Any of them could do it, and they are all good workers.

Despite his nod to a new tradition, Guoxi was aware that his children longed for a different life. Because some in Sandhill do escape, they had some hope. Despite Guoxi's claim that he would depend on whichever child treated him best, it was clear that did not have his daughters in mind when he spoke. In fact he would not pass his animals to his third daughter.

No, I have sons! If you have sons, you can't have your daughter and her husband live with you. You only do that if you don't have sons. If your daughter marries, and if she's home and has little work of her own, then she can come over to help out. But to have her husband marry in, that wouldn't be right! Neither family would be willing to see such an arrangement. The groom wouldn't be willing, his parents wouldn't agree, and since you have sons of your own you'd be unwilling as well.

The future looked uncertain. When we first chatted with the Fus, we realized that if both his youngest sons found jobs elsewhere, and with his wife chronically ill, there would be no way for him to care for his herd. But two years later, one twin had failed the entry examination for Sandhill's junior high school, and went to work at his father's side. Guoxi's future prospects were looking brighter, and he eagerly talked about expanding his herd. He expected his second twin to join them after junior high school. His sons' academic and occupational failures were the platform for his own future pastoral success.

My third son is still in school, just midway through, but his grades are not so good. He probably won't pass the high school entry examination. Anyway we only have rural registration, and 80 percent of our rural kids have no other road to take. If he ends up working at home, then we will raise more cows! His twin brother didn't pass the exam. He was smart enough to pass it but he wasn't very keen on school. So he's already working with me, and he's a good worker.

Making a Living

Fu Guoxi worked hard to build a good sized Sandhill herd. He takes great pride in this and would like to see even further growth. It was therefore all the more frustrating to think that he might have to cut back because of his offsprings' success in finding jobs.

I bought my first calf in 1963, when the commune let every family own one. When that cow calved, we turned it over to the team. They didn't want us to develop private herds. We were allowed to sell our milk, but the price was very low. As time passed we could have more than one cow and keep their calves. Still, only when we shifted to the responsibility system were our family herds secure. Before that we never knew when our animals might be taken. My herd actually started from an animal I bought in 1979 for 500 RMB. One good cow can start a large herd. As our saying goes, "If your cows produce female calves, in three years one cow will give you five head." Many people actually achieve that.

I've always been keen on building my herd. We Han have never been much given to raising sheep. Shepherding is usually done on a contract basis. Certain grassland families tend our sheep. They've been doing that since the commune ended. Although we did get some sheep when the changeover took place, we couldn't possibly have raised a large flock. I simply didn't have the manpower. We would have needed at the least two experienced men. But my sons were young, and I didn't have any brothers here. My wife's younger brothers all had jobs, so they couldn't help. I chose to build my herd of cows.

By 1987 I had 16 head, but there have been many calves since. Only one died, I gave another to my wife's younger brother. His cows aren't very good, they give too little milk. But I pay attention to breeding, so mine always have lots of milk. That's why he wanted one. And we sold a six year old for 1,900 RMB. So now my herd has grown to 32, all descended from my first cow!

Some day, when I have a larger herd, I hope to have pasture of my own to graze them in, and then I'll do it myself. But right now, like most people, I give 14 of my animals, those without milk, to a cowherd who grazes them on the open grassland all summer. Then there are my nine milkers. A day herder takes them to graze in the morning after they have been milked, and brings them home again in the evening. I put the calves out myself, in pastures at the edge of town. They just graze on their own. I can do that in under half an hour, because the place is very near.

A couple of years ago, mutton got too expensive to buy, so I bought a few sheep. They were old, weak, thin animals that were very cheap. A good one cost 150 RMB, but I bought mine for 120 RMB. Even if I had wanted to buy better ones, people aren't eager to sell quality animals. But there's a real risk doing what I did. Weak sheep get sick easily, so you have to worry about what they're eating. And if they get ill, you have to give them medicine, just like children. That's why shepherds are willing to sell older and weaker animals. Nonetheless, even those I bought may be useful. They can bear healthy lambs, and if I take care of them, they themselves may regain strength. My idea is that, eventually, they will multiply and become a reasonable flock, big enough to tend myself. So I will gradually develop a flock.

When you visited me the first time I had only 10, which we can't consider a serious flock. This year I have 20, but that's still too few to bother with myself. If you intend to shepherd in earnest, you should have about 400. I've given mine to a grassland shepherd with whom I have a special arrangement. He tends them with his own. They'll stay until I want to take them back. In exchange, I help him shear. Last year I gave him 10 days of labor. I can only spare that much time, because I have to return to cut winter fodder for my animals.

Labor and Other Problems

Older folks can tend a small herd of cows on their own. Unfortunately Guoxi and Meilin both have health problems. She is not strong enough to do anything more demanding than milking. She cannot clean the cow pens, or feed and water the animals in winter. A painful hernia keeps Guoxi from doing heavy work. They have cut down, and increasingly rely on their children. It has been a long struggle for them, only now are their children coming of age to do the work of adults.

When you were here last, I really had a serious problem. I had to do everything myself with only the help of my third daughter. After you left, my health worsened. I got really sick that September, a flare up of an old problem, one that started when I was 20, during the Great Leap Forward. That was a time of really heavy labor. I got my hernia back then, and it has never really gotten better. It flared up so bad that I needed surgery, and I stayed in hospital for 43 days. My stay there cost us a lot, over 1,000 RMB for the whole thing -- the operation, the hospital stay, and my wife's visits to Manzhouli. After I returned, I couldn't do much, I had to rest for a long time. I tell you, that operation wasn't a success. It's supposed to take only half an hour to do, but it took much longer. I've recovered somewhat, but I still have to go for injections. It's still hard to do heavy labor. But things are somewhat better, because there are more of us to work, and I'm actually considering enlarging my herd.

Now that it's summer, the women are busy. My fourth daughter and wife get up at 5 AM to milk. My third daughter helps them before she leaves for the milk processing factory. It takes the three of them an hour to milk them all. In summer, when they can eat fresh grass, they yield more, about twice what they produce in winter, when we feed them hay. So there's more milking to do.

After one of my sons delivers the milk to the collection station, my wife puts the cows out. Usually she and I work in the garden. But during grass cutting season, when we men are gone for six weeks, my wife and youngest daughter do everything here on their own. And we have a fairly large garden, so there's a lot of putting up to do. We begin that in August. Now my daughter does most of it, my wife taught her to do that early on.

We also have to clean our cow shed every day, and do it differently in the winter and summer. Because the animals are out all day in summer, one person can finish the work in an hour. But because they spend most of the time in sheds during winter, it takes two people an hour to finish. It takes an another hour just to water them, and I do that. Watering can't be entrusted to kids. I'd worry. It's heavy, and it takes understanding kids don't have. For example, a newborn calf has to have warm water, only an older animal can drink cool water. And they have to have the right amount, you mustn't give them too much. An adult always has to keep an eye on what the kids are doing with livestock.

Grass cutting season is the hardest. We have more cows than most, so our needs are greater. My eldest son takes a month off from work to help us, and my brother-in-law helps too. Although they're only 16, even the twins go with us. So far, I haven't had to hire anyone to help. My brother-in-law works with us because he needs hay for his cows, not for the money. You can't feed money to cows. He takes grass in exchange for his labor, and even then he still has to buy some grass. Although my health wasn't good last year, I went to cut grass. I did some of the lighter work, and the cooking out there.

Right now my grass cutting machinery is enough for my needs. But in future I'd like to buy a more powerful tractor, so I can cut enough to feed a larger herd. I can't finance it just now, so I only work with my small (12 HP) one. In 1985, I paid about 6,000 RMB for a machine that would now go for nearly 7,000. I borrowed 4,000 RMB from friends and kin, most from my wife's younger brother. Of course he was interested in helping us, since he cooperates with us to get grass for his animals. Some of the people who lent me money have their own machines, others don't. I repay those without tractors by cutting grass for them.

The only other income producing activity for me is fishing. I recently began to cooperate with five or six friends and relatives to do some ice fishing. We work as a team. I earn about 800 RMB from that, but I have to be away for two months or so. During that time, my children help my wife manage chores here.

Dairying remains Guoxi's main work. Since his family labor and grassland are limited, he tries to improve the milk yields of the animals he has. Selective breeding and better feed will help. But even with resort to modern techniques, there are roadblocks.

Last year I had two cows artificially inseminated. Both succeeded. This year, four out of five were impregnated. It costs 25 RMB per cow, but if it doesn't take, they return half. It's worth it, but only if the calf resembles the male! In my opinion, calves produced this way can resist the cold well enough. Cows from the south of China may not be adapted to conditions here, but our local cows have longer coats which protect against the cold. So we choose bulls from Denmark and Canada. We also raise our animals to help them resist the harsh climate here. For example, when we milk them by hand we are sure to leave some for the calves. We also feed them extra. If you feed them better, they'll grow larger and realize the full potential of their breeding.

But there are some drawbacks. These bred cows also produce milk lower in fat. Our local cows yield less than the better breeds, but their milk is richer. It all balances out though. For instance, if a local cow give you 10 kg of milk with 3 cm of cream per kg, you have 30 cm of cream in all. But if you have a higher quality animal that yields 25 kg of milk, even if the cream content is only 1.5 cm per kg, you still end up with 37.5 cm of cream and a lot more milk. That's still better than local cows can do.

So I do try to improve my animals, and if I had both my twins at home, we could raise more than we do. Perhaps next year we'll have 40! But you know, we Sandhill people can't enlarge our herds endlessly. There are real limits. Recently, when the head of our banner government came to investigate the situation in Sandhill, we had a talk. He asked how many cows I thought I could raise. I told him that, within three years, I hoped to have 50 head. But, you know, if we all had so many cows there simply wouldn't be enough hay, and we'd have to buy what we need outside. The two of us figured what that would mean if I really ended up with 50 head and had to buy hay for them. The way we calculated it, if I didn't cut more for the added animals, but bought it, I wouldn't be able to make much more than I do now.

Well, there are other ways to manage dairying, but we're not prepared for them now. If we were fully mechanized, we could handle more animals with less labor. We've been hearing about how the Australians do it. There's a young woman here that married a man in Hailar and then emigrated to Australia with him. She wrote home and told her family about a farmer there who raises over 50 cows with milking machines, and very little help. All his children went to college, only one daughter stayed home to help. She went to college, too, after one of his sons graduated and returned to replace her. Like us, he has limited pasture and has to buy fodder. But there it's easy to buy good feed. And milk collection comes to him! We're not up to that standard here.

If my herd does increase over the next couple of years, I'll have to depend on my own family resources. Naturally, I'd spend more time cutting hay, as much as two months a year, but I would do it. And if I didn't have enough grass, I'd get it from others, not buy it. We have a good reputation, so if I need hay I simply go from house to house with my wagon and borrow what I need. Last year, because I was sick, we couldn't cut enough and I had to borrow some hay from seven different households. In some cases, they had enough for their own needs, and simply sent some over to help me out, because our relations were good. It's like getting steamed buns to eat. You get a piece from this person and another piece from that person until you have the whole bun.

But my problem is not only marginal labor. I don't have enough of the feed nutrients you need if you want to raise better stock. Feed has always been a problem here, hard to find and poor in quality. Our cadres have always distributed it. When we had the commune, and you returned a two or three year old calf raised at home, they gave you some feed as a reward. Five or six years ago they started handing feed supplements out in return for fixed quantities of milk, as a kind of incentive. But that didn't last long. Since 1988 they give us free supplements only during long droughts.

Now we buy our own supplements, and mainly for our calves. We are entitled to seven catties for each head we have. In other words, we're allocated some for each animal we pay tax on. But the supply is still far too limited, and the quality not very high. Of course if you know the right people, have the right connections, you have a better chance of finding what you need. Because I can't get all I need, I grow some of my own. We have a sizable garden. This year I'm mainly using it to grow carrots, which I add to the grass I feed my animals in winter.

But even when you work hard to raise the quality of your animals there are always problems and expenses. Last year oil, diesel fuel, and spare parts for the tractor alone came to 1,600 RMB! Then I had to pay the cowherd 800 RMB to put them out to pasture. On top of that, there was 600 RMB for feed supplements. And no matter what you do there are animal losses, especially if someone is ill and you are short handed. When my wife was sick, one of my cows wandered onto the tracks and a passing train struck her. When I was in hospital we lost four that way. And I'm not the only one. From the beginning of this year, Sandhill people have seen 30 head killed like that! As things are now, we can only keep on what we are doing. The only thing I can hope for is to increase the size of my herd and concentrate on improving the quality and yields of the animals I raise. But that will all depend on whether I have the labor and feed I need.

Qi Fusan: Fishing the Grasslands

Because they decided to raise sheep and then suffered a major setback, the Qi family turned to fishing, and found it more rewarding than herding. Nonetheless, their new enterprise is no substitute for a pastoral life. This family illustrates the uncertainty of well being and how they innovate their way to better times.

Family Background

Qi Fusan, his wife Qing, and their four young children earned over 10,000 RMB in 1987, twice the Great Pasture average. Fusan had built in 1986 a fine, four bedroom brick house with tiled roof, at a cost of 12,000 RMB. The things they bought, like their home, reflected their economic accomplishment -- a TV, sewing machine, washing machine, and a tractor. Fusan's 21 cows were the basis of his livelihood, but fishing brought in almost half his income. Like many other migrants, the Qis had begun simply. Originally Shandong farmers, settling here called for some adjustment. Qi Qing recalled her own arrival.

> My husband and his father came a long time ago. When he was 17 (in 1966), he went back to his native place to find a wife. The two of us returned that same year. I had a special reason to leave home at that time. That was during the Cultural Revolution, and my family had real problems because my father, the commune Party Secretary, came under fierce attack by the Red Guards. The family decided it would be better for me to leave. So I came then, but we didn't actually marry until 1970, when we were 21.
>
> At first I couldn't get used to this place and I cried often. Great Pasture seemed primitive, I was so unhappy. But eventually I got used to it. Later, when I was three months pregnant, my father asked us to come back. By that time, the Cultural Revolution was over, and he had been restored to respect-

ability. He said he could arrange a job for me. I didn't know what to do. If I'd been a man, it would have been alright. But bringing my husband with me would have been humiliating for him. I'd have a job, but he would have nothing. Anyway, I was used to it here.

Although I didn't return, I haven't lost touch with my family. Over the last 20 years, I've managed to visit three times. Both my parents passed away. Only my younger brother and his family are still there now, so I don't return so often. We also have family on my husband's side here. He has an elder sister in Great Pasture, and an elder sister and younger brother in Chenqi.

The Qis have done so well that they arranged an exceptional marriage for their eldest son. The girl has urban registration and cadre family background. Since children follow their mother's registration, Fusan's grandchildren will be advantaged. They are preparing an elaborate wedding to mark the event, and will build a fine home for the couple to live in. Through her son's marital connections, Qi Qing also hopes to send her younger children to an urban school.

My eldest (age 20) is engaged to a girl who works at the Great Pasture railway station. Her father is a cadre. She very much likes our son. We hope to see them marry soon, and when they do, we'll give them at least two milk cows to start them off. Of course they'll move out then, and live on their own. We've already spent 26,000 RMB to build a house for them. Although they'll have their own animals, we'll continue to fish together.

Our second son (18) also fishes with his father. Then there is our daughter (14), and our youngest son (11). I would really like to see our youngest children continue their studies. In fact, our daughter has already changed her registration to Hailar and is starting school there this year. My youngest son is in fifth grade, but when he graduates from elementary school, we are thinking of sending him to live with my brother in Shandong, to continue his schooling there. The level of education here is too low. Students can't pass the college entry exams.

So we're saving for that. As long as we're in good health, we'll work to make it possible. I consider education very important. I graduated from junior high school in Shandong, but I think that my level is about the same as that of high school graduates here. My husband has no formal education at all. He can't express himself very well and isn't very polished. Even if my two youngest can't pass the exams for college, I still want them to go as far as they can.

We have a hard life, especially us women. When we get to be 40 or 50, most of us already have leg or back problems. That's why I want my children, and especially my daughter, to avoid this way of life. Moreover, because kids have so little education here, they often get into trouble. That's why I'm so strict with my older ones -- they have little education, but I pay close attention to them. That's rare here. I'd say that only one out of 10 manage to stay out of trouble. There's a lot of drinking and fighting and wasting time.

The Turning Point

Like others, the Qis saw the responsibility system as a chance to find a better life. Unlike most Great Pasture Han families, however, they opted to take the shepherd's route with all its risks. The choice was a mistake.

> When the responsibility system began, my husband was a shepherd, who tended others' sheep as well as our own. Not many Han made a living that way here. But then we were struck by a "white disaster," and lost many of our sheep. Because most of the flock belonged to others, we were deep in debt. The calamity was ours, not theirs. We had to repay them for all the animals they had put in our care. The only thing to do was to give them our own sheep and what money we had. The basis of our livelihood was suddenly gone! We had a few cows, but not enough to live on.

To recoup in a season, without the long build up that animals require, Fusan turned to fishing. Since he had no experience when he started, he joined a group of fishermen. After a year, he had the skills needed to go off on his own.

> At that time we didn't know much about fishing, so it was chancy. Even then, contracts cost a lot. Each site is different, but the cost of all of them has been going up. In 1986, we contracted one for 800 RMB. The next year we paid 1,200 RMB, and in 1988 more than twice that. Last year we paid 6,000 RMB for a good one, but this year we bid on a less desirable one for 3,700 RMB.
>
> At present there are 30 to 40 families that fish in Great Pasture, but we earn more than any. Of course, Mongols rarely fish. I know of only one family in this brigade. But he doesn't do very well at it. He's paying 8,000 RMB for a site, but he doesn't get much, because he's lazy and drinks too heavily.
>
> Fishing is a risky way to make a living, but the rewards can be good. We can't control conditions. When the weather's too warm, the fish die too fast and rot. Dead fish aren't easy to sell. In 1987, there was a heat wave and little rain, so we caught very little. Last summer there was a lot of water and we caught lots. In winter, the ice is thick and it's hard work. After expenses, my husband's group earned 30,000 RMB fishing! But we can't always earn that much. Fishing's so unpredictable.
>
> When my husband started out on his own, he bought a boat, nets, horse cart, and a 12 HP tractor. But that was not the end of it. Repairing old nets and buying new ones runs about 2,000 RMB a year. Then we pay a business fee of 3 RMB per 50 kilos of fish caught.
>
> My husband, our two eldest sons, and a hired hand fish from mid-July to the end of the year. Women never fish. It's heavy labor, and you have to be away from home. The brigade prohibits fishing before mid-July to prevent over fishing, but the men go live there in May to make sure no one comes to

poach. They stay there until the end of the year when the contract period ends. They live in a shelter cut into the earth and fish through ice. It's really cold out there in winter.

We don't catch all we could in summer because the weather is so hot that fish spoil, and we can't get rid of them all fast enough to the brokers who buy, transport, and market fish. October and November are good months, and you don't have to worry about catching too much then. It's already cold enough that the catch won't spoil so quickly.

Division of Labor

The Qis now have a sizeable herd of cows but once they found they could combine dairying and fishing they had little incentive to rebuild their flock of sheep. It would be hard to combine fixed fishing with mobile shepherding. But a dairyman can turn his fishing profits to offset added dairying costs.

We have 29 cows now; 10 give milk. But now that we fish more, we can't cut grass for them. We have to buy the hay we need. When the men are all working elsewhere, I have more work to do as well. I do most of the milking. We put the mature cows in the care of a professional herdsman each day. He takes them out to graze for 3 RMB per head per month. But we can save on the calves because they graze nearby. I put them out each day myself, and often they come home by themselves. If not, I go bring them back. I keep them nearby, because I have to bring them home in the afternoon to give them water, and then I put them back out until evening. I also make all the clothing we wear. In winter I must change all the cotton padding in our clothing. I take care of the house, and plant and tend the vegetable garden.

Still, as hard as she works because of her husband's fishing, Qi Qing does less outside the home than most farm woman. Fishing and most of the heavier dairying work belongs to men, family or hired. Her work, like that of other women here, is largely confined to the home and barnyard. While women's work takes them away from home less often than among the farmers, their burdens are nonetheless heavy, especially since the men help little.

We work harder than the men. Having worked hard outside, they can come home and rest. But for us there is no rest. Of course in our family the men are also often busy, even when they are at home. For example, they return from fishing at New Year, and a month later they prepare for the next round of fishing -- repairing nets and other things. But we women work every day!

Future Prospects

The Qis expect to continue their dual lines of work. With two grown and experienced sons, the fishing gear required, and a large herd of cows to back him up, Fusan can afford the risk of fishing. It will reward him better than anything else. Qi Qing summarized their thinking this way:

> Unless the government policy changes, we'll keep on as we're doing now. If we wanted to be satisfied with an ordinary standard of living, we could get along quite well on the income we earn from our cows alone. Each day they give us 60-70 kg of milk, which averages out to something like 700-800 RMB each month throughout the year. But that's not enough for us. We're willing to work harder, to fish as well, because we want a better living.

While fishing may be unpredictable, the costs are less than grass cutting. They do not have to raise the fish they catch, and the taxes they pay on their catch are set by what they themselves declare. No one checks on their catch, which is why one neighbor could observe that, "Whatever the Qis say they earn from fishing, you can probably multiply by 150 percent." This family has turned adversity into advantage, by taking advantage of new possibilities and making best use of labor. In that way, they have begun to move upward from the turning point.

10

Pastoral Families: The Have Nots

Given the important work men do, herding families with only ill or elderly men are in trouble. From two such families we learn how folk with few hands adjust their livestock and work to scrape by.

Gao Bingan: Struggling with Catastrophe

The Gaos had reached a decent standard of living by Great Pasture standards. They built the simple earthen home they live in a decade ago and, as income improved, bought a TV, sewing machine, bike, and clothes washer. They bought a 12 HP tractor in 1987, the year that their 22 cows, 100 sheep, and fishing earned them an income twice the community mean. Milk sales alone brought in about 5,000 RMB, fishing another 2,000 RMB. But there were many dependents, so the Gaos actually only earned 1,014 RMB per person, less than the Han mean.

The burden on Gao Bingan (age 51) was heavy. In 1988, six of his seven children lived at home, only his eldest daughter had already married out (in 1983). His second daughter was 19, his eldest son only 17. The rest, three daughters (15, 13, and 11), and a son (8), were all too young to help much. He and his wife, Anru (age 44), were supporting a large family with little labor. The problem was especially pressing because they were among the few Han in Great Pasture trying to do everything -- raise sheep, tend dairy cows, and fish. Not only were there few workers, but because most were female, they did not herd or fish.

For that reason, Bingan put his eldest son, young as he was, in charge of their flock. He and his wife managed the cows, and he cut some grass. He was trying to do too much, and when he developed a serious heart condition in 1990, and could no longer do hard work, the delicate balance was shaken. Then, when his son's inexperience cost them the family flock, the Gaos suddenly found themselves among the poorest Great Pasture households, with few prospects.

Early Arrival and Commune Life

The Gaos were born in Liaoning Province. When both his parents died in 1953, Bingan and his younger brother joined his elder sister, who had married a Great Pasture man. In 1962 he made a short visit home to Liaoning to claim the wife arranged for him there by an elder brother.

When I first came to Great Pasture, there was still no collective. First I learned to drive a horse cart and made my living transporting things. I also cut some grass for Mongols living out on the grassland. That's when I first raised animals and built houses. When the commune was organized, the cadres of each brigade classified all workers, assigned them, and rewarded them according to their skill, experience, and "way of thinking," (political attitudes). For a number of years I was a shepherd. In 1963 they introduced a new system to reward effort and penalize failure. A fisherman was supposed to catch a daily quota. If it was 40 kg of fish, and he caught that much, he earned 8 work points. If he caught more you got a percentage of the extra value, if less he'd lose some of the standard points for that work.

But when the Cultural Revolution began, they not only stopped the incentives, but punished all private enterprise. If a commune member dared to go fishing on his own, cadres would accuse him and lead him through the streets so everyone could see he'd "stolen" fish. In those years you couldn't earn more by doing more, so no one saw any reason to work hard. Things didn't get much better until 1977, when they returned to a system of bonuses and penalties.

The value of work points fluctuated a lot, because of sidelines. In our brigade, one point was worth about 0.25 RMB. But it doubled when we started to transport locally mined nitrates. I myself worked in the mine for a while, but, unfortunately, it closed (in late 1960). Then the value of our work point dropped again.

Toward the end of the 1960s, many students were sent down to the countryside. Since we had more people whose output was low, our work points were worth even less. But who would have dared to object? Hadn't Chairman Mao himself proposed sending them to the countryside? And besides, we actually got to like those kids. They lived with us, and we formed close bonds with them. So we actually gave little thought to the fact that they reduced the value of our work points.

My wife and I both went out to work. I earned eight points a day driving carts, and she brought in seven working in the common gardens. She had to work. We needed whatever she could earn. The brigade didn't require women to work, and most didn't. But if a family earned too little, then they might send a married woman out to work during the summer months. Even when they did work outside then, however, women couldn't earn much because in winter there was nothing to do in the gardens, and less milking. Only a few unmarried girls worked outside in winter.

Making a Living the New Way

In those days we put in an eight hour day, but we didn't have to work hard. That really changed when the new system started. We decided for ourselves what we would do, and how we would do it. And we owned what we produced. So, people were willing to work a lot harder, and there was more to do as well.

I already had a milk cow that the brigade had put in my care earlier. The brigade divided me 108 sheep, some cows, a horse, and two large bulls. But I had a problem. While I knew how to manage sheep, I was the only worker in the family. So I put the sheep in the care of a Mongol shepherd. We agreed that he'd care for them and give us one to one and a half sheep for each person in my household every year. We gave him the wool and lambs for meat. So we actually began with only three cows, and only one of them was a milker. It wasn't worthwhile for me to take them out to graze all day by myself, so I paid a cowherd to do it. I was free to use my horse and cart for transporting. Then I began to fish as well. Little by little my herd grew.

Arriving at the Turning Point

It was at this point that what seemed a smooth road upward took a sudden and unanticipated turn.

That was the way it was when you were last here. But things have gone downhill since. With my eldest son of age to work, I took my sheep back from the shepherd to raise. The timing looked good. My son could now do a lot, and the price of mutton was going up quickly. So, two years ago, we began shepherding our own flock. I spent nearly 4,000 RMB to buy another horse, a new yurt, and all the equipment we needed to shepherd properly.

The effort might have worked, but Bingan became ill soon after reclaiming his sheep. The illness effectively removed him from the family labor pool, and put too heavy a burden of responsibility on his son.

The year before last I had a serious heart attack and had to stay at Hailar hospital for over 40 days. I was in no condition to stay on the grasslands in winter to help with the sheep. So in December I hired a shepherd to replace me, someone my eldest daughter introduced. I paid him 70 RMB a month, plus food and clothing. And that was my problem in the end. My son was just too inexperienced, and the hired man turned out to be unreliable. Because of our shepherd's carelessness, wolves rushed into the flock and attacked many animals. We found more than 80 of them dead, animals worth nearly 10,000 RMB! Many were pregnant with lambs, so we lost both the sheep and their lambs.

You know, wolves don't actually eat the sheep, they just bite. There's some sort of poison on their teeth that kills the sheep. Anyway there were two or three bite marks on each of them. It was horrible! The animals were still edible, but we couldn't sell them. They were all still thin from the long winter. All we could do was shear the wool to sell.

It wasn't really my son's fault, he wasn't responsible for the shepherd's failure. Because of what happened, our hired man will work without salary for two years. We only give him food and clothing. But, that can never make up for what we lost. I lost all the profits of two years of work. And we didn't just lose those animals and their unborn lambs, but also all the generations of animals they would have produced. I really thought of giving up, but I couldn't do it. The only thing I could do was to put one foot in front of the other, watching each step.

Now I have over 30 cows but only about 100 sheep. I also own two horses, which I need for shepherding. We keep all our livestock on the open grassland, about 5 km from town. Three of my children live out there in a yurt. I have to keep my daughters out there in summer, I have no choice. They milk the cows every day, and the elder one bikes the milk back to Great Pasture. If the weather turns bad, we drive the milk into town on our tractor. My daughters milk and cook, but they also help take care of the sheep. Both can ride horses.

My wife and I stay home and tend our garden. But once in a while I go to look in at the yurt. And in summer, when we have to move our flock, I help as well. The girls can't really do that work. In winter we bring all the cows home to our pen, the sheep stay out there. I also bring my daughters home, only our shepherd and my son remain out there all winter. It gets too cold out there for the girls.

I bought a tractor to cut grass. But I don't have enough labor so I've never really used it for that purpose. During hay cutting, I lend the tractor out in return for three carts of grass. I mainly use it to move the yurt, and to carry supplies out there. I also use it to carry water, and to bring branches home for fuel or to use in fences.

With me ill, and only my son out on the grassland year round, there's no way we can cut fodder. I sell my cutting rights to others. Last year the selling price was 5 RMB per meter. The year before it was only 3 RMB per meter. As the number of animals goes up, so does the demand for fodder and cutting rights. But having sold my rights, I need to spend 2,000-3,000 RMB on hay. So that's my problem. I don't have enough labor to increase the size of my herd or flock, and I can't cut grass. While I have no way to increase my income, everything we buy costs more. Even the animal head tax has been going up.

My neighbor and I used to pool our labor, equipment, and money, contract a site for about 8,000 RMB and then fish it. We divided up what we earned by who put in what. Fishing earns good money, but I'd never give up herding. Animals are basic. This year I'm not going to fish at all. I lost so much money because of what happened to my sheep that I couldn't bid for a site this time round. And I'm not sure I could have won this year anyway. You have to have connections these days, to use the "back door."

Lots of people want to fish now, so arrangements are now formal. We have to register our rights at the brigade, township, and banner. And the cadres watch closely. They control when, where, and who may fish. If they catch you fishing out of season, they fine you. And when we're not allowed to fish, buyers don't come so there's no one to sell to. Even the train won't take our fish. So we can't fish when we're not supposed to.

I don't know what we'll do in future. My original idea was to build my flock and herd, and continue fishing. But now I can't do any of it. Everyone that can work is doing so, and still it's barely enough to keep what we have. It's discouraging.

Raising Children

The Gaos began their married life poor by village standards. Living on their own, short handed, they expected hard years ahead. Anru had to work as much as she could to earn the extra work points to sustain them. The arrival of children created an urgent need for her labor. She worked in collective gardens some distance from home, so she had problems reconciling the need to earn work points with her domestic duties as more children were born, a problem familiar to the cultivators we have studied. Anru described her plight:

Working in the gardens took me further from home and kept me away longer then women who only milked cows. They worked short periods each day, but I worked all day. And the gardens were nearly 4 km from home, so it wasn't convenient to go home for lunch. I brought my lunch to the gardens and ate there. So when my first was born I couldn't work. I had to stay home to take care of her, there was no one else to do it.

I nursed her a long time and then, eventually, went back to work. About six years later, my second daughter was born. I put her in the care of her elder sister and went back to earn the extra points we would need to raise our children. So long as I worked in the gardens, nursing wasn't easy. I had no choice but to give her cow's milk, steamed bread, rice and noodles instead of mother's milk. Because we needed the points I earned, my eldest daughter had to replace me at home very early. She handled many household chores and later, as she grew up, could earn points of her own. When she was 16, she went out to the lambing place to help her father. They classified her as half labor then.

In 1983, their eldest daughter married a Hailar lad, and the two of them managed a plastic bag factory. They had a three year contract with the local government. Her escape to the city pleased the Gaos.

When my eldest married, people didn't spend a lot. Poor families like ours only gave girls simple things, like a couple of suitcases, and no money. The groom's side wasn't wealthy either. Poor marry poor, so neither side spent much.

In fact our condition was worse than theirs. So we made an agreement with her husband that the two of them would send us 10 RMB every month as long as we lived. We needed the extra help because our other (six) children were young, and four were girls. Besides, I wanted to set an example for the rest. When the two of us are old. we'll certainly need help. Of course we'll depend more heavily on our sons since married daughters are no longer family. Still, we feel that all of them should help, even the girls.

Bingan lamented the rising cost of marriage, another burden to which he must adjust:

Now, as people make more, even daughters' marriages cost more. That means I must save a lot for the rest of my kids. When a son marries, his parents may spend nearly 20,000 RMB. Even for a daughter it's common now to spend 4,000 RMB! So we all have to work harder just for that. You earn more nowadays, but you spend more too.

Life has changed a lot. Before, it was hard to imagine that a family like ours, with seven children but only one male worker, could buy a tractor or a TV. With all my troubles, I still make enough from my cows to buy what we need. I don't need to borrow to buy grain. I can even pay for my children's education. I'm raising sheep now mainly to marry my kids off. Only one daughter has married, we have three more to think about. And there are two sons we will have to find wives for. So we really need to save a lot.

Their difficult position calls for innovative arrangements, like adding sheep and fishing to dairying, and looking to their daughters for help and security. Although he insists that daughters are ultimately members of other families, Bingan has made the uncommon decision to tie his future to theirs, at least until his sons are full labor. He has taken advantage of the forthcoming marriage of his second daughter to add helping hands.

Two years ago, through the introduction of our eldest daughter in Hailar, our second daughter (then 20) got to know a boy. She liked him well enough, so from her point of view the prospect was good. And the fact that he had urban registration pleased us. When they met he was unemployed, but we thought that with urban registration he'd find a good job.

The match looked good to Bingan, but Anru saw it differently. She leaped into the conversation, cutting him short:

Well, he thought the fellow was okay, but I didn't approve of him from the start. Even though he had urban registration, he came from too poor a family. But my husband agreed to the engagement. Within the year, our daughter changed her mind and regretted her engagement! She wanted to call it off, and I supported her in that. But my husband thought that we would lose face if we were to break off the engagement.

During the two years since their engagement, he has only brought us watermelon, some canned food and a few things like that, nothing of real value. And his parents have only prepared two sets of new quilts for the marriage. I've already gotten ready many fine things for them. I bought her clothing, two leather suitcases, a grandfather clock, a bicycle, a washing machine, a pair of leather boots, and a tape recorder. I spent nearly 4,000 RMB! To make matters worse, he never found a job. In fact he's living with us! He wants to learn fishing from my husband.

During the collective era, the community as a whole would have absorbed the Gaos' economic calamity. That is no longer the case. Nonetheless, Bingan still firmly supports the responsibility system. By his account, his living standard has improved, even with this recent setback. He can afford many conveniences that would have been impossible before, and still feed themselves easily. Just as he accepts that he alone is responsible for his present predicament, he is also persuaded that it is within his power to overcome his difficulties. He expects his children to be part of the solution even though, at present, they are also part of the problem.

The Zhangs: Going It Alone

From the Zhangs we learn how an older couple can live alone. Zhang Zhongmin (62) and his wife, Yuxia (58), live alone in a small mud house in Sandhill. With six cows they can do alright. By combining meager pastoral earnings with some wages, they are self sufficient, and proud of it. Their household income was only 2,504 RMB in 1987, but since they had no dependents, they earned more per capita than many.

Their home, now dilapidated, was built in the 1940s. Furniture was sparse and, apart from the TV, we saw few of the other conveniences now increasingly common in Sandhill. There was no sewing machine, clothes washer, bike, radio, tape recorder, or sofa. Although the Zhangs had few conveniences, they did not lack essentials.

Family Background

Like others, Zhongmin and Yuxia knew nothing about raising animals when they first came to Sandhill from Shanxi province. Their families had

been peasants. They are among Sandhill's earliest migrants. Zhongmin
arrived some 41 years ago. Both have spent most of their lives here.
Zhongmin recounted the family background:

> My parents passed away when I was only seven, my grandmother brought
> me up. I've never really had the experience of living in a large family. My
> grandfather had only one child, my father, so there were no uncles or aunts
> on his side. I have no brothers or sisters either because they all died a few
> years after I was born. So I was "a single plant," one without shoots, without
> a future.
>
> When I first came to Inner Mongolia, the Japanese "devils" and the "old
> hairy ones" (Russians) were both still here. I lived in Hailar first, where my
> uncle (grandfather's brother's son) had a business. I couldn't find regular
> work, so I did whatever I could.
>
> I got married (in 1947) before coming here to Sandhill. We have some
> family on her side -- two younger brothers and two younger sisters, all farmers
> in Shanxi. Neither of us have had much education. I went to school for three
> years, but my wife is completely illiterate.
>
> When my uncle came to Sandhill (in 1958), we came with him. He wanted
> us to come because he needed our help. His wife had recently died and there
> was a child to care for. So we lived with them here in this house, which had
> belonged to a Russian family. There weren't many people in Sandhill then,
> and all around there was only grassland.
>
> Because we came from farming families, we didn't know the first thing
> about animals when we first arrived. So in the beginning I did some trading.
> Then I joined the commune and became a member of the pastoral team.
> That's when I learned to raise horses, sheep, and cows, and I've been raising
> animals ever since. I worked for the collective, and Yuxia charged 15 RMB
> a month to take care of the child. I only earned 30 RMB myself, and we had
> a child of our own to care for. We almost couldn't make it.

Children and Family Relations

We found it curious that Yuxia had only one child. Zhongmin was the
single son of a single son, and now he too had a single son! It was not
intended, as Yuxia explained:

> In fact we wanted to have more, but I've always been in poor health. I
> conceived them, but none survived. They were all stillborn. Even this one
> isn't my own. We adopted him from someone here, a person from our home
> place in Shanxi. We took him when he wasn't even an hour old, and raised
> him. Of course I couldn't nurse him, I had to feed him cow's milk. At first
> he had no idea he was adopted. But you know, people here have "long
> tongues" so, eventually, he discovered the truth. He even knows who his
> natural father was, because his brother lives nearby. In fact my son and his

brother are neighbors. When he first learned that he was adopted, he wasn't upset. It didn't really matter because, all that time, we'd been good to him.

Zhongmin spoke with some irritation of the problems parents have bringing up children. Although they would like to see their son leave pastoral life, there are few ways out, especially since his son went to school during the Cultural Revolution. Education then was highly politicized. Besides, the Zhangs have rural registration, and most regular jobs are reserved for lads with urban registration.

After my son graduated junior high school he had no desire to go on. Maybe you don't know that the school level here during the Cultural Revolution was very low. The teachers were badly trained and couldn't teach, and the school day was a joke! The kids went to class at 8 in the morning and came home by 10! What sort of education can you get like that? Children are better off now. They go to class morning and afternoon, and their teachers are better trained. They all come from Hailar City.

Although he started early to prepare for his son's marriage, he could not afford to do everything at once. He had enough for a simple wedding, but not a house. It took another year to make that possible. And Zhongmin determined to pay all these expenses himself.

They married in 1984, and moved out a year later. I paid for everything. I spent over 4,000 RMB on furniture and clothing for them. And then there was the 1,500 RMB I spent for their house. If you add it all up the whole cost of him married came to about 6,000 RMB. Still it was what we call a "travelling wedding." He took his bride and went off to Beijing on a 10 day honeymoon. After they came back, they were here a couple of days, and then went to visit his wife's family. Let me tell you, I really like the idea of "travelling weddings." They open the mind to new places, new ideas. They're also very practical. Frankly, I didn't have the money for a big wedding feast. I just invited my grandfather's brother's son to a meal in my home, that was it. Even so I spent a lot of money. But you know, I only have this one son. If I don't give what I have to him who will I give it to? I would just die with it!

Zhongmin assured us that the prompt departure of his son after marriage was not precipitated by any discord. But Yuxia's complaints about her daughter-in-law suggest otherwise:

She's always trying to extract money at New Year's. Every New Year since they moved away, she's tried to get us to give them 800 RMB! But except at New Year, we hardly ever see her, she never comes around. You know, her

248

attitude isn't all that uncommon. I would guess that perhaps 20 percent of Sandhill daughters-in-law think like that!

Whatever they may think of their daughter-in-law, they consider partition at marriage perfectly normal, not necessarily a reflection of family conflict. Indeed, proud of his present self-reliance, Zhongmin eagerly told us how, despite limited means, he continued to help his son. Furthermore, he was secure in the knowledge that his son's independence would not be permanent. He fully expects that his son will care for him in his twilight years, when he can no longer work. Then, parents and son will once again become a single family and household.

They live apart right now, and that's fine since my health is still good. The way I see it is that so long as parents are O.K., sons should partition when they marry. That way you avoid arguments and problems. Why did they choose to move out just then? No special reason. We had no problem with her, her temperament is O.K. But why shouldn't they move out? We were fine, we could take care of ourselves. When the time comes that I can't move anymore, then they can come back to live with me. There's no need for us all to be together now.

But that is a prospect about which Yuxia has certain misgivings, since she still has problems with her daughter-in-law:

They are in a position, financially, to take pretty good care of themselves. They're certainly not in any need. She's a high school graduate. A year after they moved out, she opened a sewing shop in their house. She had never sewed anything for me, so naturally I was surprised. I really don't know where she learned to sew. But now that she has had her second child, she doesn't do much apart from taking care of her kids. If someone comes to seek her out, then she may sew something from time to time, but she's no longer actively in business.

Family division did not reduce the involvement that Zhongmin and Yuxia had in their son and his family. To the contrary, they paid close attention, and even pressured them to have a second child, Zhongmin in particular was anxious:

"One child policy" or not, we urged them to have a second. Here in Sandhill they don't want us to have a second now unless the first is female. He already had his son, but we just couldn't bear the thought of his having only one, after generations of "single plants." My grandfather, my father, and I had all been in that situation, and I just didn't want to see it happen again. I really wanted him to have two. Long ago I said, "Son, have another! Your father and grandfather had only one. Neither my father nor I had a brother or sister to talk to! Don't let that happen to your child. Male or female it doesn't much matter. At least they'll be able to talk to each other." I repeatedly said that to him.

So they did have a second. It turned out to be a daughter! And on top of it the authorities wouldn't register the kid. Because she was not authorized her name has still not been entered in the household register. As I understand it, the birth control section wants 150 RMB to write the necessary letter of authorization, but he won't pay it. So, she's still not registered. Well, it doesn't matter all that much. Eventually she'll be in the register. These days if you have money, you can buy anything.

Although Zhongmin and his son head separate families now, each with its own budget and property, they still help each other. Zhongmin and his wife care for their older grandchild, although they complain that he is too active and energetic for them to control. But their continued attention to the child will bolster their own claim for support later, by grandson as well as by son. Yuxia described the part they play in bringing up their grandson:

He actually lives with us now. He came to live with us when he was eight months old and has been living with us ever since. Now he's five. You could say that I really raised him. In fact we even bear the expense of it, our son doesn't give us any money. Actually I don't want his money. It costs me 20 RMB a month just for soda pop and ice cream. That child has no interest in real food! But never mind, spending money on a grandson is fine, your grandson is your own. This grandson of mine doesn't want to go to nursery school. You know it costs 50 RMB to send a child to nursery school. We paid the fee and sent him to the Han nursery here, but he ran home after only three days.

He's really naughty. We have to keep an eye on him all the time. He can easily decide to run over to the train station by himself. That's too much! Even when he wants to go home, I always make a point of taking him there myself. I'd worry if he were to walk home on his own, because of the train tracks nearby. And he goes home every couple of days to see his sister. Then he comes back here.

Making a Living Alone

Cut to the bone, pastoralists' labor needs are not overwhelming. Zhongmin and Yuxia care for a few cows, few enough that Yuxia can milk them, and Zhongmin can do most of the other work. What they cannot furnish themselves, they buy. But of course that means that they must live frugally and cut back on their expenses. But there are always unforeseen expenses that can threaten the balance:

250

We've been raising cows for eight years. At first I couldn't afford to buy a cow, so my cousin gave me a female. Now we have six, three give milk. We have quality cows. They're "test tube" cows. If we could only feed them well, they'd be really good milkers. But we can't afford it, so we get low yields. In fact they've been ill for several months now. They've been eating too much green grass and too little feed. They have soft bones because of their poor diet. Cows are like people, if we eat only vegetables we get sick too. The diet should be more balanced. You know, I've heard that about 40 percent of the cows here in Sandhill are ill this way. They all have bad legs.

I have to use my milk earnings to cure them, I don't know what else to do. These days, even if you have the money, you can't buy good, healthy, animal feed. We've had them injected more than 10 times already, and each time I spent 30 RMB. Anyway, they're somewhat better. They can walk and don't need injections or medicines now. And a few days ago we paid 60 RMB to get some better feed.

To reduce his workload, Zhongmin hires a cowherd to graze his cows. He no longer cuts hay, but buys what he needs from his son. He does not think of the transaction as a true payment. In his mind, family division is never complete or irrevocable.

It's not so easy to raise cows if you don't have a tractor to cut fodder. Buying hay from others is an expensive way to raise cows. I certainly couldn't afford to raise them if I had to pay for hay. But my son cuts his own grass, and when he does, he cuts enough for my cows as well. I give him a bit of money for it.

He bought his tractor three years ago. Before that, the two of us used to cut grass together by hand. When I got too old, he decided to buy a tractor. He didn't have the money, so he borrowed what he needed from the bank. He still owes 1,000 RMB. Well, he has an arrangement with them. They're building a new office and he uses his tractor to transport stones for them. That way he's working off some of his debt. In Fall he'll sell a cow to pay the rest off.

I'm helping him pay it off as well. I think it's only natural since I only have this one son. If I die, what good is my money? I should help him! What do we old timers need money for anyway, so long as we can eat and drink that's enough. After all, we may have separated to live apart but we're still one family. He doesn't give us any money right now, but he's not really in a position to. After all, he has two children to raise, and besides we don't want his money. But he needs our help to buy fuel for his tractor. If he had wages, and if my cows were not ill and were more productive, we could actually live quite well on our own. As it is we manage to live on 1,800 RMB a year.

After he married, I told him, "You ought to be satisfied, now you can live by yourself." He has six cows, three large and three small. He can now milk the one I gave him last year. And he's a hard worker, able to eat bitterness, to struggle. So I have no hesitation giving things to him. In fact, when I give him things, I'm only giving him things that are his anyway, just a bit early.

But their help can hardly be substantial, since they themselves have very little. They have reduced the work they do to manageable proportions, but they have also had to reduce their consumption. Although they are not in need, their lives are spartan, as Yuxia describes:

We rarely eat meat. We could raise a pig or two to eat in winter, but we couldn't afford to feed them. Each bag of feed costs 57 RMB. It also costs money to have them injected, and then you have do a lot of work to care for them. In the end, it's simpler to buy a little meat. We don't eat meat in summer anyway, because of the heat. We eat some in winter because you need the nutrition then, and pork stores better in winter. We don't buy much, about 100 catties lasts us the winter. We don't buy fish either, it's too expensive.

We can meet most of our other needs ourselves. We grow beans, cucumbers, squash, and some corn in our garden, so we have enough vegetables to last the winter. Those we grew last year were good, this year too. Our garden is well drained and we have a well nearby. It's pretty good land, and we apply compost to it. So we're able to feed ourselves alright.

Although their livelihood is marginal, Zhongmin does not yet feel endangered. To the contrary, he feels a sense of accomplishment that he and his wife are able to care for themselves.

We can still manage on our own, we don't have to ask anything of our son. I think it's important that older folks work as long as they can. Idleness leads to illness, and it's downright boring to just sit around on the *kang*. So, if I can raise a few cows, and have a little money to spend, well that's good enough for me.

Of course there are always unavoidable expenses. For example, we pay about 100 RMB a year to take the animals to pasture. And if you have to pay for what you don't do yourself, then you have to be very careful about expenses. We old timers try as hard as we can to use as little fuel as possible, to save money. We grow our own vegetables, and that's mainly what we eat.

I've never fished. It's a dangerous business. Have you heard that just yesterday a 17 year old kid drowned while fishing in the river? Every year someone is killed either by the train or while fishing. We lose a lot of cows to the train as well.

Let me give you some idea of some other living expenses. I drink 3 *liang* of alcohol a day, perhaps 10 catties a month. I can't drink more than that because of my low blood pressure. So if you add what I spend on tobacco and wine, I must spend 30 RMB on those things in the course of the year. My wife doesn't drink or smoke. In summer the two of us probably spend 70

RMB a month on food, a bit more in winter because then we eat some meat, around 80 RMB a month then. The main thing for us is to eat properly.

Her blood pressure is high, mine is low. When mine drops too low, I just have to lie down and stay there. So that's a problem. And she takes a Western medicine for her condition that costs us more than 20 RMB a month. It's more expensive than food! The clothes we wear are simple. And you can wear the kind we have for a good number of years, they're very durable. We're old, so we don't give much thought to style or brand. We're only concerned that what we wear not have holes, not be drafty, that's good enough for us.

My son buys most of our grandchild's clothing, but from time to time I also buy him shoes, or socks, or a hat. Right now he's small, so he still doesn't know to want things. But wait awhile, when he's a bit older that will surely change. He'll know then how to ask for things!

Every three months we have an electric bill to pay, about 10 RMB each time. I don't understand how it works, sometimes it goes to 26 RMB. I think someone's stealing electricity from the town and the government is simply dividing the loss up among us. We only have five bulbs in our house, and we never have them all turned on at the same time. As a matter of fact, when we watch TV we make it a point to turn all the lights off.

Although we live in town, we only have rural registration and that makes things tough. People with jobs, and urban registration, have the best of everything. We even have to pay 3 *fen* more to buy wheat! But we're too old to get upset about all that now. We're alright anyway. Our old house is small, but it takes less coal to heat it in winter. We couldn't afford a larger house. We only burn 5 tons in winter. At 60 RMB per ton that comes to about 300. That's all the fuel we buy. We cook with cow dung.

When we used figures the Zhangs gave us to calculate their annual budget, we found a shortfall. The expenses they reported came to 3,050 RMB, but they only earned 1,800 RMB from milk sales. They may have exaggerated some of their expenses, and underestimated their income. The 1987 survey data we have for this family showed 650 RMB income from "other" sources (such as from selling an animal to raise needed money). We know that fellow townsfolk, aware of the their marginal income, occasionally hire them to do small jobs. This year both worked in some of the newly opened private restaurants. Yuxia described that work but, to her mind, their contribution was a favor given rather than one received:

Someone opened a small restaurant and needed a cook. They came many times to ask for our help. They're neighbors, so we decided to help them out. My husband does a lot of work around the house here, so he wasn't eager to go, but eventually he did. He's still working for them. I myself can cook, but I react badly now to too much heat, so I don't do it much anymore.

Yuxia and Zhongmin's acceptance of the future flows from the more limited needs and desires that come with age. But it also reflects their underlying security. Zhongmin expressed it this way:

> So long as she and I can eat, we're alright. We can milk three of our cows, enough to keep the two of us busy. I can't cut grass anymore, but my son brings us what we need. You know, even if he didn't, we'd survive anyway. I could sell a cow and use the money to buy grass. Of course that wouldn't be ideal, people would certainly gossip about it. If I had to sell a cow, my son would lose face.
>
> It wouldn't make sense for another reason. Think about it, the cow I would sell to buy the grass would not even be my own! If I raise cows now, it's less for me and my wife than for my son and for my grandson. He gives me the grass I need now, but soon I will give him all the cows I have. I think that's a fair trade. In fact, he's got the edge in the exchange. He gave me 10 carts of grass, each worth 80 RMB. But I've already given him a cow worth more than that!

Most of the aging and elderly people, in all the sites we visited, live in stem families. That makes it possible for them to pass the heaviest work on to younger people. But some pastoralists, like the Zhangs, live on their own until they are quite old. Sometime later, when they are no longer able to fend for themselves, they will once again live with a son. When that time comes for Zhongmin and Yuxia, they will turn their animals over to their son. For that reason Zhongmin can properly claim that he is, even now, working for his son.

> His livelihood isn't bad now, certainly better than ours. Of course we want them to be well off. If I die, don't I have to give it all to them? Before I die too, I try to think of ways he can earn more. That's why I want to give them things, so they can live better. That way they won't be looked down upon by others.

The Zhangs are in a phase of family development more common among pastoralists than cultivators. To the extent that family planning is strictly enforced in future, their situation may become even more common. Still, it remains a temporary stage. Ultimately they will find their way back to the stem family. They are presently living alone, on their own, but even now they envision a time when divided families will reunite.

11

Conclusions: Ecology and Society on the Inner Mongolian Frontier

The Han share a set of cultural patterns they see as distinctly "Chinese." There are, of course, National Minority peoples recognized as different. But for the rest, whether they speak Mandarin, Hokkien, Hakka, or another Han dialect, they all claim to themselves a model of common behavior. "The Chinese Way" symbolizes appearance, features, body gestures, the unified written language, a lengthy history, and shared goals and values. Chinese expect to form families based on the male line of descent and maintain strong kinship ties beyond the immediate family (Cohen 1991; Ward 1989). A long history of state rule endorsed an ideology that further pressed cultural homogeneity upon the people.

Under communism, pressure for uniformity increased. People everywhere took their place in a similar hierarchy of groups. Children learned "putonghwa" (Mandarin) in schools throughout the country. Collectivization, which set up a framework for the standard deployment of land and labor, shaped behavior deeply. By eliminating private productive property, regulating marriage, and stimulating class struggle within families, the state tried to redirect individual orientations from family to nation. Differences of wealth, life style, and opportunity narrowed. People married, formed families, and bore children in like ways.

When China restored family based production, the potential for cultural variation increased. In our study of changes in the family economy of farmering and herding communities, we sought in the work people do the origins of past and current variations. We compared four settings, two in each ecoarea. We began with pure cultivators who use north Chinese farming techniques. Some raise dairy cows in sheds. Then, moving west across the mountains, we found Han Chinese who gave up farming for a pastoral way of life. Much like their Mongol neighbors, they raise dairy cows, and cut grass for use and sale. Those that herd sheep even live in Mongol yurts.

Reports from all regions of China, including ours from Inner Mongolia, make it clear that communism did not eliminate the Chinese Way. But a range of patterns emerged as Han adjusted to different environmental challenges. Chinese themes played on, along with their variations, but the mix of voices shifted. This book has been about these voices. Just as we assume something distinctive about being Chinese, so we are impressed by the forms the Chinese Way takes. Paradoxically, homogeneity and heterogeneity coexist. In a country as varied as China, with its multitude of climates, topographies, crops, and uneven access to natural and commercial resources, it could not have been otherwise.

The Ecological Variables

To understand how the work of Han herdsmen and farmers shapes their family lives, we compared ecology and the division of labor. We began with economic resources. Since they cannot expand their plots, Tranquillity and Middle villagers can only work their land more intensively. In contrast, where people have vast expanses of grassland resources, family flocks and herds can increase. We found this most in Great Pasture, blessed with abundant pasture and grassland.

Next, the use, timing, locales, amounts, and quality of labor, along with the range of tasks performed, differ. For dry field farmers, each major phase of the agricultural cycle -- field preparation, planting, crop maintenance, harvest -- calls for a special kind of effort. The different stages of the farming cycle also give rise to marked peaks and troughs in labor need, some quite arduous. Each phase of the cycle requires varied work, and at the end of each day farmers normally return home. In contrast, herdsmen work steadily at the same kinds of work every day, often far from home. Skill and experience are more crucial than great strength in raising livestock.

For most farming tasks, women and youth can help or even replace men, and our third variable is division of labor and flexibility of labor use. Although aging farmers do not become idle, as their physical powers wane they gradually pass the heaviest tasks to younger household members, on whom they depend. In contrast, because herding takes him away from home for long periods, the ideal herdsman is an adult male. Women remain at home and milk the family cows. Since carelessness can menace generations of animals, inexperienced youngsters contribute less to the pastoral economy, while the elderly have more to offer. They remain self sufficient longer than among the cultivators.

Limits of Communist Transformation

The differences between farmers and herders in resources, demand for labor, and the work of women and men, old and young began before the commune and outlasted it. Collectivization changed the way property and labor were used, and the state did extend its administrative apparatus and control deeper than ever before. But differences rooted in ecology blocked a uniform way of life even during the commune era. Cadres took advantage of the flexibility farming allowed. They pressed women and the young to work. Even the elderly had their place at the margins of labor. They could babysit and do chores to relieve younger family members for work outside. In the pastoral area, however, men did most of the herding tasks, so cadres assigned little work to women or youngsters.

In both ecoareas, people remained at the mercy of nature. Since risks were diluted, the collective protected against failure. But since they shared rewards, there was little incentive for farmers or herders to work hard. This disjointing of effort and reward weakened commitment. Since collectivization aimed to maximize returns to labor and minimize investments of capital, the loss of worker enthusiasm was costly. Large scale management in the herding area caused the most problems. When responsibility shifted from worker to worker and diluted the identification people have with animals, herdsmen gave them less attention, which resulted in much loss.

In both areas, living standards remained close to subsistence and there was little collective welfare. Peasants continued to look to their families, and to rely on family-based strategies for their well-being. They put their best efforts into whatever work they could do at the household level, rather than for the collective. The communities we have described support a view of "rational" peasants.[1] The "moral economy" approach to peasant behavior predicts that villagers should favor collectivization because the moral imperatives of the collective provide individual security (Scott 1976). The "political economy" model attributes greater force to a rational calculation of what is good for the individual family (Popkin 1979; Nee 1985). Consistent with this, we found fine-tuned calculation of family interest during the commune years. Yet it was only when they got the chance to earn money by directly participating in external markets, that rural families could truly maximize their incomes.

The New Economy, Ecology, and Profits

When the collective economy gave way in Inner Mongolia in 1982, pasture and grassland remained common property, while animals and machines were sold to individual families. The government's call upon people to find new ways to increase their incomes through private enterprise has affected both the environment and the family economy.

In the farming area, the division of collective property, family partition, population growth, and losses from flood erosion fragmented household plots. In Tranquillity this led to further land reallocations and uncertainty. Many hesitate to invest labor and capital in land they may not use next year. Peasants are willing to sacrifice soil conservation for short term profit.

While farm plots are small, and labor, credit, and investment capital are hard to get, farmers still profit from the new economic changes. When they are short on workers, farmers cannot sell their land. Lending or abandoning it would menace their livelihoods. But they alter the mix of crops they grow, till fewer labor intensive crops, and cut back on sidelines. Because they farm close by home and have a flexible division of labor, they can also draw more on women and children. While farmers with increased family labor cannot add land, their sidelines do not compete with farming, since they take advantage of slack periods and the substitutability of labor. Still, in both farming communities, lack of funds and skills, and distance from markets, limit sidelines.

In the pastoral area, privatization took a different turn. Livestock became fully alienable private property, an expandable and disposable capital resource. Animals are investment capital and the principal source of income. The more a family has, the more wealth and income it enjoys, and the greater its ability to weather shifts in expenses or income. The dramatic increase in cows and sheep threatens pasture. This problem is likely to increase because Han think of livestock as capital.

In contrast to farmers who adjust labor to basic resources, herdsmen fit their productive resources to their labor. With enough pasture and male labor, they can increase their animal numbers, mix different kinds of livestock, cut hay for sale, or fish. When short on labor, they can sell some animals or join their herds with others. Even a few head can keep a family going until they have the help to handle more. Thus, farming and herding households maximize the labor of their family members in distinct ways.

The expandable nature of basic resources, the sharper division of labor, the distance of many tasks, and the profits of pastoralism get in the way of full time employment and sidelines unrelated to livestock. Hard enough to combine different animals and pastoral activities, it is even less rewarding to divert workers to less well paying sidelines. Instead, to increase income, herdsmen will raise more animals of the same type, combine livestock, or do other rural work. However, a family that expands in these directions must have plenty of men or work with others. This is a departure from the commune years, when men were assigned to work teams so that no family had to do everything on its own. While a family need not expand or add to its pastoral activities to survive now, it can become well off if it does.

The risk is great, but so too are potential profits. In these ways, with onset of the responsibility system, farming and herding household economies have diverged.

All the people we studied have a wider range of economic choices than they did during the commune era, but they still do not control nature or the environment, and it is still hard to set long term goals. Government policy remains uncertain and, as families evolve, their number of working members changes as well. And even when they do have sufficient labor to meet the challenge, families have little capital.

The patrilineal stem household, with its equal division of property among sons, early marriage, and movement away of daughters and all but one married son, further channels choice. There are families sorely in need of labor that are nonetheless willing to see children marry out early, and sons partition out. Similarly we found parents encouraging children to seek a better education that kept them out of production longer and jobs that meant leaving home and village entirely. In many instances, their offsprings' success puts a break on family economic momentum (see Diane L. Wolf 1991; Folbre 1986).

Nevertheless, there is more room now for strategic planning, for the short term. The people we met were responding to the new possibilities rationally, measuring their limitations and moving in new directions wherever they could. And there were new directions in which to move.

Income, Inequality, and the Family

The pastoralists, especially those that combine haying with herding, have benefitted most from the new changes. Farmers with only simple sidelines have the lowest incomes, the fewest wealthy households, and lowest living standards. There are other sources of inequality within areas. The distribution of resources was itself linked to family size, so families did not start out on an equal basis. Of course, if a family began with more land or animals but many dependent children, then it had to tread water until the children could work. But even today, the wealthier households are generally larger, have more workers, and support fewer dependents.

A good start with much family labor does not alone turn into higher income. Much depends on what people do. Farmers and herdsmen who use their ample labor to expand and diversify, do the best. But by allowing that, the new system provides a basis for greater income inequality. Some families work harder, at a greater variety of tasks than before, and see their incomes rise as a result. While inequality appears on the increase, especially among the herdsmen, it is associated with a general rise in prosperity and living standards. People spend more on consumer items and on their children's marriages, especially the herdsmen. There is no evidence yet of an increase in poverty in the sites we studied.

Economy and Family Complexity

During the commune years, farmers and pastoralists drew their income only from the work points members earned. Households earned the most during phases of the cycle when there were more workers than dependents. It was not necessary, however, to have enough workers to handle the full range of farming or pastoral work, since collective work teams drew from many different families.

In the farming area, where there were ample opportunities for all family members to earn work points, the more workers a farm family had, the more it might earn. Collectivization encouraged early, patrilocal marriage, delayed family division, and enlargement to the stem family. Nevertheless, with productive property transferred to the collective and private enterprise discouraged, there was no reason for families to become more complex than that. In that sense, collectivization undermined traditional sources of family complexity. Under the commune, the family pulled back, but endured.

In the pastoral area, in contrast, demand for labor was lower and more evenly spread out during the year. Herding mainly called for male workers, so family labor was not fully used. Some women did earn work points milking collective cows or working in collective vegetable gardens, but many remained at home. Having more than one man in the household might be useful, but not several woman. Since the pastoralists did not need to mobilize as much labor as the farmers, they married later, more often lived in neolocal households, and had simpler families.

With the privatized economy, the family has once again become the basic unit of production and consumption, as it was before collectivization. Responsible now for the full round of agricultural and non-agricultural work, families are likely to adjust their structure, composition, and dynamics to best take advantage of new possibilities for diversification, the key to income improvement.

Whether farmer or pastoralist, families all have more to do on their own in a family-based economy. Farmers have a special need for able family workers because their labor needs are not only varied, but also distributed unevenly during the year. Families also cooperate to get work done during cyclical peaks in demand. Such cooperation works well only where a small number of families are involved and their relationship is close enough to ensure reliability (see Parish 1985). But they place primary reliance on the family itself. And to meet the increased need for family labor, farmers freely allow women, the elderly, and children to work alongside the men.

All labor can be used in one way or another. Thus, farmers still favor early, patrilocal marriage, and stem families with one women to work outside, and another inside the home.

Family division sets farmers back. Their holdings, small and fragmented to begin with, are smaller still after division. Parents must give a few pieces to the young couple that leaves. Neither of the resulting families can easily recover the land, labor, tractor or draft animal they lose. They cannot always continue sidelines after partition. Stem families also help aging farmers tailor their work to their capabilities, and enjoy some security at the same time. Now that families limit their childbearing, parents live longer, and there are few public services, the stem family has become even more important. Thus, farmers favor early, patrilocal marriage and stem families and delay partition even more than they did in the collective period.

Herdsmen also prefer patrilocal marriage and stem families, but they depart from those traditional forms more often. Like the farmers, they must respond to the growing, more diversified labor requirements of the new economic order. However, since they use male workers most, they need not marry early to get more women. On the other hand, they can divide their families earlier than farmers because partition sets them back less. While a departing son takes along some of the family livestock, animals can multiply in a way that land cannot. The family head can partition his family, knowing that the resultant independent households can recover quickly.

Labor need does not increase in direct proportion to animal numbers, and a family that only raises dairy cows has a flat labor demand. So long as they keep their enterprise simple, then, a young couple can expect to make a better living than a farming couple after family division. With care and attention, and some cooperation with others for grass cutting, their few animals will multiply as their families grow. Similarly, the aged can decrease the number and types of livestock they raise, buy the fodder they need, and make a living on their own until they are quite old. For these reasons, herdsmen partition sooner after marriage, and more often marry neolocally, than the farmers. Neither the young nor the elderly suffer as a result.

Since economic diversification can encourage even more complex families than the stem form, some look for a resurgence of the joint family (Cohen 1976; Croll 1987a). But few families in our communities can resist inherent tendencies to divide. Markets are undeveloped here, capital and opportunities for investment not so bounteous as in other parts of China. Further, there are other ways to increase income that suit any family form. Where the market is monetized, people can improve earnings by specialization, share holding, or by collaborating with other families (Croll 1987b; Howard 1988).

The new economic possibilities may in time change things, but powerful forces encourage simplicity. Further, these are still adaptations to the earlier reproductive patterns that supplied the personnel for large families. If strict family limitation continues, stem families will remain the most complex form in which most people will have lived. In sum, for these cultivators and pastoralists, stem families suffice to diversify the household economy and to integrate the elderly.

Family Reproduction

As elsewhere in China, the government encourages people to delay marriage and limit family size. These policies should have levelled differences between ecoareas in age at marriage and in the number of children women bear. In fact, they have not. Legal restraints on marriage age have not had a great impact. Since their daughters and daughters-in-law make an important economic contribution, farmers want to replace departing daughters and begin family reproduction as soon as possible. Parents arrange the marriages of their children close to the legal age. Thus, there has been little change in average age at marriage in the farm area over the past four decades.

Herders do not rigidly adhere to the marriage laws either, but they do delay marriage longer than the farmers. This is because their marriage more often coincides with family division and loss of the irreplaceable labor of grown sons. Their weddings cost more, and parents need to build homes for the sons and endow them with livestock. The increasing cost of marriage, a reflection of greater wealth, thus simultaneously delays marriage and family division without increasing family complexity.

Regulations limiting childbirth shape the reproductive plans of younger women. In all our sites they bear fewer children than did older women. But farmers of all ages have more children than herdsmen, and not simply due to effective family planning. Higher farmer fertility exists despite stricter family planning, and predates it. We believe that the difference in the way herdsmen and farmers use labor has had a great impact. Because their labor is needed, farm women marry earlier, nurse less often, and are therefore more fecund. Thus, the intended and unintended consequences of the farm economy have been higher fertility as well as larger households and families.

When infant and child mortality were high, it was vital to have more children, upon whom to depend for support in old age. And when the collective subsidized medical care and education, raising them did not cost much. While support in old age weighs even more heavily on the family today, mortality has declined dramatically, while the costs of raising and marrying children have increased. Couples are now willing to stop with two or three. They would restrain childbearing even without state regulations.

While neither pastoralists nor cultivators are eager to have as many children as before, neither are they content with one. Childbearing exceeds state recommendations in all sites. But since the costs of bringing up their children are lower and children are useful sooner, farmers are more likely than the pastoralists to resist state strictures on reproduction (Greenhalgh 1988). In these ways, childbearing differences between pastoral and farming women, rooted in ecology and economy, carry forward to the present.

Women's Work and Status

Many have argued that where the non-domestic contribution women make is greater, so too is their influence and status (Blumberg 1978; Friedl 1975; Whyte 1978). The communist emphasis on mass participation in labor and politics brought large numbers of women into the labor force (Andors 1983). Huang (1990:202-203) believes that peasant women increased their labor during the collective period. And by earning labor points, women enhanced their personal value in their households. Their families could not make ends meet without the work points they earned, and the collective depended on their contribution.

If women enhance their value and voice by adding to family income, farm women should have the advantage. In the family-based rural economy, a household with enough female workers can take on more tasks. As non-farm sidelines gain in importance, farm women may increase their contribution to the family economy, by sifting sand in Tranquillity and dairying in Middle Village (Huang 1990; Croll 1984:62).

Among the pastoralists, however, even during the collective era there were fewer ways for women to earn work points, and women less often worked outside the home. Pastoral women still largely confine themselves to milking cows and tending the home. Men do the heavy work of cleaning pens and cutting grass. They alone spend long periods on the open grassland. Men and women cannot stand in for each other. Further, it is unlikely that non-pastoral sidelines will attract women in any significant way. Pastoralists see women as having less to do.

Have recent reforms enhanced the way people value women? We might expect farm women have more status because of the work they do. But the connection between input and status is hard to specify (Stratton 1981; Whyte 1978).[2] Women do not automatically have control over their work, their product, or their income (Blumberg 1978). Even when village women work outside the home, what they produce, whether in work points or things, is usually delivered to the family. Furthermore, for their labor to be considered "important" it must be visible and clearly linked to them.

In neither ecoarea do people consider the work that women do central to the household economy. Pastoralists believe that women's work complements, but is peripheral to the main tasks. When asked who did the most important work, they mentioned the grass cutting, not milking. Thus, their work did not bring herding women much status. While the farmers did not make so clear a distinction between the farm work of men and women, Blumberg (1978) has proposed that even when men and women do the same work, the status of women may be low. Despite her more varied and more substantial contribution, even the farm woman's labor is seen as secondary, lighter, or as domestic and therefore not labor in the true sense (Gates 1989). Further, with demise of the collective, women who would once have brought work points home now find themselves confined to work for the family. Family work is usually thought of as subsidiary. Thus, some doubt that the new reforms will enhance women's value and influence (Davin 1991).

To raise the position of women, changes are needed in the family as well as work outside the home. Yet rural socialist institutions have reinforced the traditional family system and its valuation of women (Anagnost 1989; Andors 1983; Diamond 1975; Johnson 1983; Young 1989; Stacey 1983; M. Wolf 1985). Collective institutions were premised on a higher estimation of male labor, on male headship of the family, patrilocal residence, and patrilineal succession. Rural institutions reinforce the traditional family system even now. Old views about the nature of women and their proper roles are still widespread and strongly held. The greater labor contribution of cultivating women may not translate into greater real control, voice, or autonomy (Croll 1981; Gates 1989). This empirical question requires study in its own right. No one has yet systematically measured the effect of work outside the home on women's status or autonomy in China. Nor have we. The clues are ambiguous, even contradictory.

Control over property is one area of ambiguity. Since they bring wealth or property, farm women should have more influence. Every child born to a farm family is entitled to an allocation of land. While technically allocated per capita, however, the land actually becomes part of a family estate. Children do not decide what will be grown on it, who will use it, or how it will be planted. Nor can a bride take it when she marries. The community calls for its return to reserve. Her husband's family can request a land assignment on her behalf, so a woman gets land when she marries as well as when she is born. But again, in the minds of family members, her land is not really identified with her, and she can not control it. We cannot simply assume that whatever land she may bring will influence the way people think of her.

While farm women have the right to property, pastoral women do not. The community assigns no animals, pasture, or grassland on their birth. When they marry, they do not get an equal share of livestock. Although a considerate parent might give his daughter a milk cow, most pastoral women come empty handed. If wealth or productive property confers status or influence, pastoral women would be clearly disadvantaged.

Other indirect indications of women's position are household appliances. Where women work and earn, their families might buy washing and sewing machines to lighten their domestic burden. The woman themselves might channel the use of family funds in that direction. We would then expect to find more labor saving devices among the cultivators, but in fact, we find them among the herders. That pastoralists have more household appliances likely reflects higher incomes rather than strong female voice.

The cost of marriage for farming and pastoral brides and grooms provides another indirect way to assess status. We might expect that where women have an important economic role to play, the groom's family would pay a substantial bridewealth while the bride's might only give a modest dowry. Among the pastoralists and farmers alike, it costs more to marry a son than a daughter. Pastoralists pay more than cultivators for both, but again have more to spend. That dowry without bridewealth is more common among the pastoralists, even more points to their need to bolster a daughter's worth.

Yet looked at another way, pastoral marriage and family structure confers some advantage. Cultivators more often marry patrilocally and women live longer with their in-laws. A farm woman is therefore more subject to her mother-in-law's judgements. Since pastoralists are more likely to marry neolocally and to live in conjugal families, would women not enjoy a greater measure of autonomy?

Finally, herding women go to school longer, work and marry later, and bear fewer children than farm women. Many are better educated than their husbands. Do these benefits give them more power in the household? Since these characteristics emerge from the lesser economic role and importance of pastoral women, we believe they do not enhance herding women's control over their own lives or increase their self fulfillment. Whatever educational advantage a pastoral girl may enjoy does not give her a better job or way of life. Most follow in the steps of their mothers.

Indeed, the lower education of farm women, their earlier marriages, and their higher parities only underscore their importance to the domestic economy. But we doubt that their earlier and more substantial input necessarily gives them any greater bargaining power. Where women can work more outside the home, this may only make their lives more difficult.

A real understanding of gender relations calls for long-term participant observation. To answer this empirical question requires going beneath the surface of structure to look at actual interactions in different family forms, and that is a matter for future research. Future researchers will need to watch relationships in families at different stages, observe what people do as well as what they say they do.

The Ethnic Equation

When Han farmers first crossed over the Great Wall looking for a better life, they found themselves in a setting where the climate was unmerciful, the land unyielding, and the local inhabitants unfriendly. Many eventually gave up, turned around, and went home. Only those prepared to alter customary behavior were able to remain. Those that settled on the Inner Mongolian frontier modified their Chinese Way to meet each challenge. Those that turned to pastoralism are still distinctly Chinese, although they are not the same as the farmers they left behind.

Han and Mongols in similar settings work and live alike. Mongols in our farming area have adopted the north Chinese mode of farming and the Han manner of life. In part because of their smaller numbers and the demands of cultivation, they live interspersed with the Han and have become culturally indistinguishable from them. In architecture, clothing, and activity, we find few indications of a major departure from the Chinese Way. They make their livings much the same way and enjoy much the same income. They often intermarry. Like the Han they favor early patrilocal marriage, two or three children, and stem families.

But the pastoral Han and Mongols west of the Daxingan mountains have dissimilar approaches to production and living. Here there are more marked cultural and political differences. Each group specializes in its own form of livestock, although increasingly that line is blurring. Pastoralists, far more than cultivators, speak their own language and marry their own kind. There are more Mongols here than in the cultivating area, and their traditional adaptation predominates.

Just as sedentary cultivation forged similarities, bringing Mongol and Han life ways closer, so pastoralism encouraged a convergence, but in the other direction. When Han exchanged farming for a pastoral life, they changed. And the specializations in livestock that once distinguished Han and Mongols are eroding, as the Han add sheep and Mongols expand into dairying. Both build housing that suits these pursuits. There are other similarities as well. The size and structure of families of both ethnic groups fit the needs of herding. Han and Mongols marry later, are more often neolocal, and have smaller, simpler families than the farmers. In these ways, pastoral Han cowboys resemble pastoral Mongols more than farming Han.

As Han moved into Inner Mongolia and adapted to the grassland ecology, they abandoned farming and many of the ethnic traditions of the Chinese Way. Making their livings on the grasslands as dairymen and shepherds shapes what they do and value. While they did not cease to be Chinese, and despite the homogenizing role of the state, the new Han cowboys of the Great Wall frontier have forged another kind of society.

Notes

1.   In a recent collection of essays on Chinese rural development, a number of authors point to problems of incentive and management during the collective era similar to those we have described. The editor notes that most of the case studies in that volume,

> tend to support the "rational peasant" model of collective farm behavior. When the collective supports a complex economy that provides many additional benefits that can not be achieved by individuals acting alone, peasants are eager to join. But in most areas, where the economy remains one of simple grain production, there are few economies of scale or other sorts of endeavors that would entice peasants into collective activities (Parish 1985:19-20).

2.   The problem has to do with the criteria of status. Is it to be measured as ability to exert control over domestic expenditures in general, or over particular types of expenditure? Is it to be measured as ability to affect other family decisions, or to participate in social and political activities outside the home? Does it have to do with who determines reproductive behavior? To equate status with autonomy is no more satisfactory since that term too requires specification.

References

Albert, Claude. 1991. *Rural China, 1985-1990: Are the Reforms Really Bogging Down?* Hong Kong: Institute of Asia-Pacific Studies, USC Seminar Series No.2.

Anagnost, Anne. 1989. "Transformation of Gender in Modern China," in Sandra Morgen, ed., *Gender and Anthropology: Critical Reviews for Research and Teaching.* Pp. 313-342. Washington, D.C.: American Anthropological Association.

Andors, Phyllis. 1983. *The Unfinished Liberation of Chinese Women, 1949-1980.* Bloomington: Indiana University Press.

Arnold, Fred, and Liu Zhaoxiang. 1986. "Sex Preference, Fertility, and Family Planning in China." *Population and Development Review* 12:2: 221-46.

Banister, Judith. 1987. *China's Changing Population.* Stanford: Stanford University Press.

Blalock. 1972. *Social Statistics.* New York: McGraw-Hill.

Blumberg, Rae Lesser. 1978. *Stratification: Socioeconomic and Sexual Inequality.* Dubuque: Wm. C. Brown, Co.

Bodde, Derk. 1959. *China's Cultural Tradition: What and Whither?* New York: Rinehart and Company.

Bongaarts, John. 1983. "The Proximate Determinants of Natural Marital Fertility," in R. A. Bulatao and R.D. Lee, eds., *Determinants of Fertility in Developing Countries.* New York: Academic Press.

Butler, Steven B. 1985. "Price Scissors and Commune Administration in Post-Mao China," in William L. Parish, ed., Pp. 95-114.

Chi Ch'ao-ting. 1963. *Key Economic Areas in Chinese History: As Revealed in the Development of Public Works for Water-Control.* New York: Paragon Book Reprint Corp.

Chung, A. W. 1979. "Breastfeeding in a Developing Country: The People's Republic of China," in D. Raphael, ed., *Breastfeeding and Food Policy in a Hungry World.* New York: Academic Press.

Coale, Ansley J. 1987. *Marriage and Childbearing in China Since 1940.* Ann Arbor: University of Michigan Population Studies Center Research Reports.

Cohen, Myron L. 1976. *House United, House Divided: The Chinese Family in Taiwan.* New York: Columbia University Press.

_____. 1991. "Being Chinese: The Peripheralization of Traditional Identity," *Daedalus* 120:2: 113-134.

Croll, Elisabeth. 1981. *The Politics of Marriage in Contemporary China.* Cambridge: Cambridge University Press.

_____. 1983. "Production Versus Reproduction: A Threat to China's Development Strategy," *World Development* 11:6: 467-481.

_____. 1984. *Women and Rural Development in China.* Production and Reproduction. WEP Research Working Paper, (March) (also in *Women Work and Development*, 11 [Geneva: ILO, 1985]).

_____. 1987a. "New Peasant Family Forms in Rural China," *Journal of Peasant Studies* 14:4: 469-499.

267

268

Croll, Elisabeth. 1987b. "Some Implications of the Rural Economic Reforms for the Chinese Peasant Household," in Saith, A., ed., *The Reemergence of the Chinese Peasantry*. Pp. 105-137. London: Croom Helm.

Davin, Delia. 1991. "Women, Work and Property in the Chinese Peasant Household of the 1980s," in Diana Elson, ed., *Male Bias in the Development Process*. Pp. 29-50. Manchester: University of Manchester.

Davis, Deborah. 1988. "Patrons and Clients in Chinese Industry," *Modern China* 14:4: 487-497.

Diamond, Norma. 1975. "Collectivization, Kinship, and the Status of Women in Rural China," in Rayna R. Reiter, ed., *Toward an Anthropology of Women*. Pp. 372-395. New York: Monthly Review Press.

Dong Lian Sheng and Xu Jan Jiang, eds., 1989. *Zhalantun Feng Wu Zhi*. Hailar: Inner Mongolia Cultural Publishing House.

Dryer, June. 1976. *China's Forty Million: Minority Nationalisties and National Integration in the People's Republic of China*. Cambridge: Harvard University Press.

Eberhard, Wolfram. 1965. *Conquerers and Rulers: Social Forces in Medieval China*. Leiden: Brill.

Ekvall, Robert Brainard. 1968. *Fields on the Hoof: Nexus of Tibetan Nomadic Pastoralism*. Holt, Rinehart & Winston.

El-Minawi, M.F. and M.S. Foda. 1971. "Postpartum Lactational Amenorrhea," *American Journal of Obstetrics and Gynecology* 111: 17-21.

Evans, Grant. 1990. *Lao Peasants under Socialism*. New Haven: Yale University Press.

Feeney, Griffith, Feng Wang, Mingkun Zhou, and Baoyu Xiao. 1989. "Recent Fertility Dynamics in China", *Population and Development Review* 15:2: 295-328.

Feuchtwang, Stephan. 1987. "Changes in the System of Basic Social Security in the Countryside Since 1979," in A. Saith, ed., *The Reemergence of the Chinese Peasantry*. Pp. 173-210. London: Croom Helm.

Folbre, Nancy. 1986. "Cleaning House: New Perspectives on Households and Economic Development," *Journal of Developmental Economics* 22:5: 5-40.

Freedman, Maurice. 1958. *Lineage Organization in Southeastern China*. London: Athlone Press.

Freedman, R., Xiao Zhenyu, Li Bohua, and W. Lavely. 1988. "Local Area Variations in Reproductive Behavior in the People's Republic of China, 1973-1982," *Population Studies* 42: 39-57.

Friedl, Ernestine. 1975. *Women and Men: An Anthropologist's View*. New York: Holt, Rinehart, & Winston.

Friedman, Edward, Paul G. Pickowicz, Mark Selden. 1991. *Chinese Village, Socialist State*. New Haven: Yale University Press.

Gallin, Bernard. 1960. "Matrilateral and Affinal Relationships of a Taiwanese Village," *American Anthropologist* 62: 632-642.

Gates, Hill. 1989. "The Commoditization of Chinese Women," *Signs* 14:4: 799-827.

Geertz, Clifford. 1970. *Agricultural Involution: The Process of Ecological Change in Indonesia*. Berkeley: University of California.

Gladney, Dru C. 1990. "The Ethnogenesis of the Uighur," *Central Asian Survey* 9.1: 1-27.

_____. 1991. *Muslim Chinese: Ethnic Nationalism in the People's Republic.* Cambridge: Harvard University Press.

Gorissen, P. J. A. and E. B. Vermeer. 1985. *Development of Milk Production in China in the 1980s.* Puodoc, Wageningen: Center for Agricultural Publishing and Documentation, Wageningen, the Netherlands.

Greenhalgh, Susan. 1988. "Fertility as Mobility," *Population and Development Review* 14:4: 629-674.

Griffin, Keith. ed., 1984. *Institutional Reform and Economic Development in the Chinese Countryside.* London: Macmillan.

Hardee-Cleaveland, Karen and Judith Banister. 1988. "Fertility Policy and Implementation in China, 1986-88", *Population and Development Review* 14:2: 245-381.

Hinton, William. 1990. *The Great Reversal: The Privitization of China 1978-1989.* New York: Monthly Review Press.

Howard, Pat. 1988. *Breaking the Iron Ricebowl: Prospects for Socialism in China's Countryside.* Armonk, New York: M.E. Sharpe.

Huang, Philip C. C. 1985. *The Peasant Economy and Social Change in North China.* Stanford: Stanford University Press.

_____. 1990. *The Peasant Family and Rural Development in the Yangzi Delta, 1350-1988.* Stanford: Stanford University Press.

Hulunbuir. 1988. Beijing: Hulunbuir Association for Cultural Exchange with Foreign Countries, Foreign Languages Press.

Hulunbuir Mengqing (Inner Mongolian Conditions). 1986. Hulunbuir League Local Annals Office. Hulunbuir: Inner Mongolia Publishing Company.

Jankowiak, William R. 1988. "The Last Hurrah?: Political Protest In Inner Mongolia," *The Australian Journal Of Chinese Affairs.* Nos. 19 & 20: 269-288.

_____. 1992. *Sex, Death, and Hierarchy in a Chinese City.* New York: Columbia University Press.

Johnson, Kay. 1983. *Women, the Family and Peasant Revolution in China.* Chicago: University of Chicago Press.

Judd, Ellen. 1989. "Niangjia: Chinese Women and their Natal Families," *Journal of Asian Studies* 48:3: 525-544.

Landa, Janet Tai, and Janet W. Salaff. 1987. "A Biography of Tan Kah Kee," unpublished typescript.

Lardy, N. 1984. "Consumption and Living Standards in China, 1978-83," *China Quarterly* 100: 849-865.

Lattimore, Owen, 1962. *Inner Asian Frontiers of China.* Boston: Beacon Press.

Leeming, Frank. 1985. *Rural China Today.* New York: Longman.

Lin, Nan and Yanjie Bian. 1991. "Getting Ahead in Urban China," *American Journal of Sociology* 97:3: 657-688.

Ma Rong. 1987. *Migrant and Ethnic Integration in Rural Chifeng, Inner Mongolia Autonomous Region, China.* Ph.D. Dissertation, Brown University.

Ma Rong. 1990. "Han-Mongolian Intermarriage Patterns in Rural Inner Mongolia, The People's Republic," typescript.

Nee, Victor. 1985. "Peasant Household Individualism," in William L. Parish, ed., Pp. 164-192.

_____. 1989. "A Theory of Market Transition: From Redistribution to Markets in State Socialism," *American Sociological Review* 54: 663-681.

Oi, Jean. 1986a. "Peasant Households Between Plan and Market: Cadre Control Over Agricultural Inputs," *Modern China* 12:2: 230-251.

_____. 1986b. "Peasant Grain Marketing and State Procurement: China's Grain Contracting System," *China Quarterly* 106: 272-290.

_____. 1989. *State and Peasant in Contemporary China*. Berkeley: University of California Press.

Parish, William L., ed., 1985. *Chinese Rural Development: The Great Transformation*. Armonk, New York: M.E. Sharpe.

_____. 1985. "Introduction: Historical Background and Current Issues," in William L. Parish, ed., Pp. 3-29.

Parish, William L. and Martin K. Whyte. 1978. *Village and Family in Contemporary China*. Chicago: University of Chicago Press.

Pasternak, Burton. 1972. *Kinship and Community in Two Chinese Villages*. Stanford: Stanford University Press.

_____. 1983. *Guests in the Dragon: Social Demography of a Chinese District, 1895-1946*. New York: Columbia University Press.

_____. 1985. *Marriage and Fertility in Tianjin China: 50 Years of Transition*. Honolulu: East-West Population Institute.

Pasternak, Burton, Carol R. Ember, and Melvin Ember. 1976. "On the Conditions Favoring Extended Family Households," *Journal of Anthropological Research* 32:2: 109-123.

Perez, A., P. Vela, G.S. Masnick, and R.G. Potter. 1972. "First Ovulation After Child Birth: The Effect of Breast Feeding," *American Journal of Obstetrics and Gynecology* 114: 1041-1047.

Popkin, Samuel. 1979. *The Rational Peasant*. Berkeley: University of California Press.

Potter, Sulamith Heins, and Jack M. Potter. 1989. *China's Peasants: The Anthropology of a Revolution*. Cambridge: Cambridge University Press.

Prema, K., and M. Ravindranath. 1982. "The Effect of Breastfeeding Supplements on the Return of Fertility," *Studies in Family Planning* 13:10: 293-296.

Riskin, Carl. 1987. *China's Political Economy: The Quest for Development Since 1949*. New York: Oxford University Press.

Saith, Ashwani, ed., 1987. *The Reemergence of the Chinese Peasantry*. London: Croom Helm.

Scott, James C. 1976. *The Moral Economy of the Peasant*. New Haven: Yale University Press.

Selden, Mark. 1985. "Income Inequality and the State," in William L. Parish, ed., Pp. 193-218.

Selden, Mark. 1988. *The Political Economy of Chinese Socialism*. Armonk New York: M.H. Sharpe.

Simpson, Ida Harper, John Wilson, and Kristina Young. 1988. "The Sexual Division of Farm Household Labor: A Replication and Extension," *Rural Sociology* 53:2: 145-165.

Simpson-Hebert, Mayling and Sandra L. Huffman. 1981. "The Contraceptive Effect of Breastfeeding," *Studies in Family Planning* 12:4: 125-133.

Stacey, Judith. 1983. *Patriarchy and Socialist Revolution in China.* Berkeley: University of California Press.

Stratton, Joanna L. 1981. *Pioneer Women: Voices from the Kansas Frontier.* New York: Simon and Schuster.

Szelenyi, Ivan. 1988. *Socialist Entrepreneurs: Embourgeoisement in Rural Hungary.* Madison: University of Wisconsin Press.

Tien, H. Yuan. 1982. "Sterilization Acceptance in China," *Studies in Family Planning* 13:10: 287-292.

_____. 1991. *China's Strategic Demographic Initiative.* New York: Praeger.

Unger, Jonathan. 1985. "Remuneration, Ideology, and Personal Interests in a Chinese Village," in William L. Parish, ed., Pp. 164-190.

_____. 1985-86. "The Decollectivization of the Chinese Countryside: A Survey of Twenty-Eight Villages," *Pacific Affairs* 58.4 (Winter): 585-606.

Unger, Jonathan, and Jean Xiong. 1990. "Life in the Chinese Hinterlands under the Rural Economic Reforms," *Bulletin of Concerned Asian Scholars* 22:2: 4-17.

Van Esterik, Penny, and Ted Greiner. 1981. "Breastfeeding and Women's Work: Constraints and Opportunities," *Studies in Family Planning* 12:4: 184-197.

Vermeer, E. B. 1982. "Income Differentials in Rural China," *The China Quarterly* 89: 1-33.

Walder, Andrew G. 1986. *Communist Neo-Traditionalism: Work and Authority in Chinese Industry.* Berkeley: University of California Press.

Ward, Barbara E. 1989. "Varieties of the Conscious Model: The Fishermen of South China," in *Through Other Eyes: An Anthropologist's View of Hong Kong.* Hong Kong: Chinese University Press. Pp. 41-60.

Wasserstrom, Jeffrey. 1984. "Resistance to the One Child Family," *Modern China* 10:3: 345-374.

Watson, Andrew, Cristopher Findlay, and Du Yintang. 1989. "Who Won the Wool War?: A Case Study of Rural Product Marketing in China," *The China Quarterly* 118: 213-241.

Whyte, Martin King. 1978. *The Status of Women in Preindustrial Societies.* Princeton: Princeton University Press.

_____. 1984. "Sexual Inequality Under Socialism: The Chinese Case in Perspective," in Watson, J. L., ed., *Class and Social Stratification in Post-Revolution China.* Pp. 198-238. Cambridge: Cambridge University Press.

Whyte, Martin King, and S. Z. Gu. 1987. "Popular Response to China's Fertility Transition," *Population and Development Review* 13:3: 471-493.

Wiens, Herold J. 1954. *China's March Toward the Tropics.* Hamden, Conn.:The Shoe String Press.

Wittfogel, Karl A. 1957. *Oriental Despotism: A Comparative Study of Total Power.* New Haven: Yale University Press.

Wolf, Arthur P. and Chieh-shan Huang. 1980. *Marriage and Adoption in China, 1945-1945*. Stanford: Stanford University Press.

Wolf, Diane L. 1991. "Does Father Know Best? A Feminist Critique of Household Strategy Research," *Research in Rural Sociology and Development* 5: 29-41.

Wolf, Margery. 1972. *Women and the Family in Rural Taiwan*. Stanford: Stanford University Press.

_____. 1985. *Revolution Postponed: Women in Contemporary China*. Stanford: Stanford University Press.

Zhongguo Tongji Nianjian (Statistical Yearbook of China). (Various Years). Beijing: State Statistical Bureau.

Zweig, David. 1985. "Peasant Household Individualism," in William L. Parish, ed., Pp. 141-163.

About the Book and Authors

We know the Chinese as villagers who carefully tend small plots of land using family labor, marry young, want many sons, and live in extended families—"the Chinese Way." Now for the first time we find Han Chinese "cowboys" who raise dairy cows and herd sheep on the Inner Mongolian grasslands. This book, based on surveys and intensive interviews, compares family lives, the economy, and gender relations among Chinese herders and farmers. The authors find that livestock have brought new wealth and opportunities that change the Chinese farming-based way of life, and they explore how privatization has altered the distribution of wealth. Although Han and Mongols still have their own cultures, those who herd livestock share a common way of life distinct from farmers that are nearby.

Burton Pasternak is professor of anthropology at Hunter College in New York City. **Janet W. Salaff** is professor of sociology at the University of Toronto.

Index

Abortion, availability of, 196

Birth quotas. *See* Family planning, national policy of
Birth rates, among herders and farmers, 191–193, 200(n38)
  parity in, 195(table), 200(n37)
"Black households," 194, 212
Breastfeeding, 80, 89(n41), 118, 212, 225, 243
Bridewealth, 73–75, 88(n25), 100–102, 104, 115, 131, 132, 185, 212

Chengbao. See Contract system
Child care, 118, 129–130, 138, 225–226, 243
Chinese government, 3–9, 25(nn 1, 4), 26(n5)
Chinese Way, 3–4, 6, 254–255, 265, 266
Class differentiation, 8–9
Climate, and pastoralism, 11–12
Collective system, 8–9, 32–40, 144–150, 254–255
  economy of, 32–34, 59(n6), 256, 266(n1)
  individual family experiences of, 107–108, 117–118, 128–129, 218–220, 224–225, 240–241
  labor division in, 34–36, 117–118, 149–150, 168(nn 1, 2)
  livestock management in, 205, 211, 219, 229, 241
Communes. *See* Collective system
Consumer goods, ownership of, 71, 72(table), 186(table)
  living standards, 184, 185(table), 186(table)

Contraceptives, 81, 84, 89(n46), 118, 196
Contract system, 37–40, 55. *See also* Responsibility system
Cowboys, professional, 154, 155
Cows, 179, 198(nn 10, 16), 230, 232–234, 241, 250, 253
  ownership of, 146, 151–154, 155(table), 168(n3)
  See also Livestock
Croll, Elisabeth, 62(n28)
Culture, effect of privatization on, 26(n6), 254

Dadusulongmu family, 216–222
Dairying, 56–57, 62(n35), 148
  examples of in individual families, 232–234, 239, 241–245, 249–250
  and the Han Chinese, 144, 149, 150, 153–154, 157, 168
  and income, 173, 175, 183
  as sideline, 55–56, 67, 69, 165–168
Disease
  black fever (*ke shan*), 92, 113(n1)
  venereal disease and fertility, 192–193, 200(n39)
Divorce, 106
Dowries, 98, 104, 115, 132, 212, 226
  increase in, 73–75, 88(n25), 184–185

Ecology, effect on family labor, 5, 9, 10
Education, 68(table), 69, 180–182, 198(n12)
  example of in individual families, 118–119, 226–229, 235, 247
  sex differences in, 99–100, 180, 181(table), 182, 264

275

280